How to Read a Dress

Lydia Edwards

How to Read a Dress

A Guide to Changing Fashion from the 16th to the 20th Century

BLOOMSBURY VISUAL ARTS

LONDON • NEW YORK • OXFORD • NEW DELHI • SYDNEY

BLOOMSBURY VISUAL ARTS
Bloomsbury Publishing Plc
50 Bedford Square, London, WC1B 3DP, UK
1385 Broadway, New York, NY 10018, USA

BLOOMSBURY, BLOOMSBURY VISUAL ARTS and the Diana logo
are trademarks of Bloomsbury Publishing Plc

First published in Great Britain by Bloomsbury Academic 2017
Reprinted 2017, 2018 (twice)
This edition published by Bloomsbury Visual Arts 2018

For legal purposes the Acknowledgements on p. 7 constitute an
extension of this copyright page.

Cover design: Clare Turner
Cover image © Victoria and Albert Museum, London

A catalogue record for this book is available from the British Library.

The Library of Congress has cataloged the Bloomsbury Academic edition
as follows:
Names: Edwards, Lydia (Lydia Jenny), author.
Title: How to read a dress : a guide to changing fashion from the 16th
to the 20th century / Lydia Edwards.
Description: New York : Bloomsbury Academic, 2017. | Includes
bibliographical references and index.
Identifiers: LCCN 2016029748| ISBN 9781472533272 (pbk.) |
ISBN 9781472534521 (hardback)
Subjects: LCSH: Women's clothing—History. | Fashion—History.
Classification: LCC GT1720 .E39 2016 | DDC 391/.2—dc23 LC
record available at https://lccn.loc.gov/2016029748

ISBN: PB: 978-1-3501-0828-8
       ePDF: 978-1-4742-8624-4
       eBook: 978-1-4742-8625-1

Typeset by Precision Graphics
Printed and bound in India

To find out more about our authors and books visit
www.bloomsbury.com and sign up for our newsletters.

Dedication

For my husband, Aaron,
and the little shadows in our lives

Table of Contents

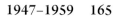

Acknowledgments

There are many people to whom I owe deep thanks and gratitude in their assistance with the completion of this book. First, I must thank my editor, Anna Wright, whose consistent expertise, support, and advice has been utterly invaluable. Frances Arnold must also be thanked for her hugely helpful and encouraging feedback throughout the last few months of writing. Editorial Assistant Ariadne Godwin has also provided helpful guidance and information throughout, for which I am very grateful.

Several museums and societies have generously offered their time and expertise as well as the use of beautiful images. Special thanks must go to Karin Bohleke from the Fashion Museum and Archives at Shippensburg University for her detailed guidance, advice, feedback, and friendship. Mary West and the team at Swan Guildford Historical Society generously gave many hours of time and care to the project, allowing me to make use of some rare and beautiful garments. Glynis Jones from the Powerhouse Museum in Sydney provided hands-on access to garments and a wealth of expertise. Thanks must also go to Kaye Spilker from the Los Angeles County Museum of Art and to all at the McCord Museum, Quebec.

Love and thanks go to my husband Aaron Robotham, for his endless advice and support—and for his beautiful photography, which has been a vital component of the book. Love and gratitude also go to my wonderful parents Chris and Julia, and dear friends Louise Hughes, Anna Hueppauff, Liz Mannering, Nina Levy, and Susan and Alice Ash.

Final thanks to the Tsoulis, Hueppauff, Levy, and Kästing families for their generous permission to use their treasured family photographs.

Preface

The story of the evolution of dress is not as readily accessible as might first be imagined. Books and articles often choose to focus on narrower areas of interest such as a particular era or style, and some function as a wider sociopolitical analysis of how dress adapted and molded to fit contemporary demands. Extraordinary museum collections worldwide are a first and highly precious resource for many researchers and enthusiasts, but most face various inevitable limitations. Chief of these are space, resources, funding, and, more specifically, the necessity (because of loans or conservation requirements) to have a significant number of garments out of the display cases at any one time. Because of this, it can be impossible for visitors to witness a continuous, chronological flow of styles, changing before their eyes in fundamental shape and small details, to produce a comprehensive vision of—quite literally—the evolution of clothes. That is the express intention of this work, which aims to take the reader on a sartorial journey through women's fashion in the Western world, explored in blocks of a few years each and spanning the years 1550 to 1970. The scarce availability of extant (surviving) garments prior to 1550 means that this date has been chosen as a starting point, but there are many publications that consider dress in detail before this point. Books such as Ninya Mikhaila and Jane Malcolm-Davies's *The Tudor Tailor* offer expert reconstructions of earlier garments and a strong background to Tudor dress leading up to the era covered in the first chapter of this book. Janet Arnold's acclaimed *Patterns of Fashion* series starts with a look at *The Cut and Construction of Clothes for Men and Women c.1560–1620*, providing coverage of the sixteenth century through an exploration of extant garments; it is a highly recommended source of further reading.

Examples from works of art and, primarily, extant collections from some of the best (and lesser-known) museums across the world teach the reader how to anticipate and "read" the details of dress, thereby developing a trained eye and enhancing their enjoyment. In a few instances, painted representations have been included, but this only occurs where it has been impossible to find full examples, a particular struggle for sixteenth- and early-seventeenth-century garments because only small fragments often remain. Paintings can also cause some confusion when it comes to using them as reliable historical indicators, and readers should be aware of their limitations as well as great benefits. One of the reasons why portraits can be unreliable evidence is seen in the following examples. First, consider Peter Lely's *Portrait of Louise de Keroualle, Duchess of Portsmouth* from c.1671 to 1674. The Duchess is wearing what came to be known as "fashionable undress": light, flimsy garments for "at home" wear that, due

to their suggestion of leisure, were a popular portrait costume of choice for the upper echelons of society. This fabric was pinned into shape and, while hairstyle and other accessories can be helpful confirmation of a broad time period, the actual "undress" itself remained similar right into the eighteenth century. Mrs. John Pigott's dress in the neighboring image is more shaped to the body in the manner of a usual gown but its wide, low décolletage and unstructured sleeves set it apart as a piece of "undress."

The ability to recognize the adaptation of fashionable details into lower-middle and sometimes even working-class dress across the centuries will be a skill the reader can take from this book and apply to their own exploration of fashion history. The garments in the following chapters come from museums in Australia, Britain, Canada, the United States, Italy and Czechoslovakia. They have been chosen for their ability to illustrate fashions from a broad Western geographical base, with European, American, and Australasian fashion being the prime focus in order to maintain a clear and concentrated overview. Some of the dresses, suits, and ensembles seen here have never been published before: those from small Australian collections such as Swan Guildford Historical Society (Western Australia) and Manning Valley Historical Society in New South Wales. These are important examples because they demonstrate the fluidity with which European fashions were taken up, and often modified, in colonial societies. More generally, it is important not to view the development of fashion through purely European lenses but to bear in mind other Western countries that had a significant impact. Wherever possible, original sources have been consulted to highlight the prevalence of certain trends and the uniqueness of others. These range from contemporary newspapers and books to theatrical reviews.

Trends in accessories—shoes, hats, purses, fans and so on—are discussed in the dress analyses themselves (particularly where it is felt that accessories are a vital part of the overall style ensemble). However, the title of this book being *How to Read a Dress*, the focus is very much on the dress as garment: the body covering worn by women in various phases through history. The aim is to recognize key changes in the cut of bodice and skirt, of overall aesthetics, embellishment, and innovation. This approach is not a universal one and, whilst staying general within its theme, is intended to emphasize the structural and decorative shifts in this very particular item of clothing. As fashion became more diverse, dresses were no longer the only option nor, recently, even the most representative. Therefore, on occasion, a single coat or suit will be shown when deemed representative of the general line of dress at that point in history. As designer Elsa Schiaparelli put it in 1936: "I wear suits nearly all of the time. I like them; they are practical in every way, and my advice to a business girl who wishes to dress smartly at all times and whose income is very limited is this: buy a good suit and live in it."[1]

This quote also exemplifies another aim of the later chapters of this book, which is not to showcase exclusively upper-class clothing. Despite a lack of extant examples, we know from pictorial and written accounts that working clothes did attempt to follow the fashionable line to however small an extent, and that those who could afford it would have had a single dress "for best" made, as far as possible, to copy the styles seen in fashion plates and on the bodies of the wealthy. It is inevitably the garments of the rich that have for the most part survived; since these clothes are most representative of the fashionable ideal, we draw the majority of our knowledge and enjoyment from them. Therefore, until the twentieth-century examples, it will be these (with some exceptions) that make up the majority of the images in this book.

An end date of 1970 has been given because, it can be argued, women's fashion after this point saw "the dress" less as their main choice of clothing, and more as just one among many. The ability to "choose" is key here: as historian Betty Luther Hillman put it, "'Liberation' came not from the actual clothes a woman decided to wear, but from the knowledge that the choice was hers to make."[2] Although dresses and skirts were still a norm for women in the 1970s, the knowledge that trousers and shorts were accepted and, indeed, fashionable alternatives, made their relationship with the dress somewhat more fluid. Added to this, the 1960s and 1970s saw a significant move forward in the production of clothes that could be worn by both sexes. Zsa Zsa Gabor wrote in 1970 that "Today is the best time in the world for women to dress like their own personalities ... A lot of adults get what the young people call 'uptight' about unisex clothes ... they say, 'It's terrible! You can't tell the difference between them.' I say, don't worry, they can tell the difference."[3]

It is, of course, impossible to cover every element of such a complex and diverse topic as fashion evolution in just one volume. The aim here is to provide coverage of some of the most important and easily recognizable styles worn by women from 1550 to 1970, and to offer the reader a means by which to identify them. Such knowledge will aid visits to costume exhibitions and allow a greater enjoyment and understanding of historically themed films, TV, and stage adaptations. It is also hoped that the student of art and fashion history or fashion and theatre design will find in these pages a handy reference guide, and a gateway to understanding dating and analytical techniques to aid the increasingly interdisciplinary arts and humanities researcher.

Introduction

Dresses were meant to make women beautiful.
Hubert de Givenchy, March 1952 [1]

Fashion history is a major component of the cultural landscape in Western societies today. Dress can be the ultimate signifier of a person's gender, age, class, employment, and religion down to more subtle indications such as aesthetic predilection, political standpoint, and marital status. Fashion, in particular women's wear, has been a source of great social and cultural importance since the earliest civilizations: inciting passion, obsession, derision, scorn, scandal, and fascination in all its many guises. Dress can hold the power to alter perceptions and opinions, to disguise and reinterpret, to heighten or lessen the wearers' very sense of themselves for better or for worse. This has been the case for as long as society can remember and, indeed, as far back as the first century B.C.E., Ovid wrote that "We are captivated by dress; all is concealed by gems and gold; a woman is the least part of herself." [2]

In the twenty-first century, fashion is as much a topic of discussion as it ever was, and historical fashion has not ceased to inspire. "A little worn, a little torn / Check the rack … what went out, is coming back" is a key lyric from Paul McCartney's *Vintage Clothes* on the album *Memory Almost Full* (2007) and illustrates the fact that, time and time again, contemporary designers have turned back to the past for stimulus. [3] Throughout much of the twentieth century and now—well into the twenty-first—there remains a deep interest in historic sartorial representation. The prevalence of historical dramas on TV and in film is testament to the current craze for vintage nostalgia and the ever-present reminiscences of a "golden age," which frequently accompany the start of a new century. Fashion museums across the world have experienced a swell in visitor numbers in recent years, but despite this there seems to be little general recognition of how and why styles have changed across time, or of an ability to pinpoint subtle changes in shape as they occurred. Even the smallest alteration in cut or the application of trimming can indicate new reactions and associations on the part of the wearer and her social and cultural climate, and an ability to recognize these increases our understanding of significant shifts and trends in the social, political, economic, and artistic world.

It is therefore of concern that the current fondness for so-called vintage style is not representative of any era in particular. The word itself is deeply problematic in the breadth and casualness of its use. In contemporary bridal fashion, for example, "vintage" can simply mean a section of lace trimming or a sparkly, antique-looking brooch placed at the center of a satin belt. Brides asking for a "vintage look" can walk away with a gown whose pretensions to nostalgia include nothing more than a lace overlay or pair of sleeves. There is a tendency to loosely align this trend with the 1930s, 1940s, 1950s, and 1960s, elements of which are often amalgamated into one. This illustrates the ever-present cyclical nature of fashion, but it does mean that anyone wishing to recognize and enjoy legitimate examples runs the risk of confusion and misinformation. The ability to date clothing and to recognize particular stylistic elements is vital if we are to distinguish and understand those same elements being recycled today. It is the author's hope and intention that this book will abate that confusion and reduce usage of the catchall vintage label, offering the reader an informed and concise model with which to read contemporary as well as historical fashion.

Many wonderful museum and gallery collections across the world offer the best way of discovering and understanding historic dress. But with old garments comes inevitable alteration and conservation across the years, and this book will also aim to highlight a few examples where contemporary intervention—however appropriate and effective—needs to be acknowledged. Some museum items will also provide a broad provenance, or one that has been debated, and this is particularly common in smaller collections and historical societies, where funds for further definitive research are not available. Two examples in this book, both from a small but valuable historical society in Australia, discuss the most likely date and background for the dresses in question.

The ebb and flow of fashionable shape makes up the fascinating and familiar styles that have dictated women's dress for the past 1,000 years. The dress—as we know it today, generally a single-piece garment or bodice and skirt—first arrived with the Plantagenets, and that basic nonbifurcated (a garment covering the legs that is not divided into two) foundation has remained. Its reaction to changing society and attitude, though, has been anything but static. In their various phases, bodices have been flat-fronted, waist cinching, intentionally baggy and androgynous, encompassing only the bust or from neck to hips. Corsets have been either indispensable or shunned. Petticoats of some sort were rarely deemed unnecessary, from the farthingale of the sixteenth century (which was to return in many incarnations at various points over the following 400 years) to the slinky satin slips of the 1930s. So despite these resurgences and the enduring presence of that garment known as a dress, gown, robe, or mantua, innovative phases—wrought by style or necessity, and sometimes both—have worked to create an extraordinarily vibrant and dramatic silhouette across the centuries.

It has never just been a simple case of studying dress as a single entity. As society progressed and as class distinctions became more concrete in the West, it became usual for wealthier women to present themselves in more than one garment during the day. By the mid nineteenth century, for example, it would be usual for upper-class (and increasingly, middle-class) women to possess gowns for morning, afternoon, tea, dinner/evening, and specific occasions such as a reception or ball. Adding to the repertoire might also be the half dress, worn for both day and informal evening occasions; the walking or promenade dress, made for particular sports (most popularly, the riding habit—in existence since the eighteenth century); and the traveling dress. Most of these varieties were also available as clothes for mourning and maternity, states of life that the majority of nineteenth-century women would experience at some point. This book will show an assortment of such garments, all chosen for their adherence to the fashionable silhouette, but also to define and discuss the many variants that existed. There may be subtle differences in the fabric or trimming of an afternoon gown as opposed to a morning dress, for example, that make further analysis necessary.

Although gender boundaries are now far more fluid than they were even fifty years ago, the dress has remained a garment that typifies femininity in all its guises. With a wide variety of daily clothing options, including, of course, trousers, women now relegate the dresses in their wardrobe to particular occasions. For many, a dress will signify "best" or "smart" outfit or perhaps a garment worn more for work than at home during the weekend. Most brides still expect to wear a dress on their wedding day, and it was only during a key period of utility—World War II—that the tailored suit often became a bridal choice through necessity, and only later by design, as can be seen in this photograph from a 1960s London wedding.

Men have worn nonbifurcated garments at various points through history, and into the nineteenth century, small boys typically wore dresses, and then shorter tunics, until they were "breeched" at around the age of six or seven. Skirts for men have included, among others, the Scottish kilt (still worn today for special and ceremonial occasions: this is a common choice of outfit for a bridegroom), the medieval *tonlet* (a metal skirt worn as part of a suit of armor for protection during foot combat, and based on tunics seen in contemporary dress), and in ancient Greece and Rome, men and women wore very similar bifurcated clothes in the shape of a long robe known as toga, himation, and chiton. Since then, however, the dress—also known across the centuries as a gown or robe—has been exclusively feminine in the Western world, and women have embraced or merely accepted it as such. Critic Quentin Bell wrote in the 1930s that "western woman's long struggle to be recognized as a biped began in the nineteenth century," [4] and this book will also document the rise and influence of "rational" dress in that century and into the twentieth, twinned with a similar movement toward "aesthetic" clothing that was largely propagated by Oscar Wilde and other prominent bohemian figures.

Whether studying or just enjoying historic costume, it is always important to consider the very physical implications of wearing particular clothing. The way people moved in, and consciously managed, their clothes can tell us much about attitudes toward gender, class, and standards of decorum and decency throughout the ages. The way elite female sitters in mid-seventeenth-century portraits were posed—for example, with exposed lower arms bent and elbows held out, slightly away from the body, with one hand on the other arm's wrist—was

not just for aesthetic reasons. It is true that, from the early years of the century, women were, at last, permitted to show their arms, and this must have influenced the choice of portrait posture quite considerably: but in the stiff bodices, it was also far more comfortable for a woman to hold her arms up and away from her body. [5] In images from the early 1840s, dresses and their narrowly cut shoulders (with sleeves sometimes set well below the shoulder line) necessitated a wearer's arms to be held much closer to the body, whereas gowns from 1900–05 had sleeves set at the "natural" armscye (armhole), just before the shoulder meets the top of the arm, and consequently allowed, in some respects, a more natural posture. The lower classes (who do not generally appear in such portraits except occasionally as favored servants) would, of course, have needed to wear clothes that enabled ease of movement and that took up as little time and energy as possible. Nonetheless, the upper classes still held the yardstick for fashion and the "correct" mode of appearance and, as stated in the Authors' Note, the lower and middle classes would have attempted to emulate this where they could. [6]

The study of dress is an invaluable methodology when attempting to understand and deconstruct the past. In the context of this book, it can also shed light on gender relations and the ways in which society perceived women but also, crucially, the way women perceived themselves and presented their bodies to the world. With clothing for so long deemed a woman's main interest and occupation, it is incumbent upon historians to fully understand the aesthetics and function of that interest and to chart the developments of dress and the changing ways that women used fashion to express, to conceal, to rebel, to protest, and to forge identity within—for the most part—a fiercely patriarchal world.

Chapter 1
1550–1600

It is rare to come face to face with surviving examples of sixteenth-century dress for the simple reason that so few complete garments remain. Even the wealthy often made new clothing (or parts of new garments) from the sturdy remains of the old, and we have no complete surviving physical record of working- and lower-class clothing. Our knowledge derives from the fortunate wealth of portraits and other artworks that remain—primarily European in origin—and that form an integral part of the analysis of this first chapter.

Many different layers made up the clothing of European women in the sixteenth century. This was partly for a very practical reason: the weather. Research has shown that the climate during the late 1500s was, on average, around two degrees colder than the twentieth- and twenty-first-century mean.[1] Coupled with the fact that both men and women were expected to be fully and neatly attired at all times, it is possible to understand the practical and moral need for fabric in excess. At the same time, a definite form and fit that moved away from the loose folds of medieval styles was emerging. Although much fabric was still used in the construction of a gown, a focus was on shaping and the accentuation of different parts of the body. From the 1550s onward, daily dress for middle- and upper-class women nearly always incorporated a smock, stays, kirtle (later called a petticoat and usually with a bodice attached), gown, farthingale, forepart, sleeves, ruff, and partlet—all of which will be defined in this chapter. Multiple layers ensured decency, especially since drawers or any other kind of undergarment was not worn under the smock. Key stylistic traits can usually be recognized through the principal garment, the *gown*, which could be either "loose" or tightly fitted to the torso. French, English, and Spanish bodices retained a conical V shape, whereas German and Italian gowns can be characterized by visible front lacing (the aforementioned styles usually fastened at the sides or back) and elaborately puffed sleeves.

Elizabeth I ascended the throne of England, Ireland, and France in 1558. Despite her masculine attitude toward politics, she took a keen interest in clothes of all European states and was the instigator of several trends during her sixty-year reign. The Spanish note in dress, which half-Spanish Queen Mary had promoted during her reign, continued into the Elizabethan period in the form of the *farthingale* and *ruff*. The triangular Spanish farthingale, or verthingale (derived from *vertugarde*), was soon joined by a new kind of skirt support, what could be termed the second farthingale of the sixteenth century: the circular roll. This stuffed tube of fabric, said to originate in France, was worn around the waist to hold out gathered overskirts creating a new voluminous swell to the skirt after the flatter, more triangular silhouette of the Tudor era. The excess of fabric needed to create this distinctive shape was famously parodied in the anonymous caricature *The Vanity of Women* (c.1590–1600), which depicts a single-minded group of women trying on "bum rolls" of various sizes. Despite the seeming luxury of such substantial usage of material, to some women, transitioning from a farthingale to a circular roll alone represented the adoption of an inferior social status.

RIGHT
Hendrik Goltzius,
Portrait of Lady
Françoise van Egmond,
Holland, 1580,
Los Angeles County
Museum of Art

DAMOISELLE FRANCHOYSE DEGMONT

Goltzius fecit

Across Europe, sumptuary laws were a prominent factor regarding choice of clothes, even for the upper classes. Prior to Elizabeth I's reign, these regulations, intended to curb excessiveness in dress, had existed—and the Queen continued to denote dress and fabric types according to the wearer's class. The reasons behind such laws were also politically biased, attempting to exercise some control over imported goods. As Elizabeth wrote in June 1574: "The excess of apparel and the superfluity of unnecessary foreign wares thereto belonging now of late years is grown by sufferance to such an extremity that the manifest decay not only of a great part of the wealth of the whole realm generally is like to follow." [2]

No woman, unless a member of the aristocracy, was to wear "cloth of gold, tissue, nor fur of sables," nor velvet, embroidery or *passement* lace of gold or silver, or embroidered silk—and the list goes on to include the use of such items as satin, damask, tufted taffeta, and silk grosgrain in gowns, petticoats, and kirtles, with different stipulations for their use in each garment. Some items could be worn by "the wives and daughters of the sons and heirs of knights" and, on rare occasions, "gentlewomen attendant upon duchesses, marquises, countesses" could wear items passed on to them by their mistresses. These demands went some way to ensure that the middle classes could not, without great difficulty, ascend the ranks to nobility—although it was very difficult to legally enforce them or to formally prosecute.[3] An outward show of wealth through clothing was incredibly significant, and restricting its distribution was an effective means of exercising social and political control. In other parts of Europe, sumptuary laws for clothing had been in existence since Ancient times and generally fell out of favor in all countries by around the middle of the seventeenth century. Dissatisfaction was starting to be expressed from prominent quarters, among them the celebrated French writer Michel de Montaigne, who objected to the unnecessary inconveniences implicit in the laws' enforcement. He believed that moral example should stem from the very source that decreed it: "Let kings leave off these ensigns of grandeur; they have others enough besides; those excesses are more excusable in any other than a prince." [4]

Throughout Britain and mainland Europe, some inspiration for women's dress was taken from that of men. An increasing focus on the separateness of the upper and lower body, and the need to clothe them accordingly, can be seen in interpretations of the masculine doublet, illustrated in this French engraving. In France, some women chose to wear a bodice in the Spanish style featuring a stiff stand-up collar, in many respects almost identical to that worn by fashionable men.[5] Ruffs, a chief accessory of the time, were practically indistinguishable for both sexes, particularly in the years immediately after Elizabeth's coronation. A prevailing image is of the large, closed, flat ruff, but during the 1500s we can frequently spot open examples, where the gathered edges of a ruff simply form a standing collar framing the sides and back of the wearer's head. Moreover, small differences in the shape and method of wearing ruffs were in evidence throughout separate countries, so we can observe substantial variety throughout Europe.

The supremely impractical French (or "wheel") farthingale from the end of the century can be seen as the epitome of elite, leisured women's wear. It is ironic that its inception should have taken place in France, given the French fondness for softer, more flexible fashions than their Spanish-style rivals. Not so long before its introduction, many French women preferred to hold out their skirts by wearing numerous stiffened petticoats. This created a cascade of irregular pleats from waist to floor, a complete departure from the smooth stretched frame of the Spanish farthingale.

A plate-like caned structure, the French farthingale formed a graduating halo shape around a woman's waist, extended out at all sides and was worn over a padded roll to hold the rear side up and push the front down, further elongating an already conical torso. The skirt simply fell to the floor from the edges of the hoop, creating the unusual effect of narrow torso and shortened legs. The skirt of this type of gown was also enhanced by the presence of verthingale sleeves, similar to the puffed, crescent shape of men's doublet sleeves, gathered at the shoulder and wide all the way down the arm. These could grow to extremes and sometimes required whalebone supports to retain their shape. At court, the bodice would usually be topped with an imposing standing collar that, at its tallest and widest, could extend behind and far above the wearer's head. In order to maintain this height and presence, the collar was often held in place by a *supportasse*, a frame that "underpropped" the ruff itself and provided the foundations for layered and complex shapes. Extra dimensions could be added by the use of a *whisk*, a curved wire frame covered with sheer fabric and ornamented with pearls and lace.

Surface decoration was an extremely important aspect of fashionable dress during the sixteenth century, often shown through the use of revers on bodices and doublets. Blackwork—a type of embroidery made from black silk thread onto white fabric—was especially representative of the era. Under Elizabeth's reign it became more elaborate than previously: rather than the more stylistic, geometric patterns favoured in the early 1500s, inclinations tended toward the floral, often accented by threads of silver.[6] But excesses in ornamentation spread much further than embroidery alone. Slashing, which had first become popular during the previous century, consisted of delicate or rough pinked slits in the surface of a fabric, showing off further luxuriant fabrics beneath.

When Elizabeth I died in 1603, her funeral effigy displayed an invaluable resource for costume historians: the corset. This "pair of bodies" contained an additional supportive measure, the busk—a long, flat strip of whalebone, wood or metal, inserted vertically down the front. Busks first came to prominence in the 1500s and gained an erotic reputation, often given as gifts by a lover and featuring secret carved messages.[7]

Silk velvet gown,

c.1550–60, Museo di Palazzo Reale, Pisa

◆

This crimson silk velvet dress (sottana con maniche), luxuriantly trimmed with gold is a rare and precious example of a surviving Italianate Renaissance gown. It was discovered on a wooden effigy at San Matteo, Pisa, and bears strong similarities to the funeral dress of Eleonora di Toledo, although whether it belonged to her—or another of her kin—is open to debate.[8]

....

The neckline is low and square at both front and back, and would often be worn with a piece of light fabric draped around the shoulders.

At the top of each sleeve is a style sometimes known as *baragoni*: panels of fabric pulled into a decorative puff when the ties are fastened. Sections of the smock are then drawn through the corresponding gaps.

These sleeves are slashed—the practice of making slits in the fabric for decorative purposes.

The skirt is gathered in deep pleats at front, back, and sides.

The skirt is composed of straight and triangular panels to achieve the flared silhouette (the discolored seams can be glimpsed from this image). It sports a significant rounded train, also edged in corresponding rows of gold trim.

Sleeves were separate at this time, fastened to the armholes of the bodice by a series of ties known as *aiguillettes*: braided cords finished with metal points.

The bodice (known as *imbusto*) is shaped at the back by two vertical rows of lacing, placed just under the arm and extending to the waist. This was the common position for bodice lacing of the upper classes: working-class women would usually have laced their bodices only at the front so as to enable the speed and necessity of dressing without assistance. Another supporting and shaping method was to stiffen the bodice with layers of felted wool or buckram. It should be noted that although stays were in existence, they were not yet stiffened with whalebone.[9]

Follower of Titian, *Emilia di Spilimbergo*, c.1560, National Gallery of Art, Washington D.C.
This Italian portrait from 1560 depicts a young woman in a similar deep red gown worn with a jewelled girdle, under a loose robe with standing ruff. This gives us an insight to how such dresses would have been worn and accessorised on a daily basis.

The skirt is composed of straight and triangular panels to achieve the flared silhouette (the discolored seams can be glimpsed from this image). It sports a significant rounded train, also edged in corresponding rows of gold trim.

Unknown, Portrait of a Young Woman,

1567, Yale Center for British Art, New Haven, Connecticut

◆

This portrait of an unidentified, but certainly wealthy, young English woman shows a dress conforming closely to fashionable elements c.1560–70. From the small, setback escoffion cap to the arch of the neckline (drawing attention to a very slender waist), this richly ornamented dress indicates high style in the early part of Elizabeth I's reign.

This elaborate necklace is long enough to loop three times around the neck and is arranged in swags across the top of the bodice. Its composition and design mirror that of the girdle.

Low, square necklines were filled in by a *partlet* until around 1570. This was a rectangular piece of cloth with an attached standing collar (in this case, a ruff) that was worn under the bodice and covered the neck, shoulders, and upper back. The fact that it is worn open at the front here suggests that the sitter was unmarried.

Increasing focus on shoulders can be seen in these padded *shoulder rolls* or *wings*, decorated with the same trim as that seen on the bodice and skirt opening.

A slender, concave waist is enhanced by a wide, conical skirt worn over a farthingale.

These sleeves are slashed, with puffs of the underlying smock pulled through the holes.

The dress is worn with a jeweled *girdle*. From the Middle Ages onward, a girdle referred to a belt worn around the hips or waist with a long chain hanging from the center, down the front of the skirt. The end of the chain would sometimes have an attachment: a larger jewel, portrait miniature, purse, or even a small book or mirror.

The gown is worn over a *kirtle*, a fitted and usually bodiced garment that covered the petticoat beneath. Kirtles often had a triangular panel of rich fabric, known as a *forepart*, attached to the front of the skirt, a display of wealth that was visible when worn with an open fronted gown such as this.

Christoffel van Sichem I, Elizabeth, Queen of Great Britain,

1570-80 (published 1601), Natonal Gallery of Art, Washington D.C.

◆

Christoffel van Sichem (1546–1624) was a Dutch woodcutter and engraver whose works mainly comprised portraits as well as more traditional biblical and narrative scenes. This image illustrates a continuing trend for ornate surface decoration and popular usage of ruff and shoulder rolls. It also illustrates the masculine influence seen in women's wear.

....

By the 1570s the bodice was often high-necked, but a low décolletage would start to become fashionable again by the end of the decade.

Vertical strips of fabric, known as *panes*, decorate substantial shoulder rolls at the top of the sleeves.

The flat torso was a result of the lack of darts used in bodices at this date, providing no extra space to accommodate a woman's bust. In this way, the female bodice was structured very similarly to a man's doublet.

The waistline is becoming lower and more pointed.

The hem of the farthingale became wider c.1575, and skirts were usually worn with hip pads as well to create the shape seen here.[10]

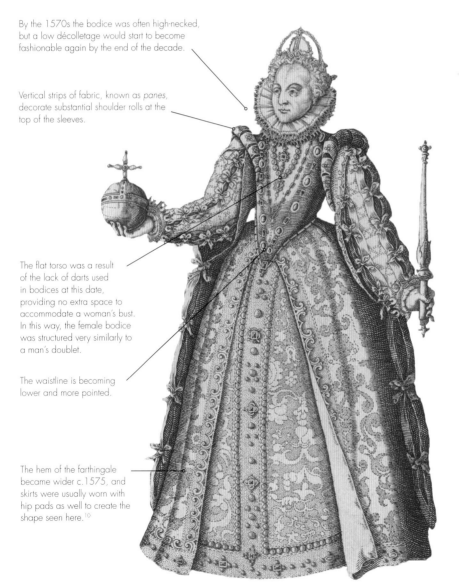

Hendrik Goltzius, *Hieronymus Scholiers*, c.1583, National Gallery of Art, Washington, D.C. This portrait from the same time period shows the similarities in cut and decoration between male and female dress. The high collar with ruff, *shoulder wings*, and *false hanging sleeves* suggest a corresponding influence.

Long false sleeves hang loosely around the bodice sleeve and are then caught by bows at intervals as they near the floor. This corresponds to the bows holding the panes of the bodice sleeves together.

Crispijn de Passe I, Queen of England,

c.1588–1603, National Gallery of Art, Washington D.C.

◆

This engraving of Elizabeth I, depicts one of the shortest-lived (yet one of the most recognizable) fashions of the sixteenth century: the wheel or drum farthingale. It was quickly discarded by most of Europe in the early seventeenth century but remained for some time in the court of Anne of Denmark, who encouraged the continuation of the style.

Rows of pearls and jewels were worn around the neck and draped in loops over the bodice.

The double halo-like structure behind Elizabeth's head was known as a *butterfly-wing veil*, made from two to four circular "wings" that framed the back of the head. These would be filled in with sheer gauze and the edges decorated with pearls and jewels. Usually, a white veil would be attached to the base of the wings and float down from shoulders to floor.

For most of the century, men and women wore similarly shaped ruffs. However, with this much lower décolletage came a large open ruff, only covering the back and sides of the neck and exposing the cleavage. It would have been positioned using a supportasse (or *underpropper*), a wire frame pinned to the bodice.

These *trunk* (also known as *cannon*) sleeves were fashionable during the last quarter of the century. Wide at the top and tapering to a close-fitting wrist, their shape was maintained through padding, boning, and wire supports.

Over the white and gold bodice and skirt, a fitted gown is worn. It is shaped to the waist and covers the back half of the farthingaled skirt.

This frill around the outside "wheel" of the farthingale was known as a *frounce* or sometimes a *drum ruffle*.[12] It created a softer, more feminine edge to a very angular structure and could be seen on dresses like this from the 1590s until the early years of the seventeenth century.

Long-hanging false sleeves drape over the farthingale behind the arm, often reaching the hem of the skirt. They were known as "false" because original variants were closed, featuring a front slit for the arm to pass through, and therefore had some practical purpose. These lengths of fabric, on the other hand, are purely decorative.

The hoop was angled forward, resting on a bum roll that was worn tied around the waist underneath the gown. This meant that it sat much higher at the back than at the front.[13]

The skirt fell straight down from the edges of the frame, usually stopping at around ankle length or just below. Unlike earlier Spanish farthingales, which contained hoops of graduating sizes, the wheel farthingale used rows of whalebone that were arranged in equal diameter from waist to hem. Because of this, skirts were made up from straight widths of fabric and did not need to be shaped.

Puffs of white silk set on cloth of gold are interspersed with jewels including rubies, pearls, and emeralds.[11]

Chapter 2
1610–1699

Due to the scarcity of complete surviving examples of seventeenth-century dress, the images in this chapter are largely made up of contemporaneous artistic depictions as well as extant pieces. Although these choices will inevitably feature wealthier examples, the artists have been chosen due to their detailed depictions of clothing. They also span a range of European countries, given that this era was one of the most diverse in terms of a continuation of specific national tendencies in dress. This includes several Dutch pieces, Holland being such a hub for creativity and innovation in dress (particularly in textile production, with a thriving linen industry in Haarlem and silk weaving in Amsterdam) as well as other areas of aesthetic, economic, and political concern.

The first example illustrates predominating Spanish styles in dress. The most prominent indicator is the extended *stomacher* that was shaped and often bolstered to jut out and create something of a shelf at the wearer's abdomen. In Spain and Portugal, such innovations remained popular for much longer (Charles II's Portuguese wife, Catherine of Braganza, arrived at the English court from Lisbon in 1662 similarly dressed, though soon afterward she adopted the English gown and hairstyle). For women in England and France, however, the decades of artificial stiffness, ruffs, and bolstered skirts of Elizabeth I's reign gave way to a softer, fresher, more natural silhouette. France caught onto the new fashion slightly more reticently, since the traditional wheel farthingale was still used for court occasions in that country well into the seventeenth century. After 1610, the neckline of dresses dropped, and sleeves became very full, gradually puffed out at various points down the arm, and fastened with ribbon ties or rosettes. Slashing of outer fabric (a common decorative feature from the sixteenth century) was also reintroduced, but much surface decoration focused upon large swathes of lace, either as sleeve cuffs or neckline trimmings. Instead of being stiffened to become ruffs, these were now usually left to fall elegantly over the shoulders, known commonly as a *falling band* or ruff, and latterly as a *van Dyck collar,* a style particularly admired by the artist and used frequently in his portraits. By 1625, the waistline had risen and stayed in its new position, just below the bust, until the mid-late 1630s. This new style comprised a bodice made with wide shoulder seams, the armholes set far into the center back to allow for very large sleeves. During the 1620s–1640s, bodices could be made with or without *basques* (tabs extending below the waist, also seen on men's doublets), but their inclusion was certainly more common—as will be seen in the examples of this chapter.[1]

Skirts were always loosely gathered at the waist, falling in heavy and irregular folds to the floor, and sometimes slightly trained.[2] A wide opening in the front of the overskirt displayed an underskirt, the front panel made of a contrasting and preferably rich, textured, costly material (sometimes the costly would be rationed to the front, with the rest of the garment made of a much plainer, cheaper fabric). The skirt itself was very full, its volume achieved by means of hip pads or bum rolls, a rounded tube of fabric stuffed with horsehair, which added

bulk to the hips and a swell to the skirt. Nearly all gowns were worn with a narrow ribbon sash that followed the high waistline and was tied in a bow, either slightly to the side or on the center front of the bodice. To preserve their modesty when adorned in extremely low-necked dresses, women often wore a neckerchief, which was folded diagonally around the shoulders and either left to hang free or closed at the throat or bosom with an attractive brooch.

One of the most significant differences during this period concerned the frequent lack of separate stays. The boned bodice generally took on that supportive role, initially encasing the bust and waist by means of a separate stomacher that was positioned inside the front panels (an alternative that provided the same fashionable silhouette was a back-fastening bodice with a closed front and no stomacher). This meant that, for much of the early part of the century, a separate shaped undergarment was simply not required, and what would later be considered "underwear" was, in effect, twinned with outerwear as a part of the dress itself. Leading into the second half of the century, bodices became very heavily boned and maneuvered the torso into a long, slim line that could only be maintained by tight lacing and the use of newly available whalebone. By this point, stays were commonly worn, but they were not universally adopted until the introduction of the mantua in the 1680s.

This "pair of bodies" (possibly the derivation of the modern word *bodice*) would be worn over a smock, the arms of which were usually visible underneath the elbow-length sleeves of the basque (the bareness of a woman's arms was a novel feature of this age, and one that attracted considerable comment from moralists). Where sleeves of an undergarment were not visible, the outer sleeve would be finished with a broad cuff, edged in lace and sometimes stiffened with starch. On those rare occasions when stays were worn, they were styled very similarly to the bodice, except for the lack of sleeves (though long-sleeved versions were sometimes worn, especially in winter—an example can be seen in the Victoria and Albert Museum). Nevertheless, because we have so few surviving garments, the truth is that we simply do not know how tightly women of the early seventeenth century were laced into their dresses. We are familiar with the idea of the corset being used principally to create a small waist, but prior to the 1800s its function was largely to alter the shape of the top of the figure. With the aid of a well-fitting bodice, stays were not necessarily required to mold the body into a shape befitting outer garments. Shaping the shoulders and upper bust would have been the chief province of the low, tightly fitting neckline that rested on the edges of a woman's shoulders. We can tell from portraits c.1620–30 that clothing in the early years of the century was looser and freer than it had been for over a century, and women must have keenly felt this freedom after the comparative stiffness of the late 1500s and early 1600s.

During Cromwell's Protectorate in Britain (1649–1660), fashion was not exclusively the black and gray somberness and restraint of Puritan ideals. Those who remained sympathetic to royalism still maintained an element of "the Cavalier" in their day-to-day dress, and for

RIGHT
Studio of Gerard ter Borch the Younger, The Music Lesson, c.1670, National Gallery of Art, Washington D.C.

women this included lace-edged collars and cuffs and the continuation of silks and satins in brighter hues such as blue, yellow, and rose. Religious, political, and, above all, class indicators were marked out by the nature of the fabric and trimmings rather than by differences in the underlying structure of the garment. This image by William Dobson depicts the clothing of a family who were adhering to Calvinist modes of dress before the overthrow of Charles I. The woman is wearing an entirely plain collar that totally covers the décolletage of her gown. No lace is present, and her hair is covered by a simple coif. For Puritan women, this type of ensemble continued to be worn throughout the Protectorate, along with the tall hats that are so recognizable of the era. Similar dress could be seen in Holland, also with a base in political concerns. The Protestant government, ruled by elite members of the bourgeoisie, accentuated its piety and seriousness by a sober and conservative uniform made up largely of black clothes. The continued presence of the ruff in Dutch fashion was the only concession to frivolity, remaining—and expanding—long after it had been abandoned in England and France.

With the Restoration came a lengthening of the bodice in England and France, the waistline finishing in a very low point. Some bodices also retained the tabs of the 1630s through 1650s, which helped to shape this "pair of bodies" to the torso. The bodice was now more universally worn with stays, but it was still heavily boned and made in fabric that complemented the skirt and lent itself well to external ornamentation.

Necklines were low and rounded and were still usually covered by collars or neckerchiefs for daywear. Sleeves remained full and set far back into the bodice; they were heavily pleated at both armhole and cuff but were gradually getting shorter as the 1670s approached. The sleeve of an underlying smock would nearly always be visible, its frills poking out at both cuff and décolletage.

Embroidery was an important addition to clothing at this time, and the types of techniques used and the patterns created could be numerous. For example, scientific discoveries of the seventeenth century and before were frequently picked out in exquisite silks and metal threads. Both flora and fauna were depicted with enthusiasm, a "great age of discovery [. . .] celebrated in the very fabric of domestic furnishings and costume." [3] Surviving women's jackets, particularly those held by the Victoria and Albert Museum and the Metropolitan Museum of Art, are evidence of the lavishness of both embroiderer's material and subject matter. Silver and silver-gilt bobbin lace was an attractive finishing to many surviving garments, and along with such aesthetic advancements we begin to see more practical innovations during the century. Hooks and eyes, for example, started to replace ribbon ties as fastenings although bows remained a common decorative feature for some time. The use of jackets as practical and fashionable accessories was seen often throughout the century in the paintings of Dutch masters Vermeer and Jan Steen and, in the example here, the studio of Gerard ter Borch the Younger. The women in these atmospheric genre scenes often wear loose coats, over their gowns. These are usually silk, and sometimes fur-trimmed or lined, suggestive of both luxury and intimacy. The jacket also had a place in far more formal attire, however, and that could be seen in the development of the riding habit. Firmly established by the eighteenth century, it was to become a woman's garment in its own right (although tailoring was seen as a purely masculine province until well into the late nineteenth century). In the 1600s, however, a habit's jacket was based extremely closely on men's styles, with very few allowances made to the female shape—the specifically male practice of left buttoning over right was in evidence, and the outfit was occasionally worn with that other singularly masculine item of clothing, a waistcoat. At times the effect could be incredibly convincing, as Samuel Pepys noted in 1666:

> Walking here in the galleries I find the Ladies of Honour dressed in their riding garbs, with coats and doublets with deep skirts, just for all the world like mine, and buttoned their doublets up the breast, with perriwigs and with hats; so that, only for a long petticoat dragging under their men's coats, nobody could take them for women in any point whatever; which was an odde sight, and a sight did not please me. [4]

Until the last twenty years or so of the century, three-piece dresses—consisting of a bodice, petticoat, and gown—continued to be popular. After this time, the one-piece gown, or *mantua*, started to be worn by most women, and this would go on to become the staple garment of the eighteenth century. Derived from a simple T-shaped piece of fabric, this extraordinary garment was fitted by a series of pleats from the shoulder down, pinned to the individual shape of the wearer, and held in place by a belt. Originally a loose informal garment, it influenced the development of the sack or *robe à la française*, one of the key formal styles of the following century.

Marketa Lobkowicz burial gown,

c.1617, Regional Museum, Mikulov, Czechoslovakia

◆

The seventeenth-century Kingdom of Bohemia (modern-day Czech Republic) was home
to noblewoman Marketa Lobkowicz, whose 1617 burial garments were restored in 2003.
This gown is a good example of how the aristocracy of central Europe would have dressed at this time,
incorporating a strong Spanish influence particularly in the continued use of the conical farthingale.

The collar is made from fine silk, edged with Italian silk lace. Much of the highest quality and costliest lace came from the Italian states at this time, giving another indication of the wearer's status.[5]

The bodice is made from silk featuring a "bird's eye" design: a geometric *diaper* (all-over pattern) in a simple dot shape resembling an eye.[7]

Twenty-two square tabs edge the waistline at front and back.

The skirt is composed of eight panels, and its conical shape was achieved through the wearing of a Spanish farthingale, a *verdugado*, which was already falling out of fashion in other parts of Europe.[8]

Also included with the burial garments was this cloak, featuring typically Spanish hanging sleeves and a standing collar. It is made from a rich silk velvet onto which a floral pattern is carved, using a knife. This painstaking technique was only reserved for the highest and wealthiest classes of society.[9]

These narrow sleeves correspond to the fashionable cut of those seen on doublets or *jubons*, worn by both men and women. These tight-fitting garments also usually featured stand-up collars and shoulder wings.

The sleeves here are cut according to the usual curved shaping of the period, which meant that in most cases movement was inhibited. However, conservators of this particular gown noted that a small wedge of fabric had been inserted at the top of each sleeve to enable greater ease of movement for the wearer.[6]

This very long, rounded waistline is a testament to Spanish style, and also recalls the popular shape for stomachers in Holland at this time. This type of bodice was sometimes worn over a padded roll to increase its protuberance, the effect of which can be seen in the portrait below.

The skirt is open at center front, although both sides meet when it is worn over a farthingale.

Peter Paul Rubens, *Marchesa Brigida Spinola Doria*, 1606, Samuel H. Kress Collection, National Gallery of Art, Washington, D.C.
This painting, of Italian noblewoman Marchesa Brigida Spinola Doria, illustrates several Spanish trends that the nobility in Eastern Europe—keen to gain equal standing with the ruling House of Habsburg—also strove to emulate.

Anthony van Dyck, *Lady with a Fan,*

c.1628, National Gallery of Art, Washington, D.C.

◆

This outfit is typical of a wealthy Italian woman at the end of the 1620s. Her costume depicts a strong northern European influence, and although the era was hailed for its comparative simplicity following Elizabethan excess, we can nevertheless observe how many and varied were the parts that still made up the clothing of a fashionable woman.

Over her skirt and bodice, the sitter is wearing a sleeveless, full-length black silk gown (known as a *nightgown* in England). This relatively short-lived trend was an optional addition to a woman's wardrobe, worn open with its sides held to the body by a sash. It reached the floor but rarely, at this time, incorporated a train.

Paned (slit, sometimes known as pansied), *virago sleeves* are fitted at the forearm. Bands of silk, in a corresponding shade to the sash, hold the sections together and emphasize the style. Randle Holme in his *Academy of Armory,* published in 1688, described the virago sleeve or "slasht Sleeve" as being "When the Sleeve from Shoulder to the Sleeve hands are cut in long slices, or fillets: and are tied together at the Elbow with Ribbons, or such like." [10]

Long, deep cuffs edged with lace were usually made from linen.

The wide, square neckline (set high at the back of the bodice) is covered with a collar of sheer silk edged with lace. Shortly before this time at the start of the decade, standing collars stiffened with wire—known in Europe as *rebatos*—were fashionable.

The bodice itself is long, the suggestion of a high waist given mainly by the presence and positioning of a sash.

In keeping with bodices of the late 1620s, the stomacher ends in a narrow point (known as a *peake*), edged in this instance with small decorative tabs and gold trim.

In her left hand she holds a closed fan, suspended from her waistband by a thick gold chain.

Anthony van Dyck, Queen Henrietta Maria

1633, National Gallery of Art, Washington, D.C.

◆

Charles I's French queen, Henrietta Maria, was a favorite subject of the court painter Anthony van Dyck and is said to have sat for him up to twenty-five times, though it is recorded that she was not overly concerned with fashion. She appears in this portrait in a silk costume that has often been referred to as a "hunting outfit," although it has been established that special clothes for hunting did not exist in the early seventeenth century. The masculine-influenced aspects of her clothes do, however, suggest an equestrian influence.

A *falling band* or collar, fastened at the neck, falls over the shoulders in a style that was also worn by men.

These sleeves are gathered into puffs, to create volume. In the earlier days of the style, they were sometimes artificially shaped with *bombast*—padding made of anything from wool, horsehair, flax, or rags.[11]

The point of the stomacher is becoming gradually rounder and softer in contrast to the previous example, creating a U shape. On a bodice like this, the stomacher would have been pinned to the front closures.[12]

The ends of this wide neckerchief are looped around and held by a narrow belt at the waist.

Deep square side tabs, closely resembling those on a man's doublet, encircle the waistline.

Layers of pinked linen create decadent cuffs. Two *knots* of salmon pink ribbon add a new color to the bodice. It was popular to use ribbon ties and rosettes as decoration on the clothes of both men and women.

The blue satin of Henrietta Maria's skirt and bodice is lightly slashed in the manner popular throughout the sixteenth century. The technique returned to favor somewhat in the seventeenth century.

Rows of gold braid edge the stomacher, tabs of the bodice and hem of the skirt, and mark the position of seams on the skirt and sleeves.

Skirts were usually closed all round during this period, and there is no train, creating a comparatively simple structure.

Full figure of woman wearing ruffled collar and wide-brimmed hat

1640, Library of Congress, Washington, D.C.

◆

The art of seventeenth-century etcher Wenceslaus Hollar (1607–1677) is incredibly valuable to dress historians because it offers such a broad and detailed view of what men and women wore in the early to middle years of the century. Hollar was interested in dress and felt it was an important medium to document. His skill in depicting different fabrics, trimmings, and accessories makes him a vital resource.

A low neckline is covered with a broad lace kerchief. As the decade continued, these round or square *décolleté* would become progressively lower (and sometimes wider, closer to the edge of the shoulders).

The waistline still sits relatively high, dipping to a point underneath the apron that is worn in this example.

A stiff stomacher fills in the bodice opening, laced from side to side to keep it in place.

Aprons without bibs, such as this one, were worn as part of fashionable dress during the day. When worn for purely decorative reasons, they were often made from either silk or fine linen. In England, aprons were particularly connected with Puritan fashions, although in those cases they were rarely made from anything other than cotton or linen and were never ornamented.[13]

In Holland especially, wide, oval-shaped ruffs were worn by married women for the first half of the decade.

Two rosettes or knots are placed at prominent positions on the bodice. This type of simple ribbon accessory was very popular.

Sleeves on gowns were very full at this date, edged with a wide cuff that finished just past the elbow. A similar effect with even broader cuffs is seen in this 1650 portrait by Frans Hals:

The skirt has deep pleats at the waist and was worn over padded hip rolls to increase volume.

Frans Hals, *Portrait of a Woman*, c.1650, Metropolitan Museum of Art, New York

"Silver tissue dress,"

c.1660, Fashion Museum, Bath

This exquisite silver-thread two-piece English gown is one of the oldest complete dresses to have survived. Despite being small in size, it is nevertheless striking, and the Museum believes the original owner was a girl or fashionable young woman who probably wore this at court and for other formal occasions.

In general, bodice sleeves were now very short but reached their shortest by the 1670s. Cartridge pleats at the back provide their volume. In this example, length is achieved by the exposure of chemise sleeves beneath, which are edged with lace, their fullness achieved through ties at the cuff. [14]

The sleeves of this bodice are *paned* (slit) to allow sections of the chemise to poke through.

The bodice still has tabs, but they are now far smaller and narrower, cut at or below the natural waistline, and hidden underneath the skirt.

Tiny cartridge pleats join the skirt to a waistband, creating the soft volume seen so often on gowns of this period. It would have been worn over a petticoat and a padded roll tied around the waist.

This beautiful fabric is composed of warp silk and weft metallic (silver) thread. The addition of the shimmering silver would have glinted in seventeenth-century candlelight, and its delicacy has given this piece the label of "Silver Tissue Dress."

The wide, oval neckline, which would have sat almost off the shoulders, was designed to encase and support the upper body, accentuating the shoulders and neck.

A square-cut falling lace collar with triangular points frames the neckline. Since Puritans were known to disapprove of starching garments, this approach had become especially common in England in the years leading up to the Restoration.

After a period of gradually lengthening bodices in the 1640s and 1650s, the extremely long and pointed waist reached its apex in the 1660s. Two angled seams run from under the arms and down into the front point.

During this period it was common for gowns to be open at the front, revealing an underskirt, but here is a good example of an exception to the rule. Similar styles can also be seen in these details from *The Card Party*, painted in c.1665 by Dutch artist Caspar Netscher. The images also give a very good impression of the back views of these dresses (note the small train and low, deep-set sleeves to the left). The red gown on the right indicates a similar type of metallic lace, which is also applied to the bodice, sleeves, and skirt.

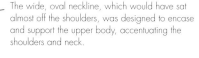

This distinctive silver needlepoint lace is placed along the seams of the garment. Needlepoint is a lace created using only a needle and thread, with many stitches making up the structure and design. Behind the lace, lengths of silver cord create a scrolling pattern. [15]

Caspar Netscher, *The Card Party* (details), c.1665, Metropolitan Museum of Art, New York

La Sage Femme,

c.1678–93, Los Angeles County Museum of Art

◆

The engravings of French artist Nicolas Bonnart (1637–1718) are useful depictions of key styles in seventeenth-century fashion. This example, depicting "the Midwife," shows an ornate gown that is starting to show the very early development of the next major innovation in women's dress: the mantua.

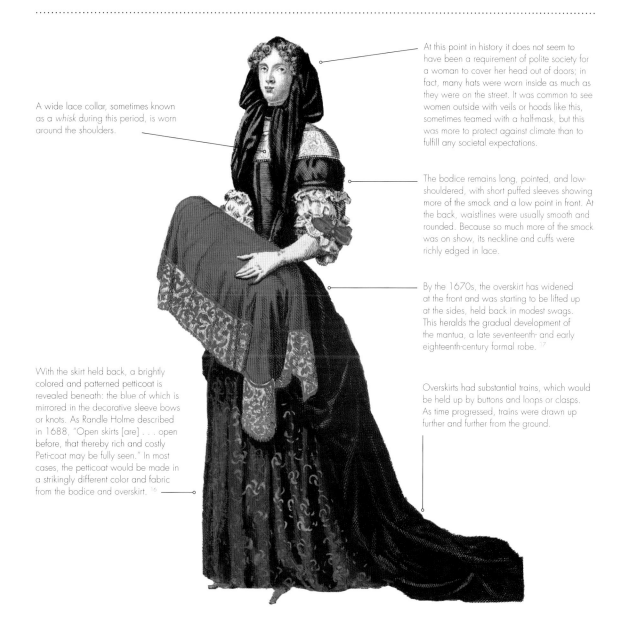

At this point in history it does not seem to have been a requirement of polite society for a woman to cover her head out of doors; in fact, many hats were worn inside as much as they were on the street. It was common to see women outside with veils or hoods like this, sometimes teamed with a half-mask, but this was more to protect against climate than to fulfill any societal expectations.

A wide lace collar, sometimes known as a *whisk* during this period, is worn around the shoulders.

The bodice remains long, pointed, and low-shouldered, with short puffed sleeves showing more of the smock and a low point in front. At the back, waistlines were usually smooth and rounded. Because so much more of the smock was on show, its neckline and cuffs were richly edged in lace.

By the 1670s, the overskirt has widened at the front and was starting to be lifted up at the sides, held back in modest swags. This heralds the gradual development of the mantua, a late seventeenth- and early eighteenth-century formal robe. [17]

With the skirt held back, a brightly colored and patterned petticoat is revealed beneath: the blue of which is mirrored in the decorative sleeve bows or knots. As Randle Holme described in 1688, "Open skirts [are] . . . open before, that thereby rich and costly Peti-coat may be fully seen." In most cases, the petticoat would be made in a strikingly different color and fabric from the bodice and overskirt. [16]

Overskirts had substantial trains, which would be held up by buttons and loops or clasps. As time progressed, trains were drawn up further and further from the ground.

La Belle Plaideuse,

c.1682–86, Los Angeles County Museum of Art

◆

The looser mantua (described in the next analysis) was becoming widely worn in the 1680s. However, because of its comparative informality, Louis XIV strongly objected to the garment and banned it from the French court. Women at court were therefore obliged to retain the stiff bodices that had gone before, and versions of this style remained as the grand habit, worn at court until the French Revolution.[18] This image shows the combination of older-style bodice coupled with some new developments in skirt drapery and arrangement.

The décolletage is very low and sweeping, sitting at the edge of the shoulders and is trimmed with a thin piece of fabric known as a *tucker or pinner.*

Bands of ribbon, tied around the arm and finished with a bow, were often worn on top of or at the base of the smock sleeve. Here, ribbons of the same color (knots) also trim the neck and waistline.

The overskirt is now draped higher, looping tightly over the hips with its draped folds flowing into a long train (a very fashionable feature at this date). This means that the ornate petticoat is visible from both front and sides.

In order to hold the overskirt out and up at the rear, false padding known as a *Cul-de-Paris* ("Rump of Paris") was required and became a primary feature of the mantua by the end of the century.

A decorated vertical slit reveals the edge of a handkerchief, indicating the presence of a separate pocket worn tied around the waist underneath the petticoat.

From the 1680s onward when hairstyles became softer and worn closer to the head, the *cornet* became a popular head covering. Not as high or structured as the fontange of the 1690s and early 1700s, it consisted of a delicate cap with long *lappets* (decorative flaps or folds) framing the face and coming to rest on the shoulders.[19]

The sleeves of the underlying *smock* create frilled cuffs.

The long, elbow-length gloves seen here would have been expected in a formal ensemble worn at court.

Fabric with stripes was popular, often arranged in vertical or horizontal rows (or both, as shown here). The silver coloring of these stripes suggests that this petticoat could have been decorated with metallic thread.[20]

Mantua,

c.1690s, Britain, Metropolitan Museum of Art, New York

◆

Derived from a simple T-shaped piece of fabric, the mantua or "open robe" was fitted by a series of pleats from the shoulder down, pinned to the individual shape of the wearer, and held in place by a belt. The introduction of the mantua heralded a significant new phase in garment production: the appointment of the female dressmaker, or "mantua maker." Working without the training given to male tailors, these women created early mantuas from simpler, T-shaped bases that had their origins in chemises and nightgowns. The garment was named for the origin of the fabric from which it was first made: a silk manufactured in Mantua, Italy.

The flat edging shown at the neckline continues into two thick revers of embroidered fabric, which meet and form the front bodice closure. It seems that, unlike many gowns of the period, this one was worn without a stomacher.

Stripes in four different tones make up the pattern of this woolen fabric, which is ornamented at central points with fronds of silver-gilt thread. This highlighting of the edges of the fabric demonstrates the skillful draping of late seventeenth-century mantuas. A similarly patterned fabric can be seen in this portrait of Queen Mary, also portraying sleeves with turned-back cuffs and a bodice that appears to close without a stomacher.[21]

John Smith after Jan van der Vaart, *Queen Mary*, 1690, National Gallery of Art, Washington, D.C.

The *fontange*, sometimes known as a *frelange*, was introduced at the very end of the century. This short-lived trend came in the form of a tall headdress usually made from lace or gauze and held in place by a wire frame. *The Ladies' Dictionary* of 1694 describes it: "A Font-Ange, is a modish Top-knot first worn by Mademoiselle de Fontange, one of the French King's Misses, from whom it takes its name." This definition arises from a story about Mademoiselle de Fontange who, whilst out riding with the king, was asked to remove her hat. Her hair had been tied up with a ribbon that fell over her forehead, and so enchanted was the king that he asked for her to wear it that way in the evening. This became popular amongst the Court ladies and soon, further afield across Europe.

The sleeve ruffles (longer versions were by this point known as *engageantes*) would probably have been attached separately, rather than belonging to a smock worn underneath. The ones shown here are made from delicate needlepoint guipure lace.

Most mantuas of this date show the skirt looped up high over the hips, revealing a large section of the petticoat beneath. Judging by the sheer amount of fabric that has been covered with gold embroidery, it is clear that this petticoat was made to be seen.[22]

Chapter 3
1710–1790

When reading about eighteenth-century women's fashion, dominant forces always seem to be France and England. This is partly due to a lack of geographical unity, which meant that countries such as Germany and Italy—the latter especially—were far smaller players on the world stage, dominated by regional influences in dress and, in Italy, by that of Austria and Spain. From being of such paramount importance in Renaissance fashion, Italy now seemed to have been pushed to the margins in terms of its sartorial output and influence. Russia, meanwhile, had long been entranced by French modes of dress, and Scandinavian countries also continued a long-standing French alliance.[1] Fashion terminology throughout the eighteenth century is saturated with French words and phrases, while the British stalwartly promoted their own ideas of style and elegance though maintaining both an admiration for—and wary distrust of—the developments of their closest European neighbor. More than once during the century, the two nations were at war, but this only seems to have increased their mutual interest and competition. Bearing this French inclination in mind, eighteenth-century fashion has been chiefly characterized by three principal gown styles; the *robe à la française* or sack-back, the *robe à la polonaise*, and the *robe à l'anglaise*. This chapter will introduce these styles, notable variations, and a brief overview of some key trends and influences that dominated women's wear during the century.

The *sack-back or sacque* was a long gown with deep-set fabric pleats hanging from between the shoulders. It was originally loose at both front and back, with the relatively unstructured pleats left unstitched and free to hang to the floor. By the 1730s–40s, the gown became far more structured with pleats and bodice fitted to the torso. The bodice was made with three-quarter length sleeves, which were typically edged with deep detachable lace cuffs known as *engageantes*. The sack gown was worn over wide *paniers* or side hoops, creating a broad skirt that sat reasonably flat at front and back. By the final years of the century, the style was used mainly for court costume or "full dress": elaborately trimmed and decorated gowns worn at royal presentations or by principal members of the aristocracy and royal family, the skirts of which could be looped up at the sides in a similar fashion to the polonaise. As court dress, the skirts of this style also reached their most extreme width—the ultimate show of wealth and leisure.

The robe *à la* polonaise ("Polish" gown, named for the partition of Poland in 1772 and also, possibly, with some connection to the popular waltz) came in the shape of an open robe with a bodice cut in one piece, the overskirt parted in front to reveal a decorated petticoat.[2] The gown would be looped up in decorative swags using hidden or displayed drawstrings, a practice often referred to as *retroussée* in contemporary French sources. The introduction of this rather elaborate-sounding garment actually heralded a more relaxed and "rustic" way of approaching dress: to depict shepherdesses and "country girls" in a romantic and carefree light, pastoral artists used the style frequently. In fact, the fashion probably originated with

workingwomen—although in greatly simplified forms—because the slightly shorter underskirt, and overskirt practically looped up away from the dusty road, would have made manual work much easier. Sometimes sections of skirt were simply looped through pocket openings in the gown. In its fashionable incarnation, mostly younger, highly fashion-conscious women wore the dress, and its additional frills and trimmings took it a world away from its sensible, practical inception.

The polonaise was in some respects similar in construction to its successor, the robe à l'anglaise: an "English" close-bodied gown, so called because its bodice was sewn close to the shape of the wearer's torso. The anglaise did not become common wear until around 1780, although because of its structural similarities—and because overskirts were often worn in the same draped retroussé arrangement—the name can be interchangeable with that of the polonaise. Until the French Revolution, the impractical sack gown had been indicative of luxury and wealth, and these two styles were worn alongside each other until the robe à l'anglaise and simple *round gown*, an early version of the Regency empire-waisted style, became common wear in the 1790s and signified an homage to the clean lines of Ancient Greece and Rome. Ironically, it was perhaps Marie Antoinette—famously dubbed Madame Déficit by the people, largely because of her spendthrift attitude to fashion—who initially did most to promote the wearing of a simpler, less-elaborate style of dress. The development of her whimsical farm at Versailles, *L'Hameau de la Reine*, in 1783 coincided with the introduction of a *gaulle*: relatively unstructured layers of muslin or cotton that emphasized the contours of the body only by the presence of a simple sash around the waist. This *chemise à la reine* ("dress of the Queen"), as it came to be known, with its strong similarities to women's *chemises* or shifts, came to prominence through Elisabeth Vigee-Lebrun's 1783 portrait of the Queen and can be seen as a clear precursor to the lightweight, figure-hugging, and initially scandalous gowns of the last years of the 1790s.

Until the middle of the eighteenth century, the one-piece gown with petticoat and stomacher (the triangular piece of fabric that usually covered the stays beneath) had been the primary staple of a fashionable woman's wardrobe. Around c.1730–1750, however, this began to change, and the individual items making up the daily wear of a lower-class workingwoman—petticoat and jacket—were also appropriated by the upper classes on less-formal occasions. Initially, the newness of this approach meant that garments such as the caraco jacket were worn more as bed jackets, but over time their practicality and potential made them more regularly seen. The *pet-en-lair* was a shortened sack gown, finishing at around thigh level and worn with a petticoat.[3] The utility of these items as traveling garments became recognized, too, with the development of the *brunswick*—a three-quarter-length hooded garment made for exactly that purpose. Winter examples were often made from a heavier quilted fabric, making them a practical and appealing item of clothing in cold European and American winters.

Silk mantua,

c.1708, England, Metropolitan Museum of Art, New York

—

This robe presents a similar silhouette to that seen at the very end of the previous chapter, and by 1700 the mantua had become accepted as formal wear. As with earlier versions, this example is composed from two uncut lengths of silk that have been draped and pleated to fit the wearer's body.

....

This mantua is an excellent example of so-called bizarre figured silk, here made from a pink damask with green detail. Bizarre silk was distinguished by its large patterns, in this case stylized floral shapes, threaded through with gold or silver highlights. Produced between 1695 and 1720, such fabrics were striking and expensive, elevating a gown from commonplace to lavish and signaling the wearer as a fashionable person aware of the latest Asian-inspired trends. The use of these designs was propagated in Britain by weavers in London's famous Spitalfields district.[4]

Digital image courtesy of the Getty's Open Content Program
This detail from a French engraving shows a lady dressed in a mantua with similar skirt drapery, wide sleeve cuffs, and stomacher edged with soft frills. This image shows the elegant arrangement of bustle and train when the wearer sits.

This ornate stomacher is held in place by multiple pins, making it a complex and time-consuming garment to put on. Mantuas were also often pinned into position at the neck, and held in place by sashes and loose stitching elsewhere (as shown in this example).

These gathered sleeves are relatively loose and full, cut separate from the rest of the bodice, and end in a wide cuff shaped by the addition of several small pleats on the top front side.

The overskirt is looped up into a bustle at the rear and then descends into a long circular train. Tiny holes left in the fabric suggest that the high-sitting bustle would have originally been stitched into place, though records of other examples suggest the use of buttons and loops to secure fabric drapery.[5]

Gathered flounces with scalloped edges, attached with the raw edges facing upward, trim the petticoat. They are made from the same fabric as the rest of the gown.

Pale blue silk mantua gown,

c.1710–20, Victoria and Albert Museum, London

◆

This gown is made from a silk patterned with fruits and leaves, elements of which are picked out in silver and evidence the contemporary fondness for natural emblems in textile design. This gown shows the gradual stylistic changes that would result in the sack-back or robe à la française.

Jean-Antoine Watteau, *Studies of Three Women* (detail), c.1716, digital image of the Getty's Open Content Program

The deep back pleats associated with sack gowns have often been referred to as the Watteau style: so called because artist Jean Antoinne Watteau (1684–1721) particularly admired this aspect of women's dress and depicted it frequently in his work. This sketch from c.1716 shows an early version (similar to the back bodice of this example) with distinctive stitched-down pleats that would later be free flowing.

A square-shaped neckline continues to dominate from the earlier mantua styles and remained popular for much of the century.

By c.1720, the mantua was more complex in its construction and was no longer T-shaped. This example illustrates how the sleeves were now made separately and set into the shoulders.

The plain, straight lengths of fabric that edge the neckline are a common feature of this era, remaining from the time when they flowed into the complex drapery of a formal mantua.

A new hoop was introduced for skirts, for the first time since the farthingales of the sixteenth century. It provided the bell-shaped silhouette that can be seen here.[6]

There was rarely a train on the mantua from around 1710. Instead, the skirt fabric was entirely caught up and stitched into position at the back.

Shot taffeta robe à la française,

c.1725–45, Los Angeles County Museum of Art

◆

By 1720, the mantua with looped-back skirt had started to morph into a comparatively simpler, looser gown known as a robe à volante. This short-lived style had free-hanging back pleats and was not shaped at the waist. What followed on from the volante can be seen here: an early example of the implementation of flattened, so-called Watteau pleating that hung from shoulder to floor but was shaped to the wearer's back.

Following on from the construction of the mantua, back pleats are stitched down to just above waist height. In subsequent examples, they are stitched to the bodice lining only so far as the shoulder blades, and sometimes not at all.

Compared to previous mantua styles, the sleeves are now tighter and narrower.

The separate *winged cuffs* of this gown are characteristic of early eighteenth-century gowns and are transformed in the coming years to become shaped and layered in graduating falls from the elbow.

A modest train emphasizes the flow of the newly popular back pleats. It now derives entirely from the body of the gown and does not feature any draped arrangement.

The stunning and precise hand-embroidered stomacher, decorated with chrysanthemums and leaves, is covered with a crisscrossed arrangement of gold cord, but dresses owned by the wealthy usually displayed far more overt trimming later in the century.

The skirt's silhouette is still rounded, gradually becoming flat at the front and wider at the sides, as the typical sack or robe à la française would come to be. Far greater and more established width can be seen in subsequent examples of this chapter.

The opulence of this gown lies its rich, changeable taffeta. Shot silks were popular throughout the century, and the fabric here is certainly a main feature, making up the petticoat as well as the gown.

Open robe, England or France,
1760–70, Powerhouse Museum, Sydney
◆

An open robe and petticoat in a deep blue satin lisere brocade (a basic weave with the pattern created from floats of warps and/or wefts).[7] The delicate floral patterning contains both natural and artificially inspired motifs, with some of the leaves simulating a dainty net or lace design. The same fabric is used for both petticoat and robe, uniting the ensemble and showing off the workmanship involved.

The cream net panel on the bodice is a later addition that the Museum has since removed. However, given the fashions at the time and the depth of the neckline, it is almost certain the dress would have been worn with some kind of neck covering.[8]

Sleeves for daywear have become longer, tighter, and simpler. They are made from two separate panels of fabric to create a slightly curved fit.

The shape of this very wide, low neckline (which sits high at the back of the bodice) is mirrored in the deep, square waistline.

It is important to note the lack of a stomacher: in this early version of a robe à l'anglaise, the bodice is closed in front and no longer requires intermediary support. However, the rectangular tab closures of the bodice, fastened with hooks and eyes, may have had a decorative as well as functional use. As seen in the dress above from the collection of the Los Angeles County Museum of Art, the trails of a fichu neckerchief could be drawn through the tab openings and displayed.

The skirt is connected to the bodice *en forreau* and would have been worn over hip pads (a bum roll) to add volume to the back. The back sides are arranged into a series of tightly gathered pleats. Inside the garment, the skirt appears to include a series of attached strings from waist to hem. When tied into different positions, these would allow the gown to be worn in the draped polonaise style.

The skirt is composed of six panels, and an underskirt made from the same fabric is visible at the front.

Silk faille robe à la française, England,

c.1765–70, Los Angeles County Museum of Art

◆

Although no less opulent in its fabric and trimming or simple in its construction, this dress does show subtle signs of progress toward a cleaner, less cumbersome shape for women's wear. Its main decorative feature lies in its patterning, with which care has been taken to ensure that the design matches across all sides of the garment.

By this date, decorative robings were usually trimmed with the same fabric as the rest of the gown, but this example features rather more elaborate metallic lace.

By the 1770s, pleats were slimmer and moving closer to the center back of the bodice. It was now rarer to see the first few inches of the pleats sewn down to the lining of the dress, as was often the case with earlier styles.

The body of this gown is made from a *faille* silk (medium weight with a ribbed texture running across the weft) with metallic thread embroidery, comprising flat metallic strips known as *lamella*, metallic thread referred to as *file*, and a silk and metallic thread called frise. [9] This effect, usually applied to the dress by a milliner rather than the mantua maker (dressmaker), corresponds with the popular aesthetic for combining applied decoration with patterned textiles. A truly sumptuous combination, it would have gleamed in the candlelight of an eighteenth-century ballroom or dining room, indicating wealth and status.

The *compere* stomacher on the bodice of this gown features further robings and covered decorative buttons, giving the impression of a front-fastening bodice. Such stomachers took some inspiration from men's wear and could be functional as well as ornamental, especially by the 1770s when stomachers were increasingly less fashionable. [10]

Treble false sleeve engageantes continue around to the front of the sleeve, where they are met with large flat bows made from the same fabric as the rest of the gown.

Smaller hip widths were often achieved through the wearing of more flexible side or *pocket hoops*, consisting of two separate hoops that were connected by tape ties that fastened at the front. When worn, they would create a smaller and rounder version of the prevailing silhouette.

There is no train on this example, matching the move to a simpler and more streamlined aesthetic on other parts of the gown.

Silk robe à l'anglaise with skirt draped à la polonaise,

c.1775, Los Angeles County Museum of Art

◆

The original robe à la polonaise featured a bodice and skirt cut as one (rather in the manner of a man's frock coat), with the skirt looped up into sections at the back. As this draped style grew in popularity, it became integrated in the skirts of other gown types. In this example, the more formal robe à l'anglaise is adapted, illustrating the choice and variety that existed in the last quarter of the century.

....

Triangular embroidered *fichus* such as this one added extra interest to the back view of the ensemble, as well as modestly shielding the exposed section of a wearer's chest in these low-necked gowns.

The placing and shape of the two swags on this skirt were a popular style but not representative of a universal trend, with some sources showing robes with no hanging sections at the front, or with an extra "pouf" at center back.

Quilted petticoats were both practical and attractive additions to a fashionable gown. Their inner layer of padding provided warmth and aided longevity, while the diamond-shaped design visible from the outside is attractive and adds texture.

The ankle-length hem of this petticoat has a practical working-class origin and, in its fashionable incarnation, has the benefit of showing off a pair of dainty floral shoes to their best advantage.

A large bergère hat balances the skirt volume, making the wearer's waist appear even smaller.

The sleeves are slim-fitting and finish just below the elbow. Along with newly popular full-length sleeves, this three-quarter style was still common during the 1770s.

The separately constructed bodice and skirt are joined *en forreau* (as a sheath), a dressmaking technique in which the skirt and a section of the bodice was cut from a continuous length of fabric. This meant that a smooth line was maintained at the center back, creating an attractive deep V as a focal point. The remaining fabric was then gathered in tiny pleats and attached to the bodice, creating the desired fullness enhanced by the wearing of hip pads as a skirt support.

The overskirt is pulled into shape by a series of ties underneath, although ties or buttons placed on the outside of the gown were also popular methods of fastening, as seen on this detail of another gown from the same collection, c.1770–80:

Another option was to draw sections of skirt up through the pocket slits, creating an effect known as *Robe Retroussee dans les Poches* (dress tucked in the pockets). This was exactly what working women would do with their skirts to make manual work easier. For fashionable versions too, such versatility was one of the style's chief advantages.

Silk twill robe à l'anglaise, France,

c.1785, Los Angeles County Museum of Art

◆

The robe à l'anglaise achieved its comparative simplicity through some cunning dressmaking techniques—one of which was to cut the skirt "en forreau" (as a sheath), described in the previous example. The desired fullness was enhanced by the wearing of hip pads as a skirt support.

By the 1780s, it was common practice to include a light neck covering (fichu) for daytime wear. This one completely covers the shoulders, and its ends are tucked into the neckline at the front.

The sleeves on this example are three-quarter length and tight fitting with little ornamentation.

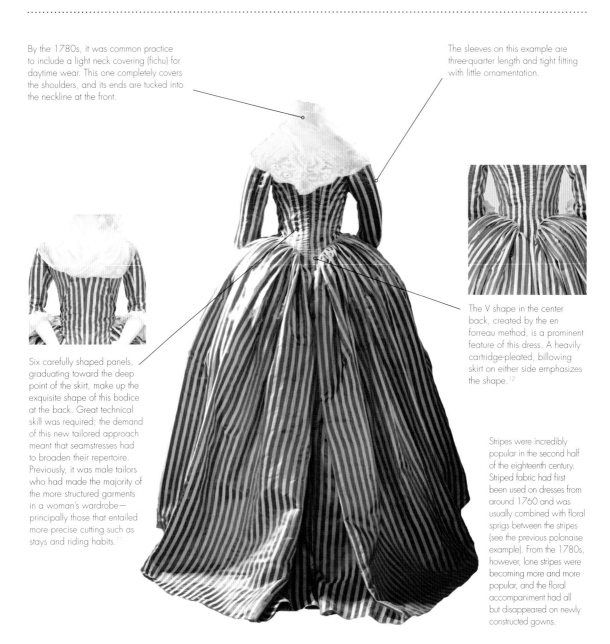

Six carefully shaped panels, graduating toward the deep point of the skirt, make up the exquisite shape of this bodice at the back. Great technical skill was required; the demand of this new tailored approach meant that seamstresses had to broaden their repertoire. Previously, it was male tailors who had made the majority of the more structured garments in a woman's wardrobe—principally those that entailed more precise cutting such as stays and riding habits.[11]

The V shape in the center back, created by the en forreau method, is a prominent feature of this dress. A heavily cartridge-pleated, billowing skirt on either side emphasizes the shape.[12]

Stripes were incredibly popular in the second half of the eighteenth century. Striped fabric had first been used on dresses from around 1760 and was usually combined with floral sprigs between the stripes (see the previous polonaise example). From the 1780s, however, lone stripes were becoming more and more popular, and the floral accompaniment had all but disappeared on newly constructed gowns.

Robe à l'anglaise,

1785–87, French, Metropolitan Museum of Art, New York

◆

It is believed that this dress may have started life c.1760 as a robe à la française or sack dress, converted around 1785 into the anglaise robe seen here. It probably underwent other alterations over the years, but in 1971 conservators brought it back to its full 1780s glory.[13]

....

The bodice features a popular cutaway (so-called zone) bodice design, similar in style to a fashionable gentleman's coat of the period. Instead of coming together with pins or buttons down the front of the torso, the zone bodice fastened at the top only and then sloped away, eradicating the bodice front and leaving a wide-open space to be filled with a waistcoat or false panel. The basic shape as described is shown in this portrait by Gainsborough:

Thomas Gainsborough, Anne, Countess of Chesterfield, c.1777–78, digital image courtesy of the Getty's Open Content Program

This *fichu* is extended and wrapped around the upper torso, its presence heightened by the addition of ruffles. The accessory could be worn in a variety of ways, and this arrangement was seen fairly frequently between c.1780 and 1800.

Simple three-quarter-length sleeves with wide plain cuffs, made of the same fabric, highlight the comparative plainness and simplicity of this style.

These self-fabric skirt ruffles hark back to earlier dress ornamentation, being seen commonly on robes à la française and polonaise throughout the century and, even earlier, on mantua gowns of the 1680s onward. Their pinked edges also reiterate a technique that had been in fashion for many years.

Underneath the bodice, a tabbed false waistcoat gives a masculine feel to the robe.

A slightly shorter skirt at the front allows for the view of dainty heeled shoes, which at this time often featured a buckle or rosette detail on the toe. The overskirt then dips down at the back to create a smooth, flowing line without a cumbersome train.

Silk and satin redingote,

c.1790, Los Angeles County Museum of Art

◆

Redingotes took their inspiration from both riding habits and men's greatcoats, with their wide cape collar and front button fastening. For this reason, they were also known as greatcoat dresses and were popular outdoors wear.[14] Redingotes continued to evolve into the nineteenth century, often incorporating military influences such as epaulettes on the shoulders and rows of braid across the front of the bodice.

....

Double-layered lapels forming a *cape collar* extend over the shoulders and into a deep triangular point at the back, also recalling the common shape of fichus worn throughout the century.[15]

The back is cut en forreau, using the method described earlier in the chapter.

These self-covered buttons on the center back of the skirt are reminiscent of those used on men's coats, placed at waist level just above the skirts of the coat.

Starched neckerchiefs known as *buffons* or *buffonts* were worn to fill in the neckline of redingotes and other low-necked styles of the 1780s and 1790s. They could reach exaggerated sizes and created a *pigeon breast* effect.[16]

Close-fitting sleeves finish just below the elbow.

The open robe shows a simple petticoat matching the substantial buffon and simple cuffs, with the skirt cut back to allow a fuller view of the deep waistline.

Being a more practical, outdoors garment, the redingote did not have a train.

Cotton dress,

c.1790s, Fashion Museum, Bath

◆

This gown is an especially interesting transitional garment, retaining the low pointed waistline of the 1770s and 1780s but introducing a skirt that is placed almost at an empire line position at the back and sides. It presents an elegant amalgam of old and new, and it is likely that this dress may be an existing 1770s or 1780s piece, restyled to fit the new shape.

Very slight pleating at the shoulder gives these sleeves a little puff, but this feature disappeared as the end of the century, creating a few years of very straight, flat sleeves for women.

The skirt has been removed from its original position at the edges of the bodice and reattached just under the bustline.

This bodice features an extremely low neckline and wide décolletage, and would almost certainly have been worn with a *neckerchief*, the ends tucked into the front of the bodice.

This bodice is sewn or pinned closed at center front.

The long, pointed waist, reminiscent of 1770s and 1780s styles, remains in conjunction with the newly placed empire line at back and sides. This type of bodice would still need to be worn with either heavily boned and conical stays (that had dictated the silhouette of the torso for so long) or the new *half stays* or *short stays*, a transitional style that encased and lifted the bust. These only reached to around the length of the diaphragm, since the fashionable waist was now rising so far from its natural position. These stays would have shoulder straps and, sometimes, tabs extending from the waist in the manner of earlier, longer styles.

In common with the previous redingote, this gown's petticoat is clean and simple, not detracting from the pattern of the dress itself.

A trailing floral design is achieved by applying the *copper plate technique* onto cotton. Developed around 1750, this was more precise than roller or block printing because of the detail that a copper plate was able to pick up. Designs were usually made by printing color against a neutral background, as seen on this dress. The process became very popular during the early nineteenth century.[17]

A low-necked bodice with pointed waist, similar to the original look and feel of this altered gown (England, 1780–90, Los Angeles County Museum of Art)

Silk dress,

c.1785–90, Los Angeles County Museum of Art

◆

Already popular in women's wear during the second half of the eighteenth century, stripes are given a new dimension here. The zebra stripe on this silk dress illustrates the keen interest in exoticism that was enhanced by Napoleon's foreign travels. But the trend did not start with revolutionary fervor: when King Louis procured a zebra in the 1780s, interpretations of the animal's unusual patterning started to appear fairly widely on fashionable garments such as this.[18]

The chemise frills visible at the gown's neckline add a touch of historicism, recalling sixteenth- and seventeenth-century styles as well as trimmings from dress of France's Ancien Régime.

Because of their soft and round silhouette, dresses like this were known as *round gowns*. The bodice and petticoat were cut as one, marking the end of separate robe, petticoat, and stomacher.[19] Front fastening enabled a smooth, uninterrupted back and placed emphasis on the very high waist. The neckline on this example is gathered on a drawstring, heightening focus on the newly fashionable empire line.

Despite the growing trend for simplicity and emulation of pure white Grecian statues, lavishness in decoration could still be seen. Surviving garments show us that the eighteenth-century fondness for gold and silver had not entirely disappeared among the wealthy. The appearance of luxurious gilt-threaded silk evening gowns such as this one, their fabric imported directly from India, married the extravagance of eighteenth-century cloth-of-gold with the flowing delicacy of the empire line.

The busy passementerie on the skirt hem is finished with gold and silver sequins and sections of clear linen net, creating an intriguing and whimsical trompe-l'œil effect.

The skirt is pleated at both front and back, creating a fullness that is enhanced by the wearing of a small pad around the waist under the dress. The significant volume that this created at the back of the dress was not seen again on fashionable high-waisted gowns after c.1800.

Straight sleeves finishing just above the elbow were extremely common on round gown styles. In this example, the arm is entirely covered by the addition of long gloves that finish where the sleeve cuffs start.

Scalloped edging had been popular on the layered sleeves of robes à la française in particular. Here, a similar effect is used to add interest to the tiny train.

Day dress (round gown),

c.1785–90, (France or England), Los Angeles County Museum of Art

◆

This dress is shown with the common decorative touch of a fichu, an embroidered shawl or kerchief. In the 1790s it was often arranged to produce the chesty "pouter pigeon" effect that would resurface in the early twentieth century. The dress is also worn with a long decorative apron and a wide red sash, showing off the new high waist. However, it still displays eighteenth-century richness in its opulent silk, providing some familiarity alongside a radical new silhouette.

Under the fichu, the gown's round neckline is gathered on a drawstring, allowing the wearer to adjust the shape and fit.

The skirt is box-pleated at the back, with fullness added through the use of a small pad worn under the dress at the waistline.

The floral and striped duck-egg blue brocade of this example is an older fabric, dating to c.1770. It is probable the dress was adapted from an earlier robe à l'anglaise.

The *fichu* is worn wrapped around the body, crossed over in front to form a prominent feature of the dress.

The gown's sleeves are slit at the back from just under the elbow to the cuff. There, the sides are joined at the wrist by a single button, allowing a small flash of ruffled muslin to be seen beneath. The front of the sleeve is then turned up into a modest cuff.

This full-length decorative muslin apron has no practical use and therefore no bib, tying around the waist under the ties of the fichu. The whitework embroidery on the front features a common symbol of love: a heart motif topped with a crown, flanked by putti. The embroidered lettering "IXXR" is a monogram for the Virgin Mary.

Each side of the apron is edged with a thin trim of bobbin lace.

Scrolling botanic motifs provide another decorative angle for this apron, depicting potted plants, bunches of grapes, and wildflowers.

Chapter 4
1790–1837

The end of the eighteenth century brought about a dramatic change in women's dress—a new, simplified, "natural" silhouette that emerged partly from the political upheaval of the French Revolution. It also had its origins in the chemise dress promoted by Marie Antoinette and other members of the aristocracy in Europe (including England's Georgiana, Duchess of Devonshire). "Naturalness" in this context meant the use of lightweight, easy-to-launder (and therefore hygienic) materials such as muslin, cotton, poplin, batiste, and linen. Meanwhile, the drape and columnar structure of dresses took its inspiration from classical Greece and Rome and the pure white statues of antiquity. Simple hairdressing, with delicate curls framing the face, complemented the look, marking a significant departure from the powdered wigs and painted cheeks of eighteenth-century high society.

In the earliest and most notorious depictions, daring ex-aristocratic French women (known as *Les Merveilleuses* alongside their male counterparts, *Les Incroyables*) were seen in Paris wearing lightweight shifts that clung to every part of their figure and were not supported by restrictive undergarments. The presence of brightly colored stockings further heightened the opaqueness of the fabric and left very little to the imagination. It was rumored that women even dampened their dresses to make the fabric cling more closely, freely displaying their breasts through the sheer fabric and low necklines, but this more extreme mode was short-lived and by no means universal.

With the ascension of Napoleon as Emperor of France in 1804, the phrase "empire-line" developed to coincide with his Directory and so-called First Empire. His frequent travels abroad, especially to Egypt, promoted an interest in foreign textiles and "orientalist" design throughout Europe (and greatly increased the import of fabrics from overseas). His wife Joséphine, too, along with celebrated couturier (or *marchand de modes*) Louis-Hippolyte LeRoy, had a considerable influence on fashion and led the way in elegance as Paris once again became an important sartorial center. [1] The cylindrical Neoclassical gown with its short bodice, small puffed or straight sleeves and long, straight skirt was by now firmly established and styles remaining from the Ancien Régime could be seen in court dress alone: by 1797, hoopskirts were still worn for presentations and other grand occasions only. Even then, the dresses worn over hoops often sported the high waistlines of the new style, making for an odd mix of influences.

The empire-line dress rapidly became very fashionable across Europe and particularly in England, where greater simplicity in dress had been encouraged for some time. While stark white and flimsy was initially the height of fashion, throughout most of the Western world (including America and Australia, which generally followed European trends) the empire-line dress was not static, evolving to become more solid first with the application of printed fabrics, and then with the increasing use of heavier materials in darker colors. Slowly, women were reverting to elements of dress that had been at the core of eighteenth-century fashions:

heavy silk and brocade fabrics, more restrictive corsetry, and greater ornamentation than had been seen in the last twenty years— an antithesis to the slim-line simplicity of Neoclassical designs. This started to become especially prevalent around 1814–15 and the event of Napoleon's exile, but for quite some time beforehand the revolutionary stirrings that had initiated and maintained the empire line had lost their place at the forefront of fashion. In a time of greater political and social security, fashion was turning to greater opulence and, as one publication put it in 1826, "to look like an hour glass, narrow in the middle [and] expanding towards each end." [2] Predictably, when the natural waist returned as a prime feature of "hourglass" fashionable dress, so did a desire to show it off to its best advantage. This meant tighter corsetry and layers of petticoats, so that the comparative freedom of the empire-line dress was quickly receding. The current silhouette was achieved first through the use of a new type of corset, longer in the body and stiffened with baleen (whalebone), with the additional support of a steel busk down the center. In order to enhance this feature, skirt and shoulder width grew exponentially into the 1830s, and large bonnets— with tall and extravagant hairstyles beneath—effectively drew more attention to the middle of the body. In this way, significant artifice was needed to align dress to the burgeoning Romantic movement (c.1815–40) and its emphasis on the dreamy, emotional, and "sublime" in contrast to the stark rationality of the Enlightenment.

Headwear was relatively varied during this era. Small bonnets and simple "jockey" caps were first introduced c.1800 and worn almost universally by women of all ages, but hats also enjoyed some popularity— particularly in the latter half of the 1810s. The aforementioned Eastern influence meant that turbans were in fashion for a time, as can be seen in fashion plates, and worn as part of an evening ensemble. Their popularity in England was no doubt also heightened by the fondness shown to the style by Adelaide of Saxe-Meiningen, wife and Queen Consort to William IV (1818–49).

This fashion plate from 1837 shows a selection of the headdresses in vogue during the mid-late 1830s. The lavender, yellow, and green bonnets show the very large-brimmed styles that were especially popular in the 1830s, reaching the point where they completely shielded a wearer's face from view if she was standing in profile. This shape had achieved its apex via the introduction earlier in the period of the poke bonnet earlier, the crown of which gradually rose higher to accommodate fashionably tall hairstyles. These examples also show what was known as a *bavolet* or "curtain": a piece of fabric attached to the back of the bonnet, covering the neck. [3] This remained popular until the mid 1860s when the *fanchon* style was introduced.

This period, full of sheer fabrics and dainty accessories, gave way in the 1830s to the silken armor that clothed women in the early Victorian era. The worldview was changing once again after the paradigm shift of the French Revolution, and the following decade was a more rigid and conservative period in dress history.

Cotton gown,

1797–1805, Victoria and Albert Museum, London

◆

This British-made gown is an excellent (and rare) surviving example of the simple Neoclassical styles that emerged in the 1790s. All surface decoration on this gown comes from "self-made" pleating and draping. In keeping with the English fondness for simplicity, there is no embroidery, beading, or lace in sight. This means that the dress achieves a certain wearability and utility, combined with classic elegance.

The deep, rounded neckline would be filled in with a fichu during the day, illustrative of the modest and practical approach of this style in England. At the back, the neckline sits relatively high on the neck.

Looped-up sleeves were a common decorative touch. In this example, the sleeves have a double layer, with an oversleeve looped up and held by a button, exposing a plain sleeve fastened just under the elbow with a drawstring.

The skirt is made with an *apron front*; slit at each side, joined to the *bib-fronted* bodice, and brought up to the waist to be tied with tapes. This complex-sounding arrangement made for a delightfully simple and fresh appearance, necessitating no break in the bodice for a button or pin fastening.

A very shallow train, in keeping with ideals of simplicity and hygiene, can be seen at the rear of the dress. It stems from a tightly gathered section of fabric at the center back.

The *bib* or *fall* (also known as *drop*) *front* fastening ensures a clean, uninterrupted bodice from whatever angle the dress is viewed. The front of the bodice is attached to the skirt; the sides are tied and buttoned into place as shown. The new high waist is indicated by the presence of a simple cream waistband made from linen tape.

The waistline at the back is slightly lower and curved, and beneath it the skirt is tightly gathered at center back. A small bustle pad would have been worn under this rear gathering around the waist to provide some fullness.

Gilbert Stuart, *Mary Barry*, c.1803–05, National Gallery of Art, Washington, D.C.

This portrait, contemporaneous with the cotton gown, shows a dress with some similar features: short oversleeves are caught up above the elbow, and a low round neckline creates an almost identical décolletage.

Muslin dress,

c.1800–05 (probably India), Los Angeles County Museum of Art

◆

Two key influences dominate this dress. First, the impact of classical Greece and Rome is seen in the effect and shape of the garment (for example, the Greek himation—a large draped rectangle of fabric—and Roman palla—a draped mantle fastened with brooches), and, second, that of India is reflected in the choice of fabric.

....

The waistline has risen since the previous example, and the bust is pushed significantly up and out. The new style of corset, designed to raise the bust and support the top half of the body, helps to achieve this prominence.

Throughout the period, Indian "muslins" were a vital part of the wardrobe of any woman with even moderate pretensions to fashion. Jane Austen's *Northanger Abbey* (1818) pokes fun at the immeasurable importance placed on the quality of muslins: "It would be mortifying to the feelings of many ladies, could they be made to understand how little the heart of man is affected by what is costly or new in their attire; how little it is biased by the texture of their muslin." [4] The fabric's fragility seems to have been one of its chief attractions; a sign of its delicacy and suitability only for those who lived a lifestyle that would allow for careful and considered elegance as well as frequent laundering.

Small beaded *reticule* purses such as this were popular accessories. They came in a wide variety of shapes and designs.

The elaborate paisley shawl is also likely to have hailed from India, made for Western export.

The popularity of woven-in designs meant that muslins in darker and more practical colors could also be obtained, and it was possible to add lighter and gentler patterns by embroidering directly onto the fabric: polka dots, for example, were a simple and understated way of doing this. But white remained popular for quite some time, and *whitework* embroidery is seen here throughout the skirt. We can see tiny, exquisite leaves and fronds, delicately worked by hand.

The main decoration on the bodice front is composed of a section of fine embroidered net. The use of net as an overlay, often for entire dresses, continued to be popular for the next twenty years.

Sleeves in these early styles were comparatively simple in gowns such as this one, straight-cut and sitting above the elbow. The bodice width is very narrow at the back, and sleeves were usually very deep-set, the edges of the armholes nearly touching at the center back of the bodice.

A *drop-fronted* bodice leaves the back of the gown fluid and smooth and provides a panel for decoration.

This *Portrait of a Young Woman in White* by the circle of Jacques-Louis David (1798, National Gallery of Art, Washington, D.C.) as well as his famous *Madame Récamier*, are good examples of this type of early empire-line style.

Until around 1805–06, trains on daywear as well as evening dress were fashionable. During the very early years of the century, a small bustle pad was sometimes worn under the skirt at the waistline, to hold out the pleats leading down into the train and enhance the soft, flowing line. [5]

Silk twill evening dress,

1810, McCord Museum, Montreal

◆

This elegant evening dress epitomizes the period between the stark whiteness of early
Regency gowns and the frills and flounces that followed at the end of the 1810s. Its color illustrates
the popular "jonquil" shade, named after the daffodil (Narcissus jonquilla) and especially popular
in the first half of the period.

The low, square neckline is typical in gowns of this era, alongside the popularity of rounded and crossover designs. Its shape is largely dictated by the use of a *drop-front* fastening. At both front and back, the bodice is gathered onto draw-tapes to allow a closer fit.

The sleeves' fullness is achieved through gathers located at the back, lending a continual smoothness to the front view.

Here, the high waist still emphasizes a pushed-up bust, although its positioning is not quite as extreme as in earlier styles. A simple cream band, met at center back with a small bow, accentuates the waistline and brings together the decorative color scheme.

Handmade bobbin lace inserts create a soft, wavy design across the front of the bodice and over the sleeves.

Delicate chenille embroidered flower motifs are featured on the bodice front and sleeves. A single pearl sits in the center of each flower, and a solid row of pearls at the cuff complement the flowers. [7]

The front of the skirt is composed from a rectangular panel of fabric, with side seams set to the back: their placement creates the appearance of a curving line at each side. This gored technique illustrates a gradual move toward increasing width, which was far more prominent from c.1813 onward. [6]

As with most dresses at this time, there is no train.

The skirt is slightly flared, an effect heightened by its stiff silk and by the tight gathering of fabric at the back of the skirt.

A slim band of bobbin lace at the hem also features the pearl detail seen elsewhere on the gown.

Spencer jacket and petticoat,

1815, Los Angeles County Museum of Art

◆

This 1815 petticoat and spencer ensemble is already starting to portray the frills and flounces of the 1820s and early 1830s, while displaying significant historical influences. In addition, despite conflict during the Napoleonic wars, French admiration for relative English simplicity in dress (sometimes referred to as "Anglomania"), meant that many styles—such as this one—also included military influences.

The wife of Napoleon, Joséphine Bonapart, has been credited with the reintroduction of certain historical elements of dress such as the Elizabethan ruff, and its early nineteenth-century interpretation can be seen in this example. The ruff would have been made as part of a *chemisette* or "habit shirt" (originally worn as part of a riding habit). [8] This was tied around the upper body with tapes, often used to cover the front of very low-necked gowns or bodiced petticoats.

Another historical influence—the Italian Renaissance—is present in the elaborate puffed sleeves, which end in a banded cuff with self-covered button.

This skirt is a *petticoat*, which at the time did not necessarily mean an undergarment, but any separate skirt worn with another item of clothing such as a jacket or gown. Here, it attaches to the inner waistband of the spencer with hooks and eyes.

The military-inspired touches on this spencer are evident in the double rows of buttons and decorative revers. They illustrate a trend that was ongoing through the legacy of the Napoleonic Wars.

Renaissance inspiration: Agnolo Bronzino, *A Young Woman and her Little Boy*, c.1540, National Gallery of Art, Washington, D.C.

"Walking Dress," 1815, France, from *La Belle Assemblée* (Author's collection)

Spencers and pelisses were very popular, cloaks and capes as an alternative could be seen throughout the period and especially in colder climates. Also influenced initially by military versions, a feminine interpretation can be seen in the mantle: a shorter cape that fastened at the neck, sometimes featuring integrated sleeves and a high collar. In this print the small stand-up collar is another military resonance, as are the tassels and pompoms. These probably stemmed from a long-standing interest in the attractive dress uniforms of the Hussars, the former cavalry of Hungary. [9]

Evening dress,

c.1815, McCord Museum, Montreal

—◆—

This evening dress illustrates the move away from stark simplicity and into silken, trimmed, and beribboned decadence. Although a relatively early example of such excess, this gown is still a clear indicator of what was to come. It would have been worn with long kid or satin gloves and accessorized with necklace and fan.

The intricate cutout silk detailing, repeated on sleeves, bodice, and hem, is a significant move beyond the simple and understated dresses of the previous ten years.

Throughout the era, sashes could sometimes be seen on evening dress, tied in a bow at the back. Here, the waistband features a solitary bow that focuses the eye on both the surface detail of the bodice and the gathering of skirt to waist. Its thickness is repeated in the padded satin cuff and hem detail.

This gown's scoop neckline sits at the edge of the shoulders, and the décolletage at the front echoes the low, sweeping, sloping shape seen at the back.

Known as *languettes* (meaning "tongue-shaped") these sections of silk adorn the center front and back of the bodice, joining the bustline at either side.[10] Their placement at shoulder and cuff emphasize the puffs of sheer organza, reminiscent of Renaissance and Elizabethan sleeve design.

With another nod to the historical, the dress is faux laced at the back with a champagne-colored length of cord. This lacing detail is simulated at the front in between a corresponding silk cutout design.

This sheer overskirt epitomizes the dreaminess of Romanticism and is embroidered with a delicate, glittering leaf design that is echoed on the sleeves. With the advent of the bobbin-net machine in 1808, trimmings or whole garments of gauze and other types of net were more accessible.[11] Tulle and crepe also became popular overlays for dresses made from satin, velvet, silk, and sarsenet.

The flat-folded satin and heavy ribbon border, which also stiffens and holds out the skirt, juxtaposes with the soft gauze overlay. The combination of these two effects highlights the oncoming transitional period between Directoire and Victoriana.

The lightly padded *rouleau* hemline is particularly resonant of developing styles that were to reach their peak in the 1820s.

Taffeta day dress,

1823–25, McCord Museum, Montreal

◆

This dress adds to the abundance of trimmings seen on the previous example and demonstrates a widening silhouette at both ends of the body. While displaying several on-trend features of the early to mid 1820s, it also references historic influences, particularly in the sleeve detail and the positioning of the waist.

The neckline is broad and square, sitting on the very edge of the shoulders and controlled and fastened with tape ties.

Puffed sleeves with satin *languettes* continue the historical inspiration seen on other garments throughout this chapter but also foretell the shape that will broaden and lengthen up to and during the 1830s. Large, highly ornate oversleeves like this were known as *mancherons* until the word *epaulette* replaced it later in the century.[12]

Decoration on the back of the dress is lighter and rather more feminine, consisting of a satin rosette at center back and flowing satin streamers.

Unlike earlier empire-line styles, here the slightly gored skirt is gathered at all sides rather than just at the back, maintaining a consistent fullness that shows the gown's surface ornamentation to best effect.

This ornate day dress is a fine example of so-called *hem sculpture*: puffed and padded sections of fabric (*languettes*) on the skirt to create a solid, architectural feel. In earlier years, this amount of embellishment would have been unseen on daywear, but the more defined bell-shape of this era lent itself well to excess in ornamentation, providing more fabric on which to display it.

The band of padded taffeta at the very bottom of the hem, a type of trimming known as *rouleau*, is another common finish of this period, adding weight to the garment and helping to accentuate and support the tongue-shaped embellishments above.

Satin bands, arranged to form the shape of a bow across the bust, enhance the widening silhouette. They are also used on the sleeves to emphasize long, flared cuffs.

Here is a slightly lower waistline, but it is not as low as most fashionable dresses of the era. It is possible that this was an altered dress or an intentional nod to nostalgia. Either way, its positioning is shown by use of a wide taffeta belt.[13]

John Bell, *Fashion Plate (Carriage Visiting Costume)*, England, 1820, Los Angeles County Museum of Art
This *pelisse* (outer garment) from 1820 shows similarly shaped languettes, decorating not only the hem but all the way up the front of the coat.

Taffeta day dress,

1825, Powerhouse Museum, Sydney

◆

The light jade color of this day dress makes the vibrancy of its deep pink embellishments all the more striking. These trimmings show a highly fashionable use of dominant ornamentation, but also look back to history, recalling triangular points of the seventeenth century—aptly named Van Dyck or Vandyke points/trimming.

....

In the early years of the nineteenth century, an interest in archaeology meant that much jewelry design—such as this gold necklace with relief patterns and small stones—was heavily inspired by ancient and Renaissance examples.[14]

The waist is now almost in its natural position and also dips down slightly lower at the back, where the dress fastens with fabric hooks and metal eyes. Many dresses of this period would also feature inner tape ties to hold the dress close to the body.[15] The waistline is subtly emphasized by the presence of a thick band in the same pale fabric as the rest of the garment body. A wide waistband or belt, a common feature at this time, was also designed to emphasize the smaller waist that was achievable through new corset styles and tighter lacing.

The padded hem sculpture of this dress, in a vibrant pink silk, picks up on the cuff detail but adds its own very definite dimension. The Vandyke point overlays are edged with three further *rouleau* in addition to the slightly wider one that edges the hem.

A high, wide circular neckline leads into broad shoulders. Across both sides, fabric is gathered and held by matching pink binding.

Demi gigot sleeves taper to cuffs fitting closely at the wrist. They show the shape and proportions that were becoming fashionable from the mid 1820s onward.

Vandyke triangular points on the cuffs and hem give a seventeenth-century feel to the dress. This style of trimming was very popular and the points could also be seen on lace, known as *frize* trimming (*cheveux de frize* in the previous century).[16]

The skirt is closely gathered at the back of the dress, creating fullness but not leading into a train.

Summer dress,

1830, Los Angeles County Museum of Art

◆

This summer dress displays some typical fashionable features of the 1830s, in particular the oversized sleeves, widening skirt, and natural waistline. The plainness of its fabric allows these characteristics to be clearly seen, and white was a popular choice throughout the decade, particularly for morning and evening dresses.

The puffed, balloon-shaped sleeve of the mid seventeenth century returned with a vengeance, reaching extreme proportions as early as 1830–31. In order to maintain the shape and hold the sleeve up and out, fashionable women were obliged to add a pair of *sleeve supports*, or *plumpers*—also known as *puffs*. [17] These would be tied to the corset straps and could be manipulated into smaller or larger sizes depending on the cut and occasion of the dress. As early as the 1820s, some dressmakers were already starting to incorporate a similar feature into the sleeves of gowns themselves—ball and evening dresses, in particular, could sometimes include an inner series of tapes and ties that, when adjusted, would alter the sleeve's size and position. The image below is a good example of the underwear that would have been worn.

The neckline is rounded and modest, exposing a suitable amount of neck for daywear. Necklines on evening ensembles generally sat much lower, revealing a good deal of shoulder.

As with the previous 1825 example, fabric on the shoulders is gathered and held by—this time—plain pieces of binding.

The emphasis here is on the large balloon-shaped *gigot* sleeves, which successfully attain the sartorial wish of having an equal shoulder width to that of the hemline.

Subtle gathering of fabric over the bust creates an attractive fan shape that draws the viewer's eye to a small waist.

Despite the prevalence of low, tiny waists in fashion plates of the era, in actual fact many women continued to wear gowns with higher waists for a considerable time to come. Fashions changed much more slowly than might be imagined from looking "high-fashion" sources, which only showed the latest new ideals from Paris. These ideas were then adapted by local and home dressmakers.

Woman's corset, petticoat, and sleeve plumpers, c.1830–40, Los Angeles County Museum of Art

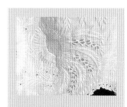

Skirt detail showing broderie anglaise (cutwork embroidery) on cotton. 1830, Los Angeles County Museum of Art.

Silk satin wedding dress,

1834, Powerhouse Museum, Sydney

This wedding dress epitomizes the historic lure of Romanticism, but its light and dainty appearance was achieved by an increasing number of undergarments. These included, in this instance, a small bustle pad worn to add a swell to the skirt.

Regency fondness for shawls continued; this example shows a distinctive geometric design at the edges.

There are strong historical elements to this wedding gown, seen primarily in the bows and *lozenge* cutout shapes on the bodice detailing.[18] These are reminiscent of eighteenth-century stomachers and the common practice of adding down the front a "ladder" of bows known as eschelles:

A broad bateau neckline accentuates the effect of the pelerine and descending sleeve puffs, here slipping gracefully off the shoulder.

Sleeves are partitioned into three sections, with tight-fitting lower and upper shoulder sections (the latter with cartridge pleating) framing the typical balloon shape of 1830s gigot sleeves in the center.

The waistline now sits closer to its natural position and, on many styles, is starting to form a sharp point in front. This would become very prominent during the 1840s.[19]

Jacques Wilbaut, *Presumed Portrait of the Duc de Choiseul and Two Companions* (detail), c.1775, digital image courtesy of the Getty's Opera Content Program

This style features a wider and stiffer hem than previous examples, creating a flare and equaling the width of the shoulders.

Ballet may have had an effect on women's dress in the early 1830s. The Italian dancer Marie Taglioni (1804–84) probably played a role in popularizing shorter skirts that showed off pointe work. Her role in "La Sylphide" showed Taglioni wearing a soft, billowing, mid-calf length skirt that made her ballet shoes impossible to miss.[19] Such costumes were similar in style to most gowns of the era, the only notable differences being the dance skirt's even shorter length and slight transparency.

Silk day dress and cape,

c.1830–40, Powerhouse Museum, Sydney

◆

Made and worn in the early colonial days of Australia (c.1835–37), this dress and cape show a strong connection with fashionable European and American styles. The cape, or *pelerine*, maintains the broad line of the shoulders and creates a smooth, rounded silhouette.

It conforms to a description given in the popular fashion paper *La Belle Assemblee*, 1831: "The dress is to be worn with a large pelerine of the same material. It forms a fichu in front, and the ends hang low; it is pointed behind, and cut in a deep point on each shoulder. A silk trimming . . . edges the pelerine."[20] Pelerines made in the same fabric as the dress, as this one is, were especially popular for a time.

The waistline is dropping and fitting more snugly to the figure. This was achieved partly through the new implementation of boning to the bodice, first in the front and, later, at the side seams as well.[21] The wide shoulders and flared hem also emphasize this svelteness.

Rectangular panels make up the simple skirt shape of this period.

The developing bell shape of skirts during this period is maintained here by the addition of padding to the hem, which adds weight and structure. In addition to the skirt's expanding width, it is also becoming longer, now reaching to below the ankle.

Under the cape, the bodice features dropped shoulders and a wide, shallow neckline. The bodice front—just visible here beneath the cape—features cartridge pleating above the waistline and below the neckline, mirroring that on the sleeves.[22]

These wide gigot sleeves have reached the proportions typical of this era. Given their size and the difficulty in making outerwear to accommodate them, capes were a popular alternative.

Tight cartridge pleats at the shoulders and cuffs add to the fullness of the sleeves.

The skirt is pleated to the waistband all the way around, adding fullness and flare.

Chapter 5
1837–1869

Gowns of the 1840s were, in many respects, far more cumbersome than those that went before and after. Although the long, fluid style was undeniably less fussy than the puffs and frills of the 1820s and 1830s, it was far more restrictive to wear. Where the 1830s featured ankle-length skirts and fuller waistlines, clothing of the 1840s introduced a transitional phase of heavy skirts and long, tight-laced bodices, which fell away at the advent of the higher waist and comparatively freer crinoline of the 1850s and 1860s. As Gwen Raverat, Charles Darwin's granddaughter, recalled in her memoir *Period Piece:*

> *Once I asked Aunt Etty what it had been like to wear a crinoline. "Oh, it was delightful," she said. "I've never been so comfortable since they went out. It kept your petticoats away from your legs, and made walking so light and easy."* [1]

From the late 1830s onward, skirts were given their shape through the wearing of numerous petticoats, and these were stiffened by various means: horsehair, cane, or padding—the latter usually in the form of a quilted petticoat. Toward the end of the decade, flounces were introduced to enhance the effect. The full, pleated skirt that this produced was paired with a long bodice, tightly laced to create as small a waist as possible. The edge of the shoulder extended onto the upper arm, and the popular *fan front bodice* design led an observer's eye down the front of the torso until the slim V of the conical waistline was reached. The skirt, gently flaring to the hem in a bell shape, complemented the shoulder line to draw attention to the waist. In a more subtle way, this shape carried on but gently modified the extreme dimensions of the 1830s silhouette. As a result, and taking into account a distinct lack of adornment (particularly on daywear), women's clothing of the 1840s can seem somewhat static. However, the practical *Workwoman's Guide*, first published in London in 1838, describes the variation available: "Gowns are high, low, three-quartered, plain, or full, open before or behind."[2] They could be made up with a "full French high body," "Grecian low body," or "plain low body," among others. These should be worn "with attention to the minutiae of dress [which] adds much to a ladylike appearance" because "an endeavour to please by an agreeable exterior . . . does not necessarily involve a disposition to vanity and frivolity." In the late 1830s and early 1840s, an "agreeable exterior" could mean, according to the *Workwoman's Guide*, "bands or rouleaux of satin, silk, gauze . . . puffings, frillings, or flounces . . . pipings, to straps of the same material on the gown . . . sometimes gaufiered or quilled ribbon or lace is employed." [3] These were usually made from the same fabric as the rest of the gown. Coupled with the preference for darker shades in dress and lack of surface ornamentation, as well as a general neatness and unfussiness—in contemporary eyes, an unremarkable-ness—was the general effect. Indeed, as the *Hand-Book of Etiquette for Ladies* (1847, "By An American Lady"), tells us, "The plainest dress is always the most genteel, and a

lady that dresses plainly will never be dressed unfashionably." [4] A sober and industrious image as being the most respectable is not a statement unique to the 1840s, but it does seem to have been particularly frequent during this decade.

Notwithstanding a plainer aesthetic there was now, ironically, more and more choice available in terms of technology and the mass creation of clothing. In Britain, the Industrial Revolution had a profound effect on women's dress and on the options available for dressmakers. Innovations made in the eighteenth century such as the Spinning Jenny and Spinning Mule paved the way for greater developments in the nineteenth, century including the power loom and steam engine (used to power textile-manufacturing mills). The advent of such machines to increase textile production inevitably accelerated the rate at which new fashions could be distributed to the public, and ever improving printing methods helped to distribute fashion papers and plates to the general public. The impact of technology was also significant where corsets were concerned: moving on from the comparatively simple stays of the early years of the century, a new cut was developed in France in the late 1840s. This style was made from seven to thirteen separate pieces, generally five on each side, and was cut without bust or hip gussets to create a fit that was far more tailored into the waist. [5] This extra support also meant that shoulder straps became superfluous, since the bust was now supported entirely by whalebone.

The 1850s can be noted as the period of a very well-known early dress reform attempt. Amelia Jenks Bloomer, along with friend Libby Smith, hoped to convince fellow American women to abandon long dresses in favor of "Turkish" style pantaloons—dubbed *Bloomers*—to be worn under a tunic. Their vision was promoted largely through Bloomer's women's newspaper *The Lily* and by in-person speeches and demonstrations of how the brave new bifurcated garment, "trowsers for ladies," might be worn.[6] Although their efforts were met with interest and, from some, a serious wish to learn more, for the most part society was simply not ready for such a drastic change. In advocating the rise of a "sensible" woman, Bloomer was questioning the mid-nineteenth-century public perception of what a woman should be. As Dickens wrote in *The Mystery of Edwin Drood*, a woman should be considered the "ministering angel to domestic bliss."[7] Such populist attitudes hardly encouraged women to follow Bloomer's example.

Despite this, small corseted waists were an abiding feature of much of the mid nineteenth century, and the popularity of tight lacing stems from this era. This would surface as a serious concern for dress reformists later in the century, but even in the 1840s some were questioning the wisdom of tight lacing. However, despite a claim by the wildly popular *Godey's Lady's Book* in 1851 that "the age of stiff stays has departed, we trust never to return, and the modern elegants wear stays with very little whalebone in them, if they wear them at all,"—"female desire for a tiny, hand span waist seemed insatiable."[8] Even those who did not tight lace to extremes retained fairly restrictive stays, seeing them as an aesthetically crucial foundation for the shape of fashionable bodices. This was in staunch disregard of medical suggestions, as well as some from the fashion world, that they should be worn with a higher degree of common sense.

Women did not exclusively wear one-piece dresses during this era. From the 1850s, the jacket-like basque bodice was separate in its construction, though it was still worn with a complementing skirt to form a "dress." In the 1860s, the wearing of separates can perhaps be partly attributed to the popularity of early leisurewear and, it has been suggested, even sportswear, with the practice of wearing a separate "bodice, chemisette or canezou" with a skirt. These "waists" look to a modern eye very much like blouses, though the word was not used until later in the century. This American photograph shows a young woman dressed in just this way, and despite the delay in America of the adoption of the latest European styles, this blouse seems right on trend. However, the original adoption of the waist in the United States was more for utility than fashion. Those living in the South during the Civil War (1861–65) had far fewer resources, and waists were worn with the recycled skirts of old dresses that no longer had functional bodices.[9] Over time, of course, this rule of function became a rule of fashion, and waists in the form of the popular *Garibaldi* (inspired by the red shirts worn by followers of Giuseppe Garibaldi, and sometimes known as a *Spencer waist* due to its similarity to Empire-era jackets) became very popular, particularly amongst young women. Often made in dark colors, they heightened the opportunities available for day-to-day variation and, therefore, allowed far greater choice in women's wardrobes. Such skirt-and-bodice ensembles were often enhanced by the addition of a *Swiss waist*, a belt pointed at back and front, often made in black, that helped to emphasize the appearance of a small waist.

In Britain, the popular Princess Alexandra of Denmark set several trends. When she married Victoria and Albert's eldest son Edward on March 10, 1863, she wore a white Worth-designed gown of English silk, lavishly embellished with Honiton lace and silver embroidery. The use of a crinoline meant that this delicate material was displayed to its best advantage. Deriving from the term *crin* meaning the horsehair originally used to stiffen petticoats, the term *crinoline* came to mean a structure made initially of horizontal whalebone hoops, graduating in size to form a wide circumference at the hem. [10] During the decade, the structure and shape of the crinoline changed according to fashion, but the basic "cage" remained in place for the 1860s. Fashions for women were starting to appear—in some respects—more extreme and impractical, and the crinoline was no small part of this, becoming one of the most enduring and fascinating images we have of the mid-nineteenth century.

RIGHT
Woman's Cage
Crinoline
England, circa 1865,
Los Angeles County
Museum of Art

Dress, c.1836–41,

McCord Museum, Montreal

◆

This barège day dress, with its slim waist and low-set armholes, foretells the restrictiveness of 1840s women's wear. Its sprigged woodblock print on the other hand is light and romantic, evoking the soft and natural designs that were so popular during the first years of the century.

This broad, deep neckline corresponds to a common 1830s shape with the edges almost off the shoulders (evening bodices would often sit at the top of a wearer's arms). The deep pleats just below the neckline drew attention to this design.

The pointed waist would become a major feature of women's bodices throughout the 1840s, 1850s, and 1860s. Here it is very definitely marked out by a double layer of green and purple piped trimming.

By this point the bodice itself is boned, adding extra shaping and support. The skirt is box-pleated at the front, with closer cartridge pleats across the back to provide volume.

A length of silk piping forms the scalloped detail to the side of the skirt, which is ornamented with silk bows. This amount of decoration is a clear remainder of 1830s taste and becomes increasingly less common into the 1840s and 1850s.[12]

These sleeves are a good illustration of the eventual demise of the large gigot style after 1836,[11] where fullness is maintained only between the upper arm and wrist. About to slip right off the shoulder, they were soon to vanish altogether. In a forecast of what was to come, on either side the fabric is pleated closely to the arm to suggest a very definite new placement. The sloping effect this provides is a major aspect in foretelling the shape of the 1840s woman. The portrait below shows a similar shape in 1835, maintaining a larger puff at the center, but nonetheless gradually making a move toward greater simplicity.

Frederick Randolph Spencer, *Portrait of Lady*, United States, 1835, Los Angeles County Museum of Art

Green silk dress,

c.1845, Shippensburg Fashion Museum & Archives, Shippensburg, Pennsylvania

◆

This recently restored day dress is composed of double-faced silk satin, dark green on one side and bright pink on the other. This creates a beautiful changeability to the fabric, and it was a highly fashionable choice from c.1845 onward.

This high neckline with standing collar was fashionable from 1848 to 1852. After this, the round collar came to dominate 1850s and 1860s daywear styles. In this example, the neckband was removed and reattached during the 1840s to allow a change from back to front opening. These types of alterations are common in extant garments and give us a good feel for how clothes were reused and recycled by ordinary people as fashions changed.[13]

Very short decorative *jockey* oversleeves were sometimes used to cover structural ruching and pleating at the top of a sleeve. In this instance, they act as a base for decoration.

A far more elongated and conical torso is evident in this example, a somewhat dramatic change from the higher-waisted gowns of only a few years earlier.

A wide *fan-front panel*, gathered from the shoulders down to the waist, draws attention to the tiny waist and low-shouldered bodice. The bodice is back fastening, allowing the smooth and uninterrupted effect of this frontal design.

Sleeves are low-set, and the shoulder seams are set relatively far back.

There was less applied trimming during the 1840s, and here the majority of the decoration is created through a multitude of pleats and gathers taken from the body of the gown itself. It was suggested in a "workwoman's guide" from 1840 that silk dresses, pipings, and other trimmings "of the same material as the gown, look well."[14] This approach has been applied here to enable a fluid, solid color scheme with no disruption.

Hooks and eyes fasten close-fitting cuffs to the wrist.

Tiny acorns covered in silk thread adorn each button. The acorn as an emblem has many associations, from hope and potential, power, to male and female sexuality and fecundity.[15]

Skirts were usually made from upwards of seven panels of fabric, and these were often quite narrow. Ideally, they were pieced together so that no center-front seam was necessary, but on some occasions this was not possible. In these instances, ornamental panels might be used to disguise the presence of a front seam. At other times they were, as shown here, purely decorative.

This 1845 daguerreotype portrait shows a woman wearing a similarly constructed dress, with jockey sleeves, high neckline, and a pleated fan-front bodice (digital image courtesy of the Getty's Open Content Program)

Dress of light blue mousseline de laine,

c.1854–1855, McCord Museum, Montreal

◆

Dresses were usually made in two pieces, bodice and skirt, during this period. This is fairly obvious here through the use of a fashionable basque bodice, cut to look like a jacket that was tight at the waist and flared out over the hips. This type of bodice was incredibly popular in both Europe and America in the second half of the decade. This dress is made from mousseline de laine, a very fine worsted fabric originally developed in France.

Dresses like this were worn with detachable cotton collars and undersleeves, which could be laundered separately to help protect the dress from dirt and wear.

These *pagoda sleeves* are wide, but much wider styles were seen, and there was lots of variation in trim and finishing. *The Belle Assemblée* monthly fashion paper reported in 1853 that "The pagoda sleeves are by no means gone bye; but for variety some are made very wide . . . sometimes they are finished by a trimming of lace or embroidery: with these, under-sleeves are worn." This last description corresponds to the arrangement seen here. [16]

The edge of the border print (discussed below) also trims the sleeve flounces and the simulated yoke around the shoulders.

The gathered flounces that make up this three-tiered skirt are very typical of 1850s trends. The printed edges of each flounce are woven *à la disposition* (border prints). This meant figured fabric with a larger, corresponding border print down one side had to be produced. It was created precisely to be displayed in this decorative way and perfectly highlighted key elements of the 1850s silhouette. [17]

Unknown, Portrait of a Woman, daguerreotype, 1851, Los Angeles County Museum of Art
This image shows a woman wearing a dress with very similar fringed, tiered pagoda sleeves.

The skirt's width is significantly increased by these three flounces, but also by the developing *crinoline or hoop skirt*, which was introduced in Paris around 1855 (see glossary and introductory text).

Two-piece dress,

c.1855, Los Angeles County Museum of Art

◆

When Queen Victoria purchased Balmoral Castle in 1852, she engendered a passion for all things Scottish. Since dress was one of the prime means of expression for most women, it is not surprising that the use of tartan-inspired fabrics—as in this 1855 dress—should be one of the main feminine outputs of the trend. The wide expanse of skirt was a perfect platform on which to display new trends in fabric.

The bodice fastens at the front with hooks and eyes. These dainty green silk tassel buttons, merely for decorative purposes, were popular during the decade and can be seen on other similar gowns of the era.

Detail, Robe à la française, 1760s, Los Angeles County Museum of Art

These *pagoda sleeves*, set low on the shoulders, are indicative of a style that appeared at around this time: the practice of cutting the fabric from large squares of fabric that hung open, sometimes right to the top of the sleeve.[18]

The surface material of the skirt is undecorated, allowing the majority of the color and interest to come from the bold plaid design.

The sleeves are edged with panels resembling *robing*, the lengths of pleated taffeta trimming that were commonly used on fashionable gowns of the eighteenth century.

Due to the domelike shape of the crinoline beneath, the skirt is consistently circular and protrudes slightly at the front as well as the back. It was not until c.1860 that skirts began to adopt a flatter front, and not obviously so until the middle of the decade, when the shape of crinolines started to change. By 1860, dresses required up to ten yards of fabric around the hem to accommodate the hoop.[19]

Wedding dress,

c.1850–60, Swan Guildford Historical Society, Western Australia

—

This homemade barège (a sheer, lightweight wool) wedding dress has a wide timeframe attributed, suggesting anywhere between 1850 and 1860, and it seems likely to have been produced at around the middle of this timeframe. The dress is a good example of a museum piece that has undergone several repairs and alterations, and these will be pointed out in this analysis.

The two brighter green covered buttons, placed over the replica lace, are also later additions provided for display purposes.

Very low shoulders—here reaching the top of the arm—were very characteristic of the 1850s and 1860s. Along with the waistline, they are also trimmed using the common decorative technique of self-piping. [20]

The skirt is box-pleated at the front and sides, with cartridge pleats at the center back. There is an inserted pocket in the right-hand seam.

The bell-shaped cuffs on the sleeves of this dress demonstrate an early and subtle widening before the popularity of the more exuberant pagoda sleeve. Here, they nicely mirror the shape and width of the skirt. Bias-cut and frilled strips of the same fabric edge the cuffs, highlighting the shape of the sleeves.

The skirt is fully lined, which, along with the pleating, helps to hold its shape and volume.

The wide lace collar is a later addition. It is likely that a separate collar would have been worn in the 1850s and early 1860s, though it would probably have been smaller and narrower than this replacement.

From the 1840s onward, bodices were often either cut with extra fullness to the front, or a separate piece of fabric was used to allow decorative pleating across the chest. In this example, the first technique has been used, and the pleats are topstitched into place. [21]

The deep, pointed waistline is self-piped, a common technique that highlights its edging and the fact that it was made independently of the skirt. This might on first glance suggest an entirely separate bodice, but the skirt is attached to the bodice lining.

The braid is probably a later replacement, attached to the center-front panel of the skirt. It surrounds the original covered buttons, the last of which (by the hem) is a replacement. The panel at center front, made from the same fabric as the dress, is thought to be an original. The gap at the top, right beneath the point of the waistline, shows either that the dressmaker ran out of fabric, or that part of the panel was damaged and removed.

Brown silk moiré taffeta afternoon dress,

c.1865, Powerhouse Museum, Sydney

◆

Despite the expanse of skirt, the style must have been quite liberating compared to the layers of petticoats that went before. The fabric would have been supported by a light cage crinoline, with one or two petticoats over that to make sure rows of steel were not visible through the silk of the skirt. It is worn with detachable lace collar and cuffs to enable easier laundering.

. . . .

The low-set sleeves are edged with bands of machine-made lace. Trimming on shoulders was very fashionable at this date, and it has been loosely sewn (tacked) into place in this example. In keeping with some other details on this dress, it is likely that this was added to an older style to accentuate the shoulders.

The bodice is stiffened and shaped with strips of whalebone, covered with linen and attached to the sides and back. [22]

The same lace that decorates the shoulders also edges the cuffs, and the black theme is picked up in this belt with two-toned rosette.

The skirt appears to have been reworked from the round dome of the 1850s to fit the oval shape of the mid 1860s. Two panels have been inserted to flatten the front, and the skirt features both hand and machine sewing, suggesting some extensive alterations as fashions changed.

The inside of this skirt features a separate bustle pad, made from cotton and roughly finished. It is attached to the waistband by two short lengths of cord, and is a later addition in line with the other alterations. It would have given extra volume to the back of the dress and created the very modest beginnings of a bustle. [23]

Auguste Renoir, *Mademoiselle Sicot*, 1865, National Gallery of Art, Washington, D.C.

This 1865 portrait by Renoir shows a woman wearing a very similar dress: low shoulders edged in lace, high neckline with white collar, front button fastening, and prominent belt. Dresses like this would be worn with a removable white collar or frill which served a functional as well as decorative purpose: to protect the neckline of the dress from dirt and wear.

Evening dress,

1868–69, Paris, McCord Museum, Montreal

◆

Significant developments toward the adoption of the bustle are seen in this example. The skirt is starting to become flatter in front, though there is still a significant bell shape created by the crinoline. A similar dress is described in an 1869 article from the Californian *Marysville Daily Appeal*: "A white dress with a panier skirt of the same material, trimmed with ruchings and fringe." [24]

Very short, puffed sleeves are edged with pleated tulle, which adds a different texture to the bodice. *Tulle*, a light silk net, was used fairly frequently as a fabric placed under outer layers to provide shape and volume. In some instances, such as this dress, it was applied as external decoration, but it was rarely used in significant amounts.

This gored *apron front* overskirt is gathered at the waistline as well as at the sides, creating a puffed effect that is particularly prominent toward the rear. [25] This shape is significant, as it marks the transition from crinoline to bustle, where the emphasis is placed on the back of the skirt. At the time, the bouffant created by such overskirts was referred to as a *panier* after the eighteenth-century style, and when open in front, it was frequently called a *Marie Antoinette* overskirt.

Self-fabric bows mark out the gathered points of the overskirt (including at the back), and it is bordered with pleated trim and silk fringe.

Gathered taffeta creates a single flounce at the hem, leading into a train.

Berthas—wide lengths of fabric encircling the shoulders and sometimes neck—were popular additions to bodices from the 1830s onward.

Here, the device is used to coordinate with the pleated and fringed trimming used elsewhere on the gown and to add some interest to an otherwise plain bodice.

The same bows used on the skirt are also placed at center front of the neckline, as well as on each shoulder.

Striped silk taffeta wedding dress,

c.1869–75, Swan Guildford Historical Society, Western Australia

◆

In some records, this dress is given a provenance of the 1880s, although it corresponds much more closely to early bustle styles of the 1870s: in particular, the dropped shoulders with piped armholes, profusion of silk fringing, and wide "coat" sleeves. Some details also suggest that it was altered from an earlier 1860s dress, hence its placement in this chapter.

....

This *Teneriffe lace* is a later addition, provided by museum workers to replace an original lost collar.

These broad coat-sleeves may have been adapted from an earlier and even more voluminous *pagoda* style. Coat sleeves first appeared in the mid 1860s, constructed from two pieces that were straight cut but with a curve at the elbow: much like those on a man's coat. [26]

The back of this front-fastening bodice is made from three pieces of fabric, with two deeply curved side back seams. This was very much a feature of the 1860s: from 1870 onward, the back seams became far straighter and more numerous. [27] This feature again points to the likelihood of the dress having been altered and reused over the years.

Legend has it that this dress was made by a bride living in the Shire of Harvey, South West of Western Australia. She drove herself to church on the morning of her wedding, only to find no groom, priest, or guests. She returned the following Sunday when the service took place: the priest and groom had been prevented from attending on the scheduled day due to the flooding of the Harvey River. This poignant story highlights the fact that artifacts like this dress do more than tell us about past fashions: they also help to provide narratives about people who wore them, giving an insight into vastly differing lifestyles, choices, and expectations. [28]

Dresses like this offer a great opportunity to explore how ordinary people made their clothes. This dress was not made by a professional dressmaker, nor was it purchased from a store. Various tell-tale signs point this out as a homemade wedding dress, particularly the lack of finishing to the top layer of box pleats at the waist, just above the *peplum*. The fabric has been roughly stitched into place leaving exposed and irregular edges:

We can also see that one section of taffeta has not been sewn flush with the cotton lining in the skirt: it is bunched and hangs slightly over the hem:

Lightweight striped materials were frequently mentioned in newspaper fashion pages, The South *Australian Advertiser* describing them as "always in good taste" when used with paler colors like this forget-me-not blue. [29]

Chapter 6
1870–1889

The years 1870–1889 can be characterized by three very distinct silhouettes: the first bustle era, from c.1870 to 1875; the "natural form" period from c.1876 to 1882, and, finally, the last phase of the bustle phenomenon, spanning roughly from 1883 to 1889. This twenty-year period saw a new inception, a brief rejection, and then a revival, which makes it a colorful, intriguing, yet contradictory time.

In the late 1860s, a gradual focus on the back of the skirt was emphasized by the changing shape of the crinoline. The area where the bustle would soon appear was marked out, almost stealthily, by subtle hints: an ornate peplum, for instance, or a bow at the center back of a waistline (a similar style is depicted in this 1870 work by Renoir). It was further suggested by the slow elaboration of drapery to the skirt—drapery that was swept up and gradually back, making the adoption of the bustle in place of the shrinking crinoline an obvious and necessary maneuver—a means of dealing with the excess fabric left behind from such voluminous skirts. Bustles can be defined as structures that were worn on the lower half of the body, tied around the waist, and that enabled the back of skirts to be thrust out, protruding like a shelf from the small of the back. They enabled skirt fabric to be caught up in elaborate drapes and folds, leading into trains and complex ornamentation.

In the very late 1860s, a smaller variety—usually featuring hoops only at the back and sides—were worn, with an extra arrangement of wires at the back to provide more support for gathering drapery. These were known as *crinolettes* or *half hoops*, and the flounced pads of horsehair tied around the waist, worn throughout both bustle eras, were referred to as dress improvers or *tournures* (the word *bustle* was thought indecent in polite society). Both devices helped produce first the softer, rounder, and higher bustle shape of the early 1870s, and then the sharper horizontal "shelf" that defined the final phase of the 1880s. This shelf was supported by structures such as that seen in the images shown here. They came in varied shapes and sizes and no longer formed part of a crinoline (though sometimes part of a frame extending down the back of the legs only), making the rest of the skirt much slimmer and narrower than it had previously been.

During the interim natural form period, when bustle frames of all types were discarded, dresses became almost skintight. They fit, sheath-like, over the hips as a one-piece *princess-line* dress, or as a skirt with separate figure-hugging cuirass bodice. All fullness was confined to the back of the skirt and the train, with the sides of the garment tightly encircling the legs. This was achieved through the use of inner ties in petticoat and skirt, which held the fabric as close to the sides of the body as possible.

In c.1883, a final bustle arrangement made its entrance. Often referred to as the shelf bustle, this style did exactly what its name suggests: it stuck straight out from the small of the wearer's back at a 90 degree angle. [1] In general, less drapery adorned this apparatus, making the effect far more rigid and architectural than it had been in the early 1870s. This was another

short-lived trend, however, petering out in the late 1880s to become only a modest bustle pad, worn to give a little fullness to the back of the gored skirts which became fashionable into the 1890s. This change was met with some relief by many fashion pages, with one Australian newspaper commenting in 1887 that "Fashion is becoming rational in the matter of he tournure. The ridiculous tournures, enormously protruding, which vexed seriously inclined spirits for the last few years, are now almost forgotten." [2]

In the popular press, satirists enjoyed lampooning early bustle styles by comparing them to the rounded exoskeletons of snails and beetles. The new princess line was not safe from ridicule either; with *Punch* magazine and similar publications suggesting that, with this slim silhouette, women were so cocooned that they could barely move. One cartoon, *Veto*, by George Du Maurier (c.1876–77) depicts a fashionable young man and woman at a ball. "Shall we—a—Sit down?" the gentleman asks. "I should like to," his companion replies, "but my Dressmaker says I mustn't!"

It was perhaps this style, in particular, that began to seriously fuel the burgeoning rational dress movement. Not since Amelia Bloomer's attempt in the 1850s had any lasting efforts been achieved, and significant widespread emancipation for women was still some fifty years away. The Artistic Dress Movement and the Aesthetic Dress Movement made certain strides, carrying similar preferences for natural fabrics and simple craftsmanship. However, both were limited mainly to the intelligentsia and "bohemian" circles, and it was the Rational Dress Society, founded in 1881, that seriously publicized reform on the basis of health and comfort above all else. Well-known reformist Mary Haweis (1848–98) was interested in the aesthetics as well as the practicalities of dress and did not believe that the two were mutually exclusive. She merely valued simple clothes that showed off the "natural lines" of a woman's figure. What she objected to was not so much the shape of fashionable dress—which, in *The Art of Beauty* (1883), she describes as "commendable because it indicates those forms of the body which have too long been completely hidden"—but to the extremes of fashionable taste:

The heavy tail or confined train is not allowed to soften and enhance the movements of the body, but in walking will jerk at each step, increasing the lady's resemblance to a clogged cow. [3]

Ordinary people reading such pieces responded by writing their own impassioned letters on the subject. One woman expressed concern in 1877 that the fine workmanship of many of these gowns was being compromised by the dictates of fashion:

> *The draping and trimming of the skirt on which so much care is bestowed, is entirely disarranged from the original design by being drawn aslant and elevated [and] a free and graceful motion of feet and hands is restrained by the burden of the heavy train, dragged together and borne constantly.* [4]

So as not to compromise the beauty of dress, rational dress advocates developed and promoted "healthy" corsets and lighter undergarments. It was hoped that these would make fashionable clothes more hygienic without making the wearer feel conspicuous. However, such innovations were only adopted by a minority, and dress reformists had longer-lasting success in the concentrated area of sports and leisure wear by encouraging women to choose more practical outfits for physical activities.

For most women, corsets remained indispensable, especially during the late 1870s when there was such focused attention on the torso in its long, lean *cuirass* bodice and princess line. Corsets were therefore cut longer in the body, and were stiffened with more strips of whalebone than previous styles. It was the development of two new technologies, however, that made the most difference to the shape and restrictiveness of corsets in this era. The first was the use of steam-molding, introduced in the late 1860s but proving particularly popular in the 1870s and 1880s. This procedure involved starching and shaping the corset on a mannequin and then allowing it to dry to the required stiffness. The second was a shaped busk known as a spoon busk, which was narrow at its tip and widened into a broad round spoon shape at the base of the corset. [5] This gave greater support, but also greater restriction, to the abdomen and kept the front of the bodice smooth.

During this period, despite the complexity of fashionable dress, it became easier and easier for all women to engage with fashion. The necessity of having fashionable pieces custom made (or in contemporary terms, *en suite*) was becoming a thing of the past. This was largely due to the fact that the textile industry's limits had been greatly expanded by the introduction of power looms and other machines that made garment cutting and assembly far more efficient (fabric-pleating machines are one example of this and were greatly in demand when this feature became so prominent on gowns of the 1880s). In the domestic sphere, more widespread use and availability of the sewing machine meant that clothes could be produced faster and in greater quantities. Paper patterns increased the level of accessible information regarding how to make and wear the latest trends, and the development of the department store allowed the consumption of ready-made garments and accessories.

By the very end of the 1880s, murmurings of doubt about the continuation of the bustle began to surface, and contemporary newspapers showed various bustle manufacturers anxiously watching to see what the outcome would be. Nevertheless, the popularity of this device intrigued one New York reporter enough to produce an article that surveyed the number of women he perceived, in different situations and times of day, wearing a bustle. What he determined initially was that the number of women with *no* kind of skirt support could be counted on one hand. However, after his investigations were complete, the reviewer was able to illustrate a gradual but definitive shift at the end of the decade. Even though a dress without a bustle was inconceivable for many, more and more women were coming forward who wore either diminutive versions ("a reed or wire fastened to the dress") or even none at all:

> A tall, stout woman, clad in a blue, tailor-made cloak … the outlines of her back denoting the entire absence of any extender. She was both handsome and stylish, and her appearance was a relief to the inspector's eyes. [6]

Though written in a humorous tone, this article is an important reminder of the real pace of dress evolution. Fashion plates and museum exhibits may lead us to believe that drastic changes—such as the three distinct styles of the 1870s and 1880s—were universally adopted by all women. Among the many followers of fashion who wanted and tried to adhere to all the newest trends from London and Paris, many would have seen little change in their personal everyday dress. Most would also have discarded or adopted new trends behind or ahead of their contemporaries. Nevertheless, the bustle dress remains an extraordinary garment: striking, provocative, immediately recognizable, and still a source of inspiration to designers today.

Silk taffeta promenade dress,

1870, American, Los Angeles County Museum of Art

◆

This was a period in which clothing modification for sports started to become more widely seen. This first image analysis of the chapter is an example of the very small changes that were permitted for active wear: in this case, the absence of any kind of train—an unusual sight at the start of the 1870s.

....

Small standing collars such as this continued to be popular throughout the early part of the decade.

The distinctive low-set sleeves of the 1860s are still in evidence here. The sleeves themselves are straight, made from two pieces of fabric, and are finished at the cuff with three fringe-edged rows of pleated trim.

The higher waist, prominent toward the end of the 1860s, has largely disappeared, and here the waistline is in its natural position.

This dress may have been produced at the very start of the first bustle period, but it already shows evidence of the great fondness for lavish trimmings during the decade. The pink silk macramé fringe on the bustle is arranged in a crossover design, which continues around to the front where it ends in two deep points below the waistline.

The skirt is still full and rounded, but a protruding bustle has been established. This suggests that the dress would probably have been worn over a *crinolette* with a wired bustle pad.

Frayed edging on the taffeta pleats add yet another dimension to the abundant trimming on this gown. The design is clearly striving to attain the latest, most fashionable ideals, keeping in line with an 1871 declaration that "A fashionable costume is a delicious melange of puffings, cross-cut tuckings, ruches, raffles, bows and flutings, kilt plaitings, side plaitings, fringes, lace and flouncings." [7]

The absence of a train on this dress evidences its suitability as a walking or "promenade" costume.

Dress, c.1870–73,

Canada, McCord Museum, Montreal

◆

This dress sports a cohesive color scheme, unlike many fashionable ensembles of the time that attempted to meld too many shades in one garment. Contrasting fabrics were also considered fashionable, and this dress is an example of that with two tones of taffeta and silk faille.

Bordered panels at the front and back of the bodice suggest a long and narrow yoke, but the effect is purely decorative.

A *postillion* extends from the back of the short-basqued bodice, resting on the bustle. This term—inspired by the uniform worn by a postillion (the lead driver of a carriage of four horses)—was applied to bodice decoration that simulated the tails of a coat, spreading out over the ledge created by a bustle skirt. This was a very popular effect in the early 1870s, with one American newspaper declaring that "the back [of fashionable bodices] is invariably a postillion." [8]

The back panel of the overskirt is gathered to the sides of the shorter front panel. This helps to create volume at the back of the skirt, with further puffs produced and maintained through the addition of vertical ties inside the overskirt. These could be adjusted to suit the wearer's preference. [9]

Jacket-like bodices such as this had also been popular twenty years before, in the 1850s. This one is short and relatively high-waisted, with the short *basques*—skirted extensions reaching below the waistline—falling open into two points below the row of buttons.

The sleeves end in slightly pointed rectangular cuffs, edged in the same deeper blue bands as used on the rest of the bodice and the apron overskirt.

The popular *tablier* or *apron* style of overskirt is seen here, divided into two sections.

A deep flounce adds flare to the hem of the underskirt. On the left-hand side, a separate panel of flat pleats, gathers, and bows adds a different texture and feel to the dress.

Evening dress,

c.1873, Paris, McCord Museum, Montreal

◆

An exoskeleton analogy, so often used by satirists lampooning the bustle silhouette, is appropriate here in this exquisite and expertly tailored evening/dinner dress. The details are typical of the gown's maker, exclusive and acclaimed French couturier Corbay-Wenzell (A. Corbay). Right on trend, this dress embodies several key aesthetics of the early bustle era.

At the front, the bodice of this dress conforms to so many of its era with a decidedly eighteenth-century-inspired square neckline, trimmed liberally with lace. The three-quarter-length sleeves, trimmed with pleated cuffs, are a manifestation of historicism in this design.

The sides of this box-pleated *peplum* are held down by artificially weighted lengths of blue silk on either side. This creates a curved "frame" above the central ruched bustle, highlighting it as a prominent feature.

Lengths of deep beige knotted trim, the ends adorned with tassels, edge the two tiers of the front of the skirt, emphasizing the popularity of multiple layers and incorporated skirt drapery. The same trim also appears on the train and neckline.

Pale blue revers separate the two-tiered front from the funnel shape of the bustle skirt. These are edged exuberantly in yet more trim—this time scrolled, scalloped silk that curves around to meet the flat-pleated trim of the train.

The silk plaid, while distinctive, is also relatively understated and sits well alongside the pale blue of the sleeves and skirt trimmings. Plaid designs were popular and frequently mentioned in fashion pages as an attractive choice, suitable for many occasions.

The bodice is slowly beginning to fit the torso below the natural waistline. By 1874, it started to descend to hip level.

The central bustle shape would have been maintained and supported not only by a bustle frame but also by separate ties within the skirt itself that pulled in the sides to create this distinctive shape. A comparatively slender silhouette is evident in the skirt as a whole, conforming to the newly popular trend of bringing the garment closer to the natural line of the body.

Silk taffeta afternoon dress,

c.1876, Australia, Powerhouse Museum, Sydney

◆

By 1876, the slim princess line and cuirass bodice were becoming firmly established, but this dress represents a continuation of the prominent bustle shape from the early 1870s. However, by this point the bustle has dropped to a lower position at the waist, soon to make way for the sheath-like princess style that was so popular c.1877–80.

The high, round neckline leads into a center-front fastening of seven buttons. These stop at the natural waist where an open-fronted peplum, edged with a frill of self fabric, extends round to the back of the bodice and rests on the bustle. [10]

The influence of menswear and military styles can be seen in both skirt and bodice trimmings, particularly the bands on the cuff and tabs edging the sides of the skirt, all with decorative buttons.

Using buttons across the entire dress was a method that came in and out of fashion during the 1870s, and a similar effect was described by the Ladies' Column of one New Zealand newspaper as "trim(ming of) the skirt, together with the sleeves, pockets, revers, &c., with very small, round, metal buttons." [11]

The bodice and skirt are in a mauve silk taffeta. Trimmings are made from a contrasting lavender shade. This mixing of similar tones in one garment was fashionable in the early to middle years of the decade. [12]

A fairly long, rounded train such as this was popular throughout the decade.

As with most skirts of the period, it is gored and gathered at the back and, in this example, falls straight to the floor over the bustle without any extra puffing or draping.

George Healy, Roxana Atwater Wentworth (detail), USA, 1876, National Gallery of Art, Washington, D.C.
This portrait shows a similar high ruffled collar along with a corsage of flowers on the bodice. The image also portrays a typical fashionable hairstyle of the decade. Made easier by the introduction of the curling iron in 1872, waves and curls were highly fashionable. Here, a portion of hair is left free to hang in ringlets down the back, while the rest is caught up in a plait with either a center parting or light fringe. [13]

Silk and satin reception dress,

c. 1877–78, Britain, Cincinnati Art Museum

◆

This three-piece dress was created in Paris by the celebrated couturier Charles Frederick Worth and is a good example of his fashion house's flair and opulence. It also has local connections to Cincinnati, the home of its wearer, where a separate evening bodice was made to be worn with the skirt shown here. The dress, therefore, has a rich history and interesting story to tell and is a good example of some of the most popular trends in women's fashion at this time.

The three-quarter-length sleeves of this day bodice were very suitable for the semi-formal function of the gown: as an outfit for receiving guests in the home.

This example illustrates a move toward the one-piece, princess line sheath dress. The separate bodice is rapidly lengthening, fitting snugly to the waist and over the hips. It came to be known as the *cuirass* after a piece of medieval armor that fit closely around the torso.

Worth, with his passion for historicism, helped to promote the return of the eighteenth-century panier overskirt, divided and pulled closely across the hips and then drawn into a low bustle at the back. These paniers continued to be popular into the 1880s, and, as one newspaper commented in 1880, although they no longer sat so flat to the hips, "they are not bunchy; in fact, Worth's paniers are not outré in any way." [14]

Two tiers of knife pleats sit above a *balayeuse*—a detachable layer of frilled muslin, often trimmed with lace (as seen here), that held the hem up off the ground, elevating it for both protective and aesthetic purposes. [15]

This deep, square neckline, edged with embroidered lace and ornamented with a bow, bears some similarity to the décolletage of eighteenth-century gowns. It brings to mind ornate stomachers such as this one, decorated with rows of tied ribbon. In both examples, the bodice ribbon is also used above the sleeve flounces.

A Mrs Mary Thoms lived in Cincinnati and bought this skirt and day bodice from the famed couturier, Charles Frederick Worth, when visiting Paris. A corresponding evening bodice was later made back in Cincinnati by local dressmaker Selina Hetherington Cadwallader. It was also lace-trimmed and low-necked, but it was made from the same floral silk seen on the underskirt. The owner purchased an additional yard of this eighteenth-century-inspired fabric from Worth when she bought the dress. [16]

Robe à la française (detail), 1750–60, Los Angeles County Museum of Art

Plaid silk dress,

1878, England, Los Angeles County Museum of Art

◆

Dresses of Scotch plaid were popular for young girls, and this dress was made for
a girl just entering womanhood. It would, therefore, be one of the first "grown-up" gowns
she would have worn, and the bold and youthful print is combined with an adult style reflecting
many of the latest trends. It is cut in a princess line, which, along with skirt and cuirass bodice,
made up the fashionable shape of the period.

Cameo, eighteenth and
nineteenth centuries,
digital image courtesy
of the Getty's Open
Content Program.

At the end of 1878, *The Young Ladies'
Journal* reported that "Plaids are come
into fashion again this autumn," going on
to describe a popular color scheme that
corresponds to the design shown here:
"Blue and green are the most usual
combination, although red also appears,
and all the Scotch clans are in requisition." [17]
Other publications recommend a revival
of plaid for all women, but mostly in
conjunction with plain fabrics on the same
bodice or skirt. The use of plaid was also
popular for trimmings, and as the fabric for
accessories such as jackets and mantles.

Rows of pleats, gathers, and bows at
the back of the skirt still mark out the
positioning of the bustle, and a structured
petticoat would be worn to maintain
fullness leading into the train. However,
there is now no protruding bustle under
the waistline, and the skirt and bodice are
cut as one with no horizontal waist seam.
Long vertical seams run from bust to hip
and create a single sheath.

Paste brooches were popular jewelry
choices at this date, as were cameos,
which were mentioned frequently in
fashion pages. Cameos could be carved
from a range of materials including shell,
stone, and even lava and often depicted
classical figures and scenes.

The long row of buttons is attractive,
but also serves a purpose in this front-
fastening design.

A large bow at center front, just below
the knees, draws the eye to the gown's
main decorative feature: a skillfully
applied two-dimensional "curtain" effect,
simulating the plaid skirt being drawn
open to reveal another layer beneath.

Even for daywear, a substantial train
was still the expected norm.

Taffeta dress,

c.1880, France, Los Angeles County Museum of Art

◆

Soft, pale colors were popular in the early 1880s, *The Queen* reporting that "the lighter the tint, the more elegant the gown." [18] The powder blue taffeta used in this dress gives the garment a youthful appearance, allowing its delicate drapery to take center stage. Expansion of the textile industry meant that it was easier and faster to produce effects such as the closely pleated kilting seen on this hem and cuffs, but introduction of power looms and other machines also made garment cutting in general far more efficient. This allowed more time for the production of elaborate trimmings that were both hand- and machine-made.

Standing collars were popular in 1880 and would later feature internal boning. Here, the collar still sits relatively flat to the neck.

The one-piece dress fastens at the front by these covered silk buttons. Such dresses usually also featured an inner waistband, to hold the fabric as closely to the contours of the body as possible.

Two coffee-colored taffeta rosettes add an extra dimension of detail to the row of buttons, most of which are functional. Two additional rosettes can be seen at the cuffs. The use of rosettes may be a historical influence, reminiscent of their popularity in the seventeenth century.

Asymmetrically draped fabric forms a kind of overskirt around the knees, making a statement at the front of the dress before disappearing into the froth of taffeta, tassel, and pleat detail forming the train.

Self-piping edges the collar and armholes.

There is no hint of a horizontal waist seam here, making the gown a great example of the engineering of a true *princess line* (allegedly named for the elegant and svelte Princess Alexandra of England). Dresses became one-piece and almost skin tight, cut to reveal the figure, and this is achieved here through the implementation of long seams on both sides, running from bust to hips.

This tiny slit reveals a built-in watch pocket, a practical consideration that is cunningly concealed.

There is now no vestige of the "traditional" bustle remaining, as seen in the previous dress. Here, the concentration of excess fabric is entirely contained to top thigh-level and below.

Mary Haweis, a promoter of the burgeoning "rational dress" movement, admired the way fashionable dress showed the "true" lines of a woman's body. However, she was concerned that long and complex trains "[deprived the limbs] of comfort (and) grace is immediately lost." She also voiced concern on the grounds of hygiene: these long, trailing skirts swept grimy city streets and brought dirt and dust into houses. [19]

Silk and wool wedding dress,

1882, Australia, Powerhouse Museum, Sydney

◆

Seen in the flesh, the gold color of this incredibly fine wool is more muted and neutral, making it appear a much softer shade of yellow. This light color scheme was becoming more popular for weddings, making the garment less practical and thereby instilling a greater sense of luxury. It is in near perfect condition, probably worn only once for the bride's wedding day. Although not made for a rich woman, the dress's significance and sentimental worth was obviously hugely important, and it has consequently not been subjected to the rewearing and alterations that are so commonly seen in bridal gowns from families of low to moderate income. [20]

Two shirred and ruched silk panels form an inverted V at the bust line. This helps draw the eyes to a very slender waist.

Eighteen satin-covered buttons create a front closure for this one-piece gown. The wide satin-edged pleated swathe of wool fabric, extending asymmetrically across the front of skirt, joins at the back of the dress to match the identically satin-edged bustle.

These rows of knife pleating, kilting, here create very precise overlapping sections. Because of the development of new machines specifically for this purpose, the technique became easier and, therefore. more readily available.

Ankle-length skirts were a common sight in the early 1880s, possibly a reference to polonaise styles of the mid-late eighteenth century.

The false orange blossom spray on the bodice, made from wax, harks back to an ancient bridal tradition where the bloom was worn as a symbol of fecundity. Wax flowers were also used on headpieces and, along with false sprays, were popular as keepsakes and can often be seen as parts of surviving trousseau.

The very long cuirass bodice is fitted to the body through a series of nine darts, morphing at the back of the gown into a ruched bustle, which is emphasized by a large, flat bow. From this emerges a train of kilted pleats, their design mirroring those on the skirt hem. [21] The complex construction and techniques shown here were made easier by the use of a lockstitch sewing machine for the majority of the ensemble. [22]

"The guaging, or shirring as it is oftenest called, is still much used on skirts of dresses," a Sydney newspaper commented in November 1882. Row upon row of tiny shirred sections of wool make up the principal skirt decoration here, and this technique was very popular during the early 1880s. It was usually only modestly applied on bodices, and this could be because, as the same article suggests, more liberal usage would be "a mistake, as it destroys the outlines of the shoulders and bust." [23]

Wedding dress,

1884, McCord Museum, Montreal

◆

This tailored wedding dress is made in a popular wine-red shade, described in a contemporary fashion journal as "Burgundy and claret reds… the colors that ladies' tailors appear to favor most." [24] It would have been worn over a petticoat composed of channels of cane or whalebone, shaped into the almost perpendicular outline that was now the accepted norm.

The overskirt, arranged in a tablier (apron) style, is looped up into three swags at the back. By this point, skirt draperies were composed of separate pieces arranged on a gored foundation skirt, which was usually gathered at center back. One newspaper fashion column from 1883 described the construction of a similar bodice and skirt: "The pointed bodice, cut short on the hips, with pannier drapery worn above a tablier… is really a tasteful mode." [25]

Here, the draped section of the apron is sewn to the foundation skirt, and a long, diagonal point covers one side, just meeting the top row of trim.

Various types of bustles could be worn, but hair-filled pads arranged in rectangular or crescent-shaped rolls were popular at this date. One American fashion column believed that they were "the most trustworthy, if lightly filled" in order to preserve "the contours . . . of the skirt" and to avoid the caricature of a "wobbling effect." If a dress was made from a fabric too thin, or with insufficient weight at the bottom of a foundation skirt, the bustle was in danger of carrying an uneven distribution of weight and interrupting the line of the dress. [26]

Rows of buttons down the front of a bodice were a common sight on dresses of this era. These eighteen metal examples add a diversion in a sea of burgundy, imprinted with a house motif.

This deeply pointed basque waistline is typical of the early 1880s, fitting sveltely over the hips but not extending past them as far as the cuirass did. At the back, it extends into a neat bustle shelf, jutting out solidly and incorporating a box-pleated peplum.

The front and sides of the skirt sit close to the legs, with extra width shifting to the back and the new perpendicular bustle.

Three rows of kilted taffeta are flanked by a line of stylized, bow-shaped sections of trim, their deep points mirroring the arrangement of the skirt drapery at both the back and front of the dress.

The skirt has no train at all—except for evening wear, they were rarely seen during the decade.

Taffeta dress,

c.1885, France, Los Angeles County Museum of Art

◆

This dress is a good example of the "separateness" of mid-late 1880s skirts, showing individual pieces coming together to form the popular line. It also illustrates the popularity of cords and braids as trimmings, here bringing the silhouette of the bustle into sharp focus. This line is also emphasised by the use of different shades of purple throughout the garment.

The 1880s saw a fashion for close-fitting bonnets like this one, but hats would soon become the prevailing style into the 1890s.

This bodice is relatively lengthy, cut in a cuirass style that extends over the hips to create a long, clean line at the front and sides of the dress.

The same cord that decorates the front of the bodice is seen again as a central embellishment on the skirt, both on the bustle itself and at intervals further down. This was a popular choice of trimming during the decade, its universality expressed particularly well by one fashion column: "Cords and tassels are . . . employed in every conceivable manner, to tie around the waist, to lace the front of the basque, to tie around the neck, to fasten in a long knot at the side of the skirt . . ." and several of those usages are applied here. [27]

The train has been looped away from the ground by a purple cord, suggesting the possibility that this gown was also worn with a different bodice as an evening or dinner dress.

Left; detail 1885, right; stomacher detail, robe à la française, c.1745, both Los Angeles County Museum of Art

The front of the bodice features a central panel, known as a *plastron*, in the same floral brocade as seen on the skirt. This panel has an effect reminiscent of eighteenth-century stomachers and is ornamented with purple crisscrossed cord (in much the same manner as the c.1725–45 robe à la française from Chapter 3). This cord is detachable, and the bodice fastens at the front through a row of thirteen studded metal buttons.

The asymmetrical "sash" encircling the knees continues the busy aesthetic of late 1870s and early 1880s dresses.

The skirt has been tightly pleated into sections lined with the lighter purple brocade, adding a flash of shimmering lilac as the wearer moved.

Dress of black Chantilly lace and pink satin,

c.1888, Canada, McCord Museum, Montreal

◆

Black Chantilly lace gained popularity in the 1880s, particularly when mounted over a soft pastel shade such as the pink seen here. Both the lace and a decorative accompaniment on this gown, jet, was popular in accessories as well as clothing, particularly hats. All the varied elements of this design agree with a comment made in a Californian newspaper from spring 1887: "Black lace dresses have not yet reached the climax of popularity, as novelties are constantly being suggested in them." [28]

The sleeves are very slightly puffed at the top, forecasting the dimensions reached in the 1890s. This is emphasized by the placing of black jet *epaulettes* at the very top of the sleeves.

Very soon after the date of this gown, the popularity of the bustle started to diminish. At the end of the decade, a small pad was worn under the skirt to slightly increase volume. In this design, three steels with inside tapes create a built-in bustle.

Scarf, Belgium, 1870s to 1890s, Los Angeles County Museum of Art
Chantilly lace was also used to make accessories such as headpieces, collars, shawls, and, as shown here, scarves.

Two bows, extending into long ribbons with corded ends, add extra decoration, and their placement picks out the front bodice closure and bustle. These ribbons (in particular their tasseled ends) call to mind sleeve ties with *aiguillettes* (cords ending in metal points) in the fifteenth and sixteenth centuries. *Demorest* magazine commented on the popularity of such trimmings in September 1887: "Ribbons ornament dresses in profusion with bows sometimes reaching from the waist to hem." [29]

Under the apron lace underskirt, the front of the gown features rows of lace flounces, which meet the pink satin openings. These are layered and edged with further flounces of Chantilly lace, flouncing being the commonest use of this particular type of lace on dresses in the 1870s and 1880s. It could also be purchased separately and used to alter an existing dress in line with fashion. In their 1886 catalogue, New York department store Bloomingdales advertised a wide range of black Chantilly lace flouncing. It was available in lengths from 12 to 36 inches wide, costing between 79 cents and $2.10. [30]

Chapter 7
1890–1916

From the end of the 1880s, the fashionable silhouette made a move away from what had been in vogue for the past twenty years. Free from the addition of some type of skirt support (except sometimes a very small bustle pad worn at the waist), women's garments of the 1890s are recognizable by their simpler flowing lines, at least on the bottom half of the body: a gored skirt with train extending from a highly structured and hourglass-shaped bodice. The disappearance of the bustle had left a superfluity of fabric at the back of the skirt and, after the extravagance of bustle drapery, skirts became almost entirely free of complicated overlay or much additional fabric. This change is one of the most important in terms of "reading" the timeline of historical fashion in this era.

With attention now shifted definitively from the arrangement of the skirt, focus for a while was on the substantial *leg-of-mutton* sleeves that dominated women's bodices for most of the decade. The idea of a leg-of-mutton is an especially helpful analogy, its shape bearing such strong relation to the way these sleeves were constructed: puffed at the top and gradually diminishing into a tight-fitting cuff, or finishing at or above the elbow for eveningwear. The style was reaching its greatest proportions by 1895, but earlier examples illustrate its prominence right from the beginning of the decade. The overall effect of these large sleeves, coupled with flared A-line skirt, was that the waist appeared even smaller.

Toward the end of the century, the leg-of-mutton sleeve began to diminish in size. In its place was left only a small puff at the very top of the sleeve, known as a *kick-up*, and often suggested in eveningwear by a separate ruffle at the shoulder. [1]

In the place of these sleeves and the hourglass torso, a new silhouette developed, the *S-bend* (commonly known as the *straight-fronted as well as the swan bill or serpentine*), which was achieved by a new corset that pushed the wearer's torso forward and hips back. This style was introduced to obtain as small a waistline as possible and, at its most extreme, made women bend forward so that they almost seemed about to tip over. This was accompanied by the "mono-bosom" effect: a very solid, front-flattened chest made possible by this new type of corset. A penchant for very large hats and high, swept-up coiffures offset the imbalance, making for a top-heavy image. At the opposite end of the body, skirts flared out from the knee and formed frothy swathes of train, made possible by numerous frills, both sewn into the hem of the skirt and attached to petticoats. This look was achieved by the widespread fondness for light, airy fabrics such as chiffon and crepe-de-chine, but stiffer taffetas and cottons made up the false hems that provided necessary shaping. Popularized by the "Gibson girl" portrayed by Charles Dana Gibson in his satirical sketches, the look became one of the most recognizable styles of the century and produced the original "It Girl," made famous by actress Camille Clifford and other popular figures. The S-bend corset remained until under-bust, hip-length styles emerged around 1908, smoothing and streamlining the lower abdomen and hips in accordance with the resurgence of the empire line.

Despite such highly idealized body types, this era simultaneously saw the introduction of significant strides in the development of more "casual" clothing for women. If a woman cycled, she had the option of wearing new forms of clothing that encouraged sport and movement. Bloomers worn for cycling were the more extreme end of this new type of sportswear and, though notorious at the time and often caricatured, were not (partly evidenced by this notoriety) worn by the majority. It was more common to see female bicyclists wearing tailored jackets and slightly shorter skirts, although it is telling that in the main, bicycles—and not the clothing of their owners—needed to be modified to allow safe riding. Models were produced with dipped frames and skirt guards, since manufacturers knew that many would feel nervous at the prospect of adopting bloomers or divided or even calf-length skirts.

Increasingly varied were the roles of women in society during the 1890s, not only as wives and mothers but also—for some—as students or professional members of society (primarily salesgirls, teachers, secretaries, and other clerical staff) with less time on their hands for traditionally "feminine" pursuits such as dressmaking. Affordable ready-made patterns, based on the latest styles from Paris fashion plates, meant that fashionable clothes could be made by almost anyone—though the fabric and embellishment used would rarely have been as luxurious as the idealized plates displayed. These changes in the role and perception of women in society correspond with ideas around the concept of the *fin-de-siècle* (end of century), associated with the late nineteenth century in the Western world. This was a phrase that came to characterize the perceived malaise, anxiety and other forms of psychological unrest accompanying the end of a familiar era. The apprehension was summed up well in a comment seen in the British newspaper the *Birmingham Daily Post* in 1899:

> *We shall make a minor event and epoch of the year 1900 . . . some (people) will be proportionately saddened and depressed . . . the great effort of the century seems spent and dying . . . the close of the century must, alas! practically witness the final disappearance from the scene of the men who made the present order . . . the next will see a new man face (new difficulties) . . . unable any longer to rest personally, as it has so long done, upon those of the old.* [2]

Merged with this vaguer expression of unease was a universal fear that the "new woman" who partook of sports—often in mixed teams with men—and who increasingly took up employment and attended college would inevitably lose interest in marriage and children. What might appear in place of these traditional values was subject to both reasoned and extreme theories, and the clothes of this era balance, on the one hand, a silhouette just as restrictive as it had ever been and, on the other, the emergence of diverse influences that permeated the mainstream as well as the avant-garde.

Nevertheless the progression of women into the workforce encouraged the popularity of more practical clothing influenced by men's tailoring. Two-piece suits composed of jacket and skirt, worn with a blouse (often known as a *shirtwaist*) including a stiff collar and sometimes a tie, made up the working wardrobe of this new, more independent woman. Even for those who maintained more traditional gender distinctions, a far more varied wardrobe was at last possible, and the wearing of separate skirts and blouses became common for nearly all women regardless of their educational or career ambitions. [3] This choice is emphasized by the fact that alongside such practical options, more overtly "feminine" frocks were always popular and available. Floral and floaty with overlays of lace and chiffon, the examples in this chapter illustrate that perennial wish for grace and elegance, abiding feminine virtues that were so well portrayed through fashion.

Just as with more unusual examples of dress reform and aesthetic dress, the reality is that by 1900 there was a waning interest in the subject of serious dress reform, even by the reformers themselves. Even though there was—to many—by no means an end to the agreement that fashionable dress needed to change, in the wider realm, any distraction from more serious emancipation issues to "frivolous" ones was perceived as dangerous. Fashion seemed to be moving in its own natural, gradual course toward an ameliorated model that would develop in time.

The period leading up to Word War I was a time of rising unrest and fevered anticipation regarding the changing political climate. As a result of the war, women witnessed perhaps the largest strides to clothing reform yet due to utilitarian attitudes and the absolute necessity to recruit women into the war effort—especially in work such as munitions manufacture. This was often a very dangerous process that for safety reasons could not be undertaken without the use of practical, utilitarian garments. Before this necessity took hold, however, the world of high fashion witnessed some of the greatest innovators it has ever seen, including Jacques Doucet, Mariano Fortuny, and Lucile. Paul Poiret, however, remains perhaps the best known among them—and is certainly the designer most commonly credited with initiating the new shape. His "lampshade" tunic and fondness for harem pants may have sat firmly on the avant-garde side of the fence, but his new tubular silhouette and flair for "exotic" sentiment— enhanced by his success with the Ballet Russe and their *Scheherazade*—were echoed across fashion more broadly.

Wedding dress

c.1890, McCord Museum, Montreal

◆

Made for a Canadian bride, this two-piece gown of ribbed and moiré silk combines elements of high fashion with more unusual additions. It bears some relation to the newly evolving "graduation gowns" worn by those who attained diplomas and degrees in the latter half of the nineteenth century. Often in a white or cream fabric, these could be given a second airing as a wedding dress later in life.

These four rows of *shirring* on the top half of the bodice allow for some movement in a stiff silk fabric, as well as provide structure and contribute to the complex diagonal drape of this dress. A New Zealand fashion column from 1893 describes the widespread use of this technique: "Shirring is extensively used . . . and not only forms the yoke, but also the cuff effect." [4] The trend had been noticeably in evidence from the middle of the century onward, and this gown is a later example of its continuing use into the final decade.

The bodice has a wrapover *surplice* front, its fabric crossing to the right and hooking closed at the center back of the dress. The *New York Times* described the popularity of this style on fashionable bodices: "The surplice waist, with many modifications, appears in costumes of every material and for every use." The small V of the neckline is created by the arrangement of the surplice and seems to have been quite a prominent shape in the early years of the decade. The *New York Times* continued to describe this effect on a similar bodice: "The fronts lap from left to right, meeting so near the throat that only a small V is left." [5]

In these early years of the 1890s, skirts fit fairly closely over the hips and flared to form a *bell* or *tulip* shape at the hem.

The dress features an overskirt with a side opening, gored in front, and draped up slightly at the back to form a small bustle. For a short time into the 1890s, this dwindling feature continued to be seen.

The fabric is draped diagonally in folds, originating from a point at the center back of the bodice and continuing over the shoulders to the bust.

The leg-of-mutton (still also known as the gigot style) reached its widest proportions by c.1895, but earlier examples such as this illustrate its prominence from the beginning of the decade.

The 1890s were an important decade for bridal fashion: wedding dresses had previously been made in any color except white, cream, and ivory (browns and purples were especially popular for much of the nineteenth century), but soft, lightly tinted shades such as this were now more synonymous with bridal wear. White, cream, or ivory accessories such as a veil, gloves, and shoes like the ones seen below were also worn:

Pair of women's Oxford shoes (wedding), USA, c.1890, Los Angeles County Museum of Art

Day dress,

c.1893–95, Swan Guildford Historical Society, Perth

◆

Here is an important Western Australian relic worn by the wife of a prominent European settler. Made by a local dressmaker, it comprises a black silk damask dress, with bodice and skirt showing firm knowledge of the latest trends from Europe and America. The leg-of-mutton sleeves are an especially recognizable feature of the era, characteristic of the more "drooping" styles seen earlier in the decade, and creating the hourglass shape that was so fashionable.

....

The bodice fastens at the front with a row of 16 shank buttons in an 8-sided, jewel-like shape that catches the light. [6] On dresses with less ornate surface decoration, button could assume a greater importance.

The bodice is stiffened with four lengths of whalebone at the back and two at the front, each encased in cotton sheaths and stitched to the inner seams. It's important to note that, in comparison to fashionable European counterparts, this is a reduced number of boning channels. They are also narrower, made to accommodate slimmer strips of whalebone than commonly used in Europe. This consideration was largely down to the climate of Western Australia.

Black machine-embroidered net is appliqued to the front and back of the bodice, forming a V shape across the center. Extra net is arranged in a circular yoke around the neck.

These leg of mutton sleeves become fairly close-fitting after the elbow, but flare out slightly at the wrist with a net insert on the outer seam.

The center back of the bodice ends in a deep point, three inches longer than that at the front. The graduating lace panel draws the eye downward and emphasizes this shape at the waistline.

Originally, a small bustle pad may have been worn at the waist to hold out the back of the skirt and show off this *silk damask* (a figured woven fabric) to its best advantage.

Six panels make up the simple shape of this skirt, which is fastened through a side-front *placket* (an opening in the upper section of skirts and trousers). [7]

There is no train to this skirt, but the slight flare would have been supported and extended by the wearing of gored petticoats, frilled at the hem.

Dress with exchange sleeves,

c.1895–96, Powerhouse Museum, Sydney

◆

This red russet day dress was purchased at department store David Jones. This establishment remains one of the oldest continuing such stores in the world and is also historically a good indicator of the position of Australia's cities as forward-moving centers of fashion despite their distance from the sartorial capitals of London and Paris. Its showrooms and catalogue were described by the *Sydney Morning Herald* in 1896 as "guarantee[ing] the satisfaction of the most fastidious taste." [8]

Silk brocade revers flare over the sleeves, extending out from the opening of this three-layered bodice. These pleated lapels were also known as *bretelles*.

Widespread use of the sewing machine made it easier and quicker to assemble complex dresses. This meant that more time could be given to handmade surface decoration like the silk rosettes and bronze beading seen here.

This gored, flat-fronted skirt, gathered at the rear into a small train, is very characteristic of the period. It would have been worn over a gored petticoat with frill and flare at the hem.

By this time, as sleeve width reached its apex, the hems of skirts widened too, often incorporating well over five meters of fabric.

By the middle of the decade, we see pronounced, extended leg-of-mutton sleeves, now wider and stiffer than those of the preceding years. To maintain this shape, extra structure in the form of stiff lining (and, briefly, wire sleeve supports) was required in much the same manner as it had been for the balloon sleeve of the 1830s.

Fashion papers during the middle of the decade spoke of the popularity of basques "long and short" and "pointed peplums," often described alongside a new passion for overskirts. Both can be seen in this example. [9]

Fashionable styles such as this one were no longer attainable only by the leisured classes. This was the era when "readymades" in clothing became more widely available than ever and started to break down the association of fashionable, well-made clothes with only the elite and moneyed. This shift came alongside the continuing development of the department store in Europe, America, and Australia, propagated by the needs and desires of a rising urban middle class. Although dressmakers (who, in contrast to seamstresses, also designed clothing) were still in high demand, the ease and availability of ready-to-wear clothing highlighted a faster pace of life and a response to growing consumer demands.

Dress,

1897, Los Angeles County Museum of Art

◆

This two-piece day dress, shown here from the back, was made by the House of Rouff, Paris: a well-known couturier described by one newspaper as a couturier that did not "make cut-and-dried gowns formed by rule: they have expression, and must be seen." [10] Along with innovation in cut comes a popular color combination—shades of light and dark mauve—on the bodice.

The very high collar indicates a growing trend from 1897–98 onward. Its long, pointed edges are a striking addition, and the shape is repeated on the cuffs.

The emphasis here is very much on the complex, architectural arrangement of pleats on the bodice, which continue over the shoulders to meet in a soft V neck at the front.

This skirt is a good example of the undecorated styles fashionable during the decade. Instead of surface embellishment, the emphasis here is on structure. The deep pleats at the center back of the skirt help to create a smooth, flowing silhouette and to add volume.

In the middle of the decade, sleeve widths reached extreme proportions. By c.1897, they were no longer as exaggerated as they had been, and this dress shows the beginning of a very slow decline. These sleeves are small variations on a gigot style, tapering to become tight around the lower arm and wrist.

A black silk sash, decorated with a black rosette, highlights the narrow *wasp waist*. It calls to mind similarly shaped *Swiss waists* of the mid 1860s (also known at the time as *Medici Waists* or *Swiss Bodies*).

Some examples from this period show sleeves made in a separate fabric to the body of the dress. Here, this technique is in evidence by use of rich purple velvet: an extremely fashionable fabric in the final years of the decade. The remainder of the dress is made from silk twill.

This example clearly shows the gored cut of late 1890s skirts, shaped through triangular pieces of cloth. This curvier shape and flared hem was to become very prominent in the succeeding decade. [11]

Day or afternoon dress,

c.1900, McCord Museum, Montreal

◆

Black tape lace is a dominant feature of this dress, made the more striking by its placement over a soft pink silk underlay. The great fashionability of lace, described by one newspaper in 1901 as being "still used in everything… blouses topped entirely by lace, and the sleeves finished by ruffles and cuffs and long pointed tabs of it." [12]

High boned collars were becoming very fashionable by the beginning of the 1900s.

These sleeves have the small shoulder puffs of the late 1890s. Shaped by only a few gathers, they no longer stand up above the shoulder line. As the 1900s continued, puffs became lower and drooping, and it was common to see sleeves caught into pouches below the elbow while the tops were slim and close fitting.

The placement of the lace leaves some sections of fabric bare. One of these, at the very top of the skirt, creates a simulated yoke, emphasizing the position of the waist and the new S-bend silhouette with hips pushed back and chest out.

The sheer overskirt is shaped to the hips by a series of darts, and the skirt is gathered at back and sides, leading into a relatively slim-fitting skirt with a modest train.

A *pigeon pouched* front of the bodice hangs a little way over the waistline and accentuates the larger *mono-bosom* and small waist (while partially obscuring the exact position of the waist). This was starting to be widely in evidence by 1898, though the longer *S-bend* corset, which enhanced this shape, had only recently been introduced. Here, a central *plastron* (a term for the front of a bodice made from different fabric to the rest of the garment), edged with petals of the tape lace, highlights the fashionable pouching.

Ruffles were a popular edging for cuffs and necklines, suggesting a historical influence and also a chance to show off interesting lace designs.

Lady Curzon's evening dress,

1902–03, Fashion Museum, Bath

◆

This sumptuous two-piece evening gown was made for Lady Curzon, Vicereine of India, by the shining light of Paris couturiers, the House of Worth—at this time run by Jean-Philippe Worth, the son of the founder Charles Frederick. It represents the epitome of early Edwardian styling: the S-bend or swan bill silhouette attained by a new vogue in corsetry, flared skirt with train, and low-set natural waistline.

. . . .

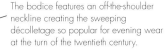

The bodice features an off-the-shoulder neckline creating the sweeping décolletage so popular for evening wear at the turn of the twentieth century.

Corset, c.1900, Los Angeles County Museum of Art
The rigidly straight front of the corset thrust the wearer's hips back, while the relatively uncovered and unsupported bust brought the chest level lower.

The bodice fastens at the front with a row of hooks and eyes. Above that, this ornate panel crosses from right to left and fastens at the side with another set of hooks and eyes, creating an unbroken line.

The detachable sash sits just below the natural waistline at the very top of the hips. This serves to emphasize the new popular shape and draws attention to the flat-fronted, highly ornate skirt.

A soft silk chiffon edging to the skirt hem echoes the trimming on the bodice. Soft and sheer fabrics such as crepe, gauze, and voile were often used as trimmings, especially for evening wear. From 1900 to 1905, these fabrics were frequently embellished with embroidery, applique, beads, and sequins.

This gown's embellishment includes more than 400 oak leaf shapes edged in cord and silk satin. The looped, forward-facing placement of these leaves on the front of the skirt draws attention to the pushed-out bust and thrust back hips of the S-bend silhouette.

Wedding dress,

1905, Manning Valley Historical Society, New South Wales

◆

This four-piece silk chiffon wedding dress from the east coast of Australia is an example of a locally made garment. Its design and construction shows a keen awareness of the latest trends from Europe and the United States, evidencing the means of wealthy families who had settled into colonial life and were reaping the benefits.

Two lengths of boning, one on each side, stiffen and support this standing collar.

The V-shaped bodice opening features a large, flat, turned-down collar (edged with the same pleated organza—a later addition—as the cuffs), and beneath this is a machine-made high *modesty neckline* that simulates a dress front. It is embellished with three small satin bows.

The wide collar slightly overhangs the waist, emphasizing the forward-leaning *pigeon* front that the *S-shape* silhouette created.

Puffed, tiered sleeves were a popular look during the first five years of the century, and a brief resurgence of the 1890s balloon shape could be seen in c.1905–07. These combine several style influences from different phases in history, as diverse as the late 1600s, 1700s, and 1820s–30s.

To preserve the pleating detail at the back of the bodice, this gown is front fastening. It closes with six brass hooks, running from the point of the V to the top of the skirt. [13]

The mixing of different colors and hues in one garment became even more popular over the next few years. There are several shades here, from ivory to coffee, mixing the ancient preference for colored wedding dresses with the newer usage of white, cream, ivory, and gold.

Bands of machine-made lace overlays along the skirt hem add some textural interest to the bottom of the garment. The back of the skirt has a flare but no train. [14]

Wedding dress,

c.1907, McCord Museum, Montreal

—◆—

The overlay of this intricate wedding dress is made almost entirely of Battenberg lace, a method of lacemaking that uses braided tapes. Other popular techniques included Irish crochet and machine-made lace. By the late nineteenth century machine-made tapes made it easier and quicker to produce the Battenberg variety, which consists of a pattern set on a lining of net or bars of thread.

....

Open-front bodices were popular around this time, allowing for the display of a decorated blouse or—as in this case—a false sheer *chemisette*. Although far more neck and shoulder was now shown on eveningwear, for daywear (including wedding dresses), women were still expected to cover their necks modestly. This practice slowly started to change from 1910 onward.

The prominent and popular *mono-bosom* effect is accentuated by a slight pigeon front to the bodice.

A wide waistband, with three large central lace flowers, draws attention to a small waist.

The round orange floral motifs that adorn several narrow, vertical panels around the skirt and bodice are set with tiny pearls, sewn directly onto a gauze background. Sections of lace are alternately broken by further vertical panels of delicate embroidery.

A slightly puffed sleeve, tapering to the elbow, still remains. It continued to be popular until c.1909–10.

These light undersleeves comprise gathered frills held by bands of peach-colored tape. The ruffled effect created is referenced in several fashion columns when discussing styles for the year 1907. It was also suggested as an easy and cost-effective way for a home dressmaker to add embellishment to a gown.

A swag motif along the hem is set above a trim of lightly pleated tulle, mirroring the neckline and upper sleeve detail.

Summer dress,

c.1904–07, Shippensburg Fashion Museum & Archives, Shippensburg, Pennsylvania

◆

Lacy lingerie or lawn dresses—sometimes known simply as whites—were popular throughout the decade and were often used for summer wear, being frequently unlined and made from lightweight fabrics. Access to sewing machines and mechanically produced lace meant that a greater number of women could wear this fashionable style.

A horizontal band of lace, perhaps foreshadowing the soon-to-come empire-line revival, breaks the center of the torso.

Here is a good example of a pouched or pigeon-fronted bodice, emphasizing the forward-leaning torso. By c.1906–07, many dresses were now made in two pieces: bodice and skirt, and bodices would fasten separately with hooks and eyes (or, after around 1903, steel poppers). [15]

A pointed yoke on the skirt gathers in excess fabric, stressing the slimness of the hips—an attribute that would soon become paramount to an even higher degree. Similar effects were sometimes achieved by the use of a wide belt or Swiss waist.

The high neck still reigns supreme for daywear. In this example, the neck leads into a simple yoke of neat gathered rows and edged with the same lace seen throughout the dress. These gathers and tucks are repeated in varying widths on the bodice, cuffs, and hem.

This dress features modest *bishop* sleeves. Fullness on the upper arms is controlled through the application of released tucks, and the lower fabric is gathered into a lace cuff at the wrist. A similar tucked effect on the bodice gives corresponding harmony to the whole ensemble.

During this period, skirts were cut long and straight in front and flowing at the back, with styles such as the *trumpet* and *umbrella* featuring gored sections to create a circular shape to the hem. This example is constructed with curved-edged gores leading into the train.

The insubstantial train is a common feature on day dresses of this era, and dress reformists of the early twentieth century relentlessly campaigned for trains to be abolished completely, believing them to be partially responsible for the spread of dirt, dust, and, therefore, disease. The rise of more practical clothing for women meant that trains naturally fell out of favor for daywear over the succeeding years. For eveningwear, however, they remained for quite some time.

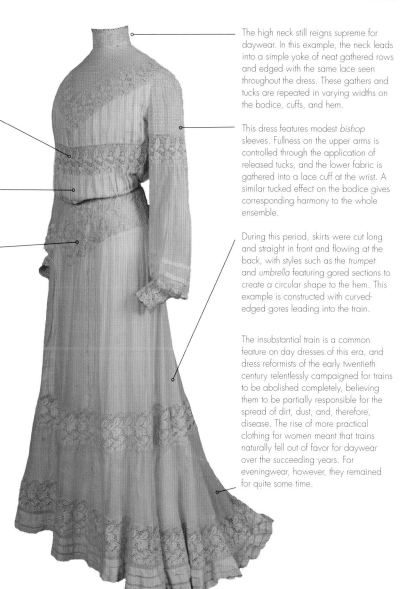

Similar light summer dresses in the German countryside, 1903

Summer dress,

c.1908, McCord Museum, Montreal

◆

More traditionally "feminine" frocks were always popular and available. Floral and floaty with overlays of lace, examples such as this illustrate that perennial wish for grace and elegance, abiding feminine virtues that were so well portrayed through fashion.

As with many dresses from the 1890s onward, the yoke was a form of trimming rather than a separately constructed piece. Here, its presence is simulated in the deliberately shaped lacework that encompasses the shoulders.

Long sleeves are slightly puffed to the elbow and then fitted from forearm to wrist. [16]

The excess fabric previously seen in the blousy pigeon pouter bodice has, in this example, moved to the sides. A gentle overhang is created through simple tucks and gathers. Two rows of horizontal lace mark out the natural waistline.

The princess-line cut is shown through these narrow bands of lace insertion, placed vertically across the front of the dress. The widest panel of lace, seen on bodice, skirt, and sleeves, features a geometric spiraling design known as a *meander or key fret*. [17] Especially recognizable as a motif from classical Greece, its ancient origins can be seen in this detail of a ceramic pot, c.800–760 B.C.

Attic Geometric Lidded Pyxis, detail, Athens, Greece, Los Angeles County Museum of Art

Its use on this dress is an early indication of the Neoclassical revival, promoting a simpler approach to dress at the end of c.1908.

The skirt is still relatively full, its hem width widened by this gathered frill at sides and back.

Black silk satin and lace dress,

c.1908–12, Griffith Pioneer Park Museum, New South Wales

◆

This dress is characteristic of the transitional styles spanning the years 1908–12, illustrating the development of the Directoire revival. Worn in eastern Australia, always a year or so behind the latest European styles, it also represents a mix of old and new in trimming and finer details.

The upper sleeves are cut as one with the surplice bodice. They reach to elbow length where they are edged with a satin band, and undersleeves of machine lace (lined with polished cotton) reach the wrist. [18]

The embroidered cotton net lace is machine-made, allowing easier creation of elaborate designs incorporating tucks, swirling floral motifs, and scalloped edges. Four small rows of tucks cover the bodice, sleeves, and skirt—a hugely popular decorative method during the period.

The bodice features a high-necked, seven-boned standing collar, molded to the shape of the neck. This style started to lose its popularity from c.1909 onward.

Sashes were often discussed in fashion columns of the time, with the *Brisbane Courier* suggesting that, due to the "plain outline of dress" currently fashionable, there is "opportunity for some originality in dealing with decorative details, and of these perhaps the sash is the most important." A cord example similar to that shown here is described: "Wide braid is also made up . . . and after being simply tied, the ends are knotted at intervals." [19]

This is a very definite empire-line waist, emphasized by the (replica) belt with a corded sash tied on top. This type of corded, braided detail, described above, recalled Japanese influences such as the *obi jime*, a decorative cord tied around the broad sash (*obi*) on a woman's kimono and seen in this nineteenth-century print.

A very similar dress is shown in this photograph taken in England, c.1909–12. The tiered sleeves and high lace collar, in particular, show the influence of some key trends across Europe to Australia.
Author's family archive

Utagawa Kuniyoshi, *Osatao and Gonta* (detail), Japan, nineteenth century, Los Angeles County Museum of Art

Evening dress,

1910–12, Powerhouse Museum, Sydney

◆

Once again, this example shows a return to the delicate proportions of classical antiquity with the empire-line silhouette. More structured and architectural than that of the 1790s and early 1800s, this c.1911 evening gown is worn over the hip-length corset and narrow petticoats so characteristic of the 1910s.

It's believed that the owner of the dress altered the neckline because she felt it was too low. It is possible that this silk and net modesty panel, matching similar detail at the back, was added to fill in the space. [20]

Double rows of flat and pleated trim on the cuffs are reminiscent of eighteenth-century dress robings. A net panel in between is spotted with silver sequins.

Trimming (robings) on the overskirt of a robe à l'anglaise, England, c.1770–80, Los Angeles County Museum of Art

The *hobble skirt*, cut very closely to the ankles and in its most fashionable form quite debilitating, was introduced in around 1910. The skirt shown here, though narrow, does flare out a little at the hem, suggesting that in general there was some versatility for women away from the most fashionable styles.

Instructions issued with commercial patterns were quick to point out that the length of a skirt was up to the maker of the dress; however, at this date, hems rarely finished above the ankle.

Kimono sleeves are cut as one with the bodice. Tucked sections of fabric, slightly overlapping the edge of the shoulders (described in one piece of fashion commentary as "draped in surplice fashion, the two sections at each side crossing far over to the sides, both back and front") was a common decorative technique. [21] Blousier effects, draped and arranged around the neckline and shoulders in the manner of an eighteenth-century *fichu*, were also popular.

The dress is front-fastening, closing down the right-hand side with a row of metal poppers. [22]

Beaded and fringed medallions focus attention on the bodice and draped overskirt. Beading was a very popular trimming during this era, and medallions were often used on evening and bridal dresses. A Tasmanian newspaper described a similar effect in September 1911: "Beaded effects are showing up among trimmings . . . Bead medallions with bead fringe show a mixture of all colors on a foundation of gold tinsel, black net, or braid or oxidised tinsel." [23] Decoration such as this would have reflected candles, gas, or electric light, creating a bedazzling jeweled effect for onlookers.

Two-tiered skirts were popular at this date, with light gauzy overlays arranged on top of plainer, more tailored *foundation* skirts. The tailored feel of this one is emphasized by a row of nine self-covered buttons, with silver beads in the center of each.

Woman's suit, wool,

c.1898–1900, McCord Museum, Montreal

◆

Suits or tailormades were often made in an almost identical fashion to a man's jacket. One "Lady's Letter," written in London in 1898 and published in various newspapers, claimed that although tailormades appeared "in all kinds of materials, what are known as gentleman's cloths are the only really suitable material for them," the dressmaker's "hand is very evident in the 'finish' of such gowns." [24]

A *shirtwaist*—a bodice fashioned after a man's shirt—would be worn, which could be made in a wide variety of fabrics and colors. This example, however, would most likely have been worn with plain white or cream and a dark necktie.

The same letter quoted above describes a tailormade of what it calls the "genuine type," aligning very closely to the example seen here: "The bodice is double breasted, with a double row of buttons set closer together as they reach the waist . . . the sleeves (are) absolutely plain, even at the shoulders." This style is described by the author as "the riding dress worn by women a hundred years ago," and it is possible to see some similarity between this outfit and the tailored habits (and increasingly, daywear styles) of the late eighteenth century:

George Haugh, *The Countess of Effingham with Gun and Shooting Dogs*, 1787, Yale Center for British Art, Paul Mellon Collection

The top lapels are inlaid with matching panels of bottle-green velvet. The rest of the bodice and skirt are made from wool, which was suggested by fashion papers as the prime fabric of choice for a tailormade. One Australian newspaper recommended "all heavy, firmly woven woollen material such as serge, Venetian cloth or cheviot." [25]

The sleeves are relatively plain, with only very small gathers at the shoulder and long, slightly curved arms finishing at a close-fitting buttoned cuff.

The skirt's simplicity corresponds to a description of a similar outfit in *The Queenslander* newspaper of April 1900: "The skirt . . . (fits) perfectly close at the top, but . . . spreads at the bottom to form a short graceful train." [26] However, this approach was not universal for tailormades, as *The Chicago Tribune* pointed out in August of the same year: "[The tailormade skirt] has gained a great deal of fussiness... the former were so near, so trim, so flat... Now we see... the tailor-mad with an applique of lace, bordered... with braid... trimmed with dozens and dozens of little taffeta ruffles." [27] This corresponds with a general call, from many fashion papers, for the use of more embellishment through the use of braid, cord, and stitching.

Woman's suit,

1912, McCord Museum, Montreal

◆

This suit, made by couturier Louis Sangan, is made from Tussah silk shantung (shot silk) in a light beige. It characterizes the long, slim line of the period and is an excellent example of a daywear alternative to the dress.

Wide collars were common on all types of daywear during the era. This shawl example continues wide and straight at the back and sits squarely on the shoulders in the manner of a sailor-suit collar. The collar is trimmed with two rows of scalloped blue and beige *soutache braid* (a flat, narrow decorative trimming also known as *galloon*). This edging is also set into the cuffs. [28]

In 1911–12, the use of buttons for both fastenings and decoration was extremely popular, the American women's magazine *The Delineator* declaring at the end of 1911 that "one can not use buttons too liberally in the present mode" [29] The self-panels shown on the lower sides of the jacket feature three domed, covered buttons. These also form the front closure of the garment.

Rounded edges to the jacket are repeated in the rounded hems of the skirt panels.

The A-line skirt features a set-in V-shaped panel on each side, decorated with the same soutache trim and button style seen on the jacket. [30]

The skirt sits just past ankle-length and would have been worn with a wide-brimmed hat and ankle- or calf-length leather boots.

Loops of braid simulating buttonholes edge the front panel of the skirt. Further rows of buttons edge the opposite back panel. [31]

Evening coat of gray satin,

Paris, c.1912, McCord Museum, Montreal

◆

This coat is included due to its representation of the fashionable line, the hugely popular kimono style, and to show the way that new high-waisted fashionable dresses would have been accessorized: in particular the puddle train and narrow hems, which became fashionable in the west in the form of hobble skirts.

The opening of Japan's trade routes with Europe in 1854 helped create a distinctive aesthetic culture with Japanese art at its center. Fashion also took its cue from these influences, bringing a shift in the direction of fashionable dress and its foundations. Despite considerable advances in female liberation, the stereotyped meek Japanese woman—portrayed in popular theatre with the Mikado and other plays—and her constructive dress, seemed to have become an enviable symbol of womanhood. At the same time, westerners admired the apparent looseness of kimono at a time when that garment was becoming increasingly less worn in Japan itself. Western dress was now frequently adopted, as seen in this 1888 print.

The weight of this straight-cut coat is supported from the shoulders, shifting emphasis from the waist for the first time in decades. Designer Paul Poiret was a key player in this change of direction.

The wide dolman sleeves finish just past elbow length. After about 1912, the poplar three-quarter-length kimono sleeves became less commonplace, making way for a longer sleeve—often a double-layered one.

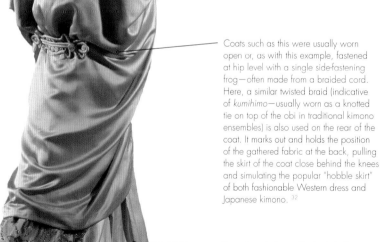

Tsukioka Yoshitoshi (1839–92), *Preparing to Take a Stroll: The Wife of a Nobleman of the Meiji Period*, 1888, Los Angeles County Museum of Art

Coats such as this were usually worn open or, as with this example, fastened at hip level with a single side-fastening frog—often made from a braided cord. Here, a similar twisted braid (indicative of *kumihimo*—usually worn as a knotted tie on top of the obi in traditional kimono ensembles) is also used on the rear of the coat. It marks out and holds the position of the gathered fabric at the back, pulling the skirt of the coat close behind the knees and simulating the popular "hobble skirt" of both fashionable Western dress and Japanese kimono. [32]

There is no train, and indeed the hem does not even reach the floor. Instead, the dress beneath is allowed to add another dimension of color and texture, perhaps echoing the separately constructed hems that were popular for certain traditional kimono styles.

Woman's three-piece costume,

c.1915, McCord Museum, Montreal

◆

From the beginning of the century, two- or three-piece ensembles known as "costumes" had been popular and became daily wear for many women, worn alongside dresses and skirt/blouse combinations. This example, dating from the early-middle years of World War I, illustrates the comparatively loose and bulky silhouette of the era. Fashion reporters described this type of fit as "sloppy" but also "rational," well suited to the modern woman and her increased responsibilities on the home front. [33]

The third piece of the ensemble is a pink satin and organza blouse with a scalloped lace applique collar (extending like a sailor collar over the jacket). It is worn under a cream-colored wool bolero with *vented* (slit) sides. [34]

A dress with a wide sailor collar, c.1917–18 (Author's family archive)

A similarly styled suit with asymmetric jacket hem and wide blouse collar is seen here in this German family portrait, c.1915–16. See also the traditional sailor collar worn by the little girl. (Kästing family archive.)

Hand-painted buttons such as these, featuring a Chinese design, were popular novelty fastenings for jackets and coats.

The jacket's high waistline continues the empire-line revival of the prewar years.

The edges of the jacket form a basque of handkerchief points, extending to the hips.

The skirt features silk cord applique on both sides, bordering a cream silk *cummerbund*—a structured belt—that fastens at the back. [35]

This costume shows a rejection of the tubular line, especially in the slightly flared skirt which features a double-stitched yoke, with a double-stitched center and back seam. [36] Such styles would become wider and more billowing in the remainder of World War I, starting to predominate around 1915–16.

Chapter 8
1918–1929

By the end of World War I, suits and "costumes" were becoming daywear staples. Newspaper reports regarding the predicted wideness and narrowness of skirts during this four-year period illustrate an aspect that particularly concerned women, and that was inevitably dictated to a large degree by rationing. As the *Daily Mail* reported in August 1917, "Women of fashion are . . . not a little alarmed by the statement in a Paris newspaper to-day that, as a result of the Government restriction of the use of woolen material, skirts are to be both shorter and narrower." [1] The article stipulates a new restriction of 4 yards and 32 inches of material per outfit, at a width of 1 ¹/₃ yards. This will be, they reassure the reader, "ample for a Frenchwoman of medium build." Given the propensity for heavily layered and somewhat solid designs during the war years, such reticence is not surprising. Fuller skirts were seen as a more comfortable and practical option after the constraint and inconvenience of hobble styles but were teamed with a continuation of the slightly higher waistlines that had been popular since c.1910.

However, in a period of wartime flux and austerity, the reality was that new fashions were not taken up immediately. An issue of *Vogue* from 1918 remarks that "The cost of the [. . .] enormous demands of the war upon stuffs and labour—all these have contributed to the cost of our clothes." It finds a silver lining, though, in the realization that "this increase has been offset . . . by the revival of the slim silhouette . . . it takes more than half the number of yards that were required in the previous season." [2] The wide skirts of the earlier war years could certainly not be seen in designs from the final years of conflict, but by the end of the war it was possible to witness a slight increase in volume. This photograph of a young couple from 1919 shows the reality for most women at this time, the wife wearing a dress with strong overtones of fashionable styles pre-World War I. The high waistline, double-button fastening, and wraparound opening conform to popular designs of that era. The main difference is the presence of an above ankle-length skirt and the sailor-style collar, both of which can be seen on many designs of this immediate postwar era. The hem length in particular suggests that the dress was probably modified in tune with shifting trends.

The low-waisted, androgynous style that was to become eponymous with the following decade is especially recognizable through its association with the "flapper" girl and Prohibition-era speakeasies of America. Although the typical flapper physique—described aptly in Evelyn Waugh's *Brideshead Revisited* as "flat-chested, leggy . . . all limbs and neck, bodiless, spidery"—was certainly seen around the western world in ballrooms, clubs, bars and even drawing rooms, most women wore clothes encapsulating a toned-down version of the look in their everyday lives. [3] However, despite popular perception there still existed strict moral codes for all classes, and many women spent the 1920s in longer, drabber, altogether more sedate variants of the high-fashion ideal.

With shorter skirts, bare arms, and cropped shingle-cut hair covered by helmet-like *cloche* hats came a suggestion of freer sexuality and speech and greater expectations from life. Following the trauma of World War I, opinion was divided on whether such optimism was appropriate or prudent. Some couturiers did respond to this hesitancy, with designers like Jeanne Lanvin and Jacques Doucet catering to older generations with the *robes de style* or "picture dress," which still featured the popular dropped waist but combined this with a wide, flowing skirt and more traditionally feminine cut. It was often, particularly for eveningwear, worn over eighteenth-century style paniers that created the familiar wide hipped silhouette. Older clients appreciated this blend of old and new, and it enabled more mature women to confidently enjoy selected aspects of the low-waisted style. Although a design more commonly associated with the 1920s, the robe de style could be seen at times throughout the 1930s, and its form and embellishment did alter to suit the current fashion. A 1939 piece by couturiere Madame Vionnet in the Metropolitan Museum of Art is especially representative of this, featuring a long, light chiffon skirt over paniers with high halter neck and subtle ornamentation. We can see the lead-up to this relative simplicity in an article from 1934, describing existing robes de style as making the wearer feel "dressed up like grandmother's plush horse . . . there are [those] who never were cut out for prima donna costumes, and know it." However, with a "rustle of romantic charm," *The Milwaukee Sentinel's* fashion pages enthuse about more demure picture frocks, with flared skirts but a slimmer fit overall. "Here," the writer says of one, "is a robe-de-style that provides the perfect setting for fragile, feminine beauty." [4] This article, and others like it, are illustrative of the fact that not every woman strived for the boyish silhouette, but also that its influence did not entirely diminish just because a new decade had arrived. "Romanticism" in fashion still seems to suggest long, full skirts and an antique charm, and variants of the robe de style appear to have catered, for some, to this demand.

In the world of haute couture, the Orientalism that had so entranced Paul Poiret and others before World War I led, during the 1920s, to the development of a new artistic movement: Art Deco. As Art Nouveau had done before it, Art Deco as a theme rejected an emphasis on historicism, moving toward abstraction as an aesthetic ideal. The "Exposition internationale des arts décoratifs et industriels modernes," otherwise known as the Paris Exhibition of 1925, had a significant impact on the spread and appropriation of Art Deco as a style. As the host city, this event also helped to continue Paris's reputation as the city of fashion post World War I, and exhibitors and visitors from all over the globe placed France at the center of this new decorative vision. Art Deco (or *Style Moderne*) had a huge impact on all the decorative arts, and in terms of clothing and textiles France was at the center of philosophy and manufacture. Couturiers like Madame Vionnet were incredibly influential and inventive, incorporating both existing "exotic" elements—from Japanese origami to

LEFT
Dress, c.1918-19,
Kent, England, author's
family archive

Chinese characters—and shapes and designs from totally contemporary movements such as cubism, Futurism, and other early forms of abstraction. Neoclassicism continued to be popular too, partly because the geometric designs of ancient Greece and Rome could be seen so clearly reinterpreted in cubist works of art.

The mid nineteenth century had seen the introduction of the first haute couture salons, elite institutions that only very rarely sold *pret-a-porter* (ready-to-wear) garments. The twentieth century heralded a change, and much stiffer competition, with designers like Coco Chanel (1883–1971) making pret-a-porter available directly from their salons. The type of clothing produced by Chanel lent itself well to this approach, being significantly simpler, freer, and more suited to the postwar woman who increasingly worked and led an independent lifestyle. Her innovative use of jersey (previously used almost exclusively for menswear, particularly underwear) was an inspired move that promoted easy-to-wear garments and an emphasis on sportswear for women. The majority of her clothing was devoid of fuss, with simple straight lines and a classic elegance that did not require the use of restrictive corsetry. This ability to marry high-end designer wear with the demands of contemporary life is a philosophy carried on by twenty-first-century designers, and the presence and celebrity of Chanel herself—perhaps the first designer to attain such a status in the world—has also had a profound influence on the designers and fashion houses of today. [5]

LEFT
Appliquéd robe
de style, c.1924,
Vintage Textile,
New Hampshire.

RIGHT
Evening dress inspired
by Poiret, Germany,
c.1918–20, private
collection

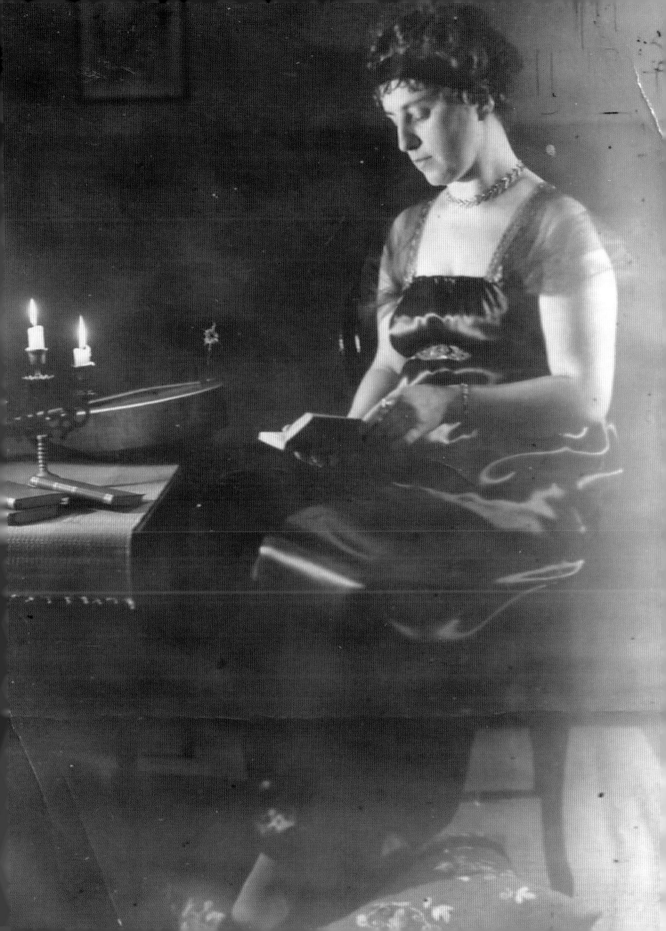

Net and silk evening dress,

1918, North Carolina Museum of History, Raleigh

◆

This gold silk and black net dress was made specifically for eveningwear. However, due to the straitened years of the war, a new evening gown was an unattainable luxury for many women. *The Chicago Tribune* suggested in May 1918 that the most economical option was to alter existing afternoon dresses. Because, the *Tribune* points out, fashionable afternoon dresses were often made "over plain satin of harmonizing shade... [overlayed] with net or lace," with the addition of a few minor embellishments, they served well as eveningwear. [6]

William Leroy Jacobs, *Woman in a blue dress*, 1917, Library of Congress, Prints & Photographs Division

This American portrait from 1917 shows a young woman wearing a similar style of dress with the same sheer sleeves, square neckline, wide sash, and ankle-length skirt. Her shoes are a typical example of the modest heels that would be worn with this type of outfit.

The Chicago Tribune suggested that "the question of skirt length is rather up to the wearer." Short or long, the writer continues, the important thing is that day and evening dresses alike are worn with heels: "[for] you look nothing whatever without a pair of trim looking heels and ankles." [7]

Two pleated lengths of black net extend from the sash and over the chest to form the shoulders. Asymmetrically draped net at the edges create light "handkerchief" pointed cap sleeves.

By 1918, deep round or square necklines such as this were popular for eveningwear, with higher necks and collars for daytime.

This wide black velvet sash meets at center back with a large bow, which sits at an empire line position directly beneath the center-back fastening of the bodice.

Decorated overskirts, often finished with a shaped hem, were very popular on both day- and eveningwear during this period. Here, deep central scalloped points at front and back are edged with gold embroidery. The fabric is pleated to the waist all around, and at the sides shorter hem lengths give width to the hips.

The gold embroidery on the overskirt is probably machine-made. This technology was commercially pioneered in Switzerland in the nineteenth century, and by the 1870s "Schiffli" embroidery machines were exported fairly widely. With the rise of ready-to-wear clothing at the end of the nineteenth and into the twentieth century, machine embroidering became increasingly popular. [8]

Tea gown by Mariano Fortuny,

c.1920–29, North Carolina Museum of History, Raleigh

◆

Spanish-born Mariano Fortuny (1871–1949) was one of the most influential designers of the twentieth century, with his clinging garments initially inspiring rational and "aesthetic" dress advocates. His signature "Delphos" dress was inspired by the Ancient Greek chiton, and this simple line, coupled with a rolled pleating technique (patented in 1909), are instantly recognizable as the designer's trademark. The example shown here was made as a tea gown, but with the new, more liberated styles of the 1920s, many of Fortuny's designs became equally popular as eveningwear.

Venetian glass beads connect the sides of the shoulder seams, continuing into the body of the sleeve. As well as adding a decorative dimension, this type of detailing is also borrowed from ancient Greek *peplos* and *chiton* robes. [9]

The wide neckline of these tea gowns was usually gathered on a silk cord.

The tunic-like bodice of this dress is a separately made piece, worn with a skirt. In many cases, though, these "tunics" were actually attached to an underdress to form one garment. Whichever method Fortuny used, the shape produced is reminiscent of ancient Greek peplos, a comparison accentuated by the addition of deep handkerchief points at either side of the tunic: [10]

Maiden from a Mirror Stand, bronze, 500–475 B.C., **The Walters Art Museum, Baltimore**

Over her peplos this statuette is draped in a *himation*, a mantle worn by both sexes into the Hellenistic period. This was a design also embraced by Fortuny and often incorporated into his garments.

Woman "Peplophoros," marble, first century B.C. (Hellenistic), The Walters Art Museum, Baltimore

The hem is edged with the same Venetian glass beads used on the sleeves, adding different texture and color, as well as giving weight to the light fabric of the dress. They also link to Fortuny's place of manufacture, the island of Giudecca in Venice where he had a studio and factory. [11]

Fortuny was interested in Eastern fashions, and created kimono-style coats with Japanese-inspired fabric. The long hem on this dress can be likened to that on formal uchikake kimono. In recent years, Fortuny's use of pleats has in turn heavily influenced Japanese designer Issey Miyake.

Black crêpe de chine day dress,

c.1920–25, Swan Guildford Historical Society, Australia

◆

Despite appearances, this is not an evening dress: sleeveless dresses, even for daywear, were becoming more acceptable by the mid 1920s: this example could potentially have been worn for any time of day.

....

A round, relatively high-set neckline was common for items of daywear.

There are two rows of *drawn thread-work* above the waistband. Also known as *pulled work*, the technique involves removing threads from the warp or weft of a fabric. Those left behind are drawn together to form various patterns. This was a popular method of decoration, partly because it was a cheap alternative to lace or embroidery—both of which it could be made to resemble. An article in the *Sydney Mail* from 1921, entitled "A Frock for Seven Shillings," enthuses: "Drawn thread insertions are the latest craze; indeed, the decorative treatment meted out to frocks of all sorts and conditions is one of the features of the summer styles." [12]

There are twelve reverse pintucks on each shoulder, all seventeen centimeters long.

Ten matching pintucks create a waistband. When worn, this waist definition would produce a "blousy" effect with the loose bodice drooping slightly over the waist.

Fine black net underskirts sit between each tier.

The tiers are finished with a hand-stitched rolled edge. Aside from the pintucks and the side and shoulder seams, the entire dress is hand sewn. [13]

A sleeveless day dress worn with brown fringed shawl in Wales, mid-1920s (Author's family archive)

Day dress,

c.1922–24, North Carolina Museum of History, Raleigh

◆

In many respects, the simplicity of this one-piece dress—in particular its dark shade, straight tubular cut, and flat collar—corresponds to popular daywear trends of the era. Beaded embroidery suggests the influence of one of the great discoveries of the age: Tutankhamen's tomb in 1922.

....

Four pintucks placed at each shoulder give a little shape to the bodice. Such details were often the only fitted elements on these simple dresses.

Wide, flat collars such as this were a practical choice for daywear and popular throughout the decade. Here, the broad lapel gives an opportunity to include beaded decoration at the back of the dress as well as at the front.

A satin sash, with shirred gathered detail to one side, highlights the fashionable placement of a low waistline.

Throughout the 1920s, one-piece dresses were frequently in fashion and, according to one column, the American girl clings to it with almost as much determination as ever her ancestors clung to their rights for freedom in another way . . . Every season . . . it becomes just as fashionable as it was during the last." [14] The same writer points out the attractiveness of panels of embroidery or other forms of decoration on such dresses, being a bold or understated way of adding texture and color to an otherwise simple garment.

The beaded animal and plant motifs on the front of the dress are only vague interpretations of ancient Egyptian hieroglyphs, though the vertical column format—with blank panels at both sides—can be described as diagnostically Egyptian in origin. [16]

An "approved" hem length for one-piece styles is given in several sources as between six and eight inches, described by Australian newspaper *Table Talk* as "a comfortable walking length, and becoming to almost everyone." [15]

Evening dress,

c.1923, Powerhouse Museum, Sydney

◆

Custom-made by notable Australian department store David Jones, this dress was purchased for use as a post wedding "going-away" outfit by bride May Camille Dezarnaulds, a recent immigrant to Sydney. [17] Its simple lines and sleeveless cut represent a classic silhouette of the era.

This wide neckline is slightly curved at the front and straight at the back, resonant of many of the most fashionable evening styles, which at this date were rarely very low cut.

The bold floral brocade from which this dress is made adds an extra dimension to the simple cut and line of a classic early 1920s style. Its rich pattern demonstrates that excesses of glitter and sequins were not always required for a 1920s evening dress to make an impact: "leave a brocade dress to tell its own story," as *The Queenslander* recommended in 1929. [18]

Shades of beige and light gold were hugely popular during the 1920s, a neutral choice favored by both young and old. As *The Sunday Times* pointed out in the last months of 1929, its popularity was perhaps down to its inherent variety: "There is beige the colour of an almond shell . . . beige that looks as if it had been mixed with green or blue . . . There is a very pale beige like sand in the desert." Such subtle yet noticeable differentiation lends itself well to this design, which combines the shades of both "sand in the desert" and "wet sand by the sea." [19]

The armholes are cut very long, almost reaching to elbow length. Such dresses would have been worn over a slip in a corresponding color.

Side folds are gathered at the front, bringing this loose-fitting dress closer to the body. They meet at hip level with a beaded applique panel, made in a bow shape.

The dress features a slightly raised hemline at the front, which accentuates the pleated detail at its sides.

Evening dress,

c.1925–29, Paris, Swan Guildford Historical Society, Australia

◆

This dress was purchased in Paris from "Th. Faroux" on the Rue Martel by its owner, a woman from Kalgoorlie in Western Australia. [20] Evening dresses like this did not always have a sewn-in and easily discernable waistline, instead accentuating the straight, free-hanging style that was by now so popular.

Relatively high, V-shaped necklines were common on both day and evening wear in the middle of the decade. At the beginning of 1924, one newspaper, forecasting popular trends, believed that "the V-neck opening is ousting all others; it is one that tends to make a figure look its slimmest." As the same publication prophesied, the fashionable silhouette was not likely to change soon, with slimness "still modish...t. it is only the slim who can do any justice to the mode of the day." [21]

Sequins were an incredibly popular form of surface decoration during the 1920s, so much so that their demand at some points outstripped supply—especially in France. Those on this example are made from both metal (black and silver) and gelatin (colored floral sections), painstakingly hand sewn onto a sheer georgette background.

A fashionable low waist is suggested only by the presence of a slim sequined belt, perhaps illustrative of the fact that the "correct" position of the waist was frequently under debate throughout the decade. From lighthearted poems—"Sometimes above, again below/The waist-line journeys to and fro"—to commentary on fashion pages— "dressmakers want to acknowledge that some sort of break is needed in the lines of the figure, but where to place it, leaders of fashion cannot agree"—the debate of the correct waistline in women's clothing continued. [22]

Floral shapes are placed at the natural waist and hemline. Designs like this were gaining popularity by the middle of the decade.

Skirts were at their shortest by 1926–27, and this knee-length example, featuring a very slight flare at the hem, is a good example of this relatively short-lived trend.

As well as sequins, bugle beads provide surface texture and ornamentation. This Parisian dress was in line with a trend that had been popular for some time, described by one 1928 fashion column: "A certain bead-madness is discernable at all fashionable frock-parades, and no frock seems complete unless plastered with beads of every imaginable color and shape." [23] Smaller round seed beads create the black leaf outlines, and edge the petals and centers of each flower.

The back of the dress also features a V neckline, and the hem length matches that of the front.

Evening dress,

c.1928, Paris, McCord Museum, Montreal

◆

This dress's designer, Lucien Lelong, was a well-known Parisian couturier of the 1920s–40s. He was known for slinky, elegant lines in eveningwear and here shows the familiar low waist of the era, still made prominent through bands of satin around the hips, but also displaying a nip at the natural waistline.

The neckline is broad and round at the front and sits lower in back, dipping to a soft V at the center.

Teardrop-shaped and diamante-encrusted embellishments, picked out in gilt thread, ornament the chest, hips, and upper thighs. As well as providing some glamour, they also pinpoint the new, curvier silhouette and the areas of a woman's body that were to become far more prominent in the following decade.

The front and sides of the skirt are cut into a handkerchief-point hem. The fabric was arranged so it appears as if the center of a square handkerchief is being held and allowed to drop into draped ends. This was a popular technique toward the end of the 1920s, and pointed hems in general were a trend on light summer and evening dresses. An example is seen in this German portrait from the mid-late years of the decade:

Very thin shoulder straps illustrate the now almost universal acceptance of bare neck, shoulders, and arms.

The broad waistline flows into a large tied bow at the rear, and extending from that are two long, broad satin streamers. The dress's date of 1928 sits right on the point at which evening dresses (particularly at the back of the skirt) started to lengthen significantly, making these streamers an indication of new styles. This worried some contemporary commentators, one expressing concern in 1927 that "Dancing... is likely to be affected, for who could Charleston in an ankle-length petticoat?" [24]

Dress, late 1920s
(Kästing family archive)

Chapter 9
1930–1946

Suits and two-piece daywear for women continued to enjoy popularity into the 1930s, with skirts now nearly always mid calf-length for daytime and, for evening, either ankle length or skimming the floor. As this photograph of a young South African woman shows, skirts were slim at the hips and down to the knees, in this case ending in kick-flare panels that created a modest funnel shape. The incredibly popular bias cut, a signature look of the 1930s, was largely credited to couturiere Madeleine Vionnet. This involved the skillful diagonal cut of fabric against the grain to produce a slinky, figure-hugging garment—a highly sophisticated innovation that Vionnet strove to protect by attaining copyright. The use of crêpe de chine to make these dresses, a fabric usually reserved for lining or underwear, created a light and floaty effect that perfectly complemented the close fit. The undeniably seductive and romantic nature of the bias cut is indicative of a larger shift in aesthetics; the return to a more overtly feminine style after the androgynous look of the 1920s. Although, *The Chicago Sunday Tribune* commented in August 1930, "feminine frills" may be more costly "than in years gone by," they will at the same time "gladden the hearts of . . . Americans" by making the wearer "a 'lady' again." [1] Similar comments frequent other fashion columns of the time, presenting a strong feeling that it was now fashionable to want to be more "traditionally" feminine.

The consumption of fashion as a status symbol and a statement of worth was certainly fueled by lifestyles depicted in the world of film. The glamorous lives of actors such as Joan Crawford and Vivien Leigh were inspirational, though their most copied garments and accessories tended to be based on costumes worn for film roles rather than personal off-screen taste. Nevertheless, the advent of the Academy Awards in 1929, and from there an increasing focus on the dazzling gowns worn to such events, only highlighted the attention and elegance that fashion demanded. By the 1930s the majority of women's magazines and journals devoted sections to screen stars and what they were wearing, presenting a fascination with fashion and celebrity that is just as prevalent today. The influence of film and burgeoning celebrity meant that a key fashion figure during the 1930s was Adrian Adolph Greenberg, known simply as Adrian (1903–59). Initially a chief costume designer in Hollywood, dressing the likes of Greta Garbo and Joan Crawford, he opened his own fashion house in 1941 and married haute couture with the glamour and "other worldliness" of Hollywood film costume. In an era when cinema was becoming so intensely popular—audience numbers reaching a peak that they have not attained since—Adrian's professional blend of costume designer with fashion designer was a recipe for success. He was also notable for bringing America into the fashion spotlight at a time when Paris was still the sartorial capital of the world. [2]

A key word for this era could therefore be *sophistication*: an elegant, mature and more restrained style, the basic figure-hugging shape of which continued well into the 1940s. This was the change, as the *Daily Mail's* Frances Maxwell-Smith put it in 1931, from "drooping femininely about" to carrying oneself straight and tall and composed. [3] However,

sophistication in the mid to late 1930s can also be twinned with a sense of ease and inherent "wearability" due to the instigation and spread of zip fastenings and easily washable fabrics including rayon and viscose, alongside variants of more luxurious silk and crêpe de chine that could be laundered and reworn for far longer periods. This practical approach was taken further in the 1940s with the widespread mass-production of military uniforms, feeding into a speedier general manufacture of clothes and accessories for both men and women.

As World War II approached, it was perhaps even more important that women were given a safe, solid, but also attractive model to stick to when it came to dress. As the following chapter will discuss, despite hardships and rationing, fashion maintained an intense importance, providing simultaneously an escapism and a normality that were sorely needed. By offering the diversion of attempting to maintain elegance amidst frugality and intense practicality, clothes were a chief aid to morale at home. The war also helped to disintegrate sartorial boundaries when it came to class. Although wealthier women already possessed wardrobes of highly fashionable and quality ensembles, nobody was exempt from rationing and other government initiatives.

In the early 1940s "utility clothing" was introduced in Britain. The brainchild of Sir Thomas Barlow, the President of the Board of Trade, this initiative aimed to produce clothing that was fashionable yet functional, attractive but not so attractive that demand outstripped supply. With the help of top-end designers such as Norman Hartnell, Hardy Amies, and Digby Morton women's wear had a simple elegance, making the square shoulders, nipped-in waist, and kick-flare skirt a staple of smart, professional clothing during the war years. The main regulation was that all garments must be cut from "utility" cloth, which had quite a broad specification but, principally, needed to be composed of the lowest possible levels of fiber content but at the highest allowable retail prices. Luckily, this stipulation did not extend to a ban on brightly colored printed fabrics, so the utility could be broken up somewhat by their use. Nonetheless, women's wear should have no more than two pockets, five buttons, six skirt seams, two inverted or box pleats or four knife pleats; 160 inches of stitching were allowed, but no excessive surface decoration was permitted for the outfit. [4] Shirring at the bust or waist was among the most popular and thrifty surface decoration. However, despite the government's endeavors, it still took some time before the British standard of living was scaled down to, as the *New York Times* put it in 1942, "a strict war-economy level." [5]

In the United States, Regulation L-85 (also known as the General Limitation Order) was issued in 1942 by the War Production Board. In a similar manner to Britain, elaborate styles that used an excess of fabric were restricted, along with certain colors and certain types of fabrics: natural fibers in particular. [6] Stories about British women who embraced the "make do and mend" attitude with a vengeance are well known, and in America a trend also began to "save scraps" and preserve as much existing clothing as possible. *The Chicago*

Sunday Tribune extolled the virtues of the British system in October 1942, reporting that as a result of make do and mend, women were "better groomed, and pick their clothes with the care an expert always gives." It was hoped by the writer that a similar spirit in the United States would encourage the continuation of more feminine fashions instead of the widespread wearing of slacks: "English women haven't slumped down into slacks, as some here show a tendency to do: Slacks are worn a lot in the country and at home, for warmth and other practical reasons, but they don't go to town, because it is considered unfashionable and unpatriotic to go about in them."[7] Therefore, if a woman was to be seen as "making an effort" where clothing was concerned, a dress—or skirt and blouse—was still considered a necessity.

Two dresses in this chapter embody that same recycling spirit present in Australia during the 1940s. Two linen day dresses, made by a bride for her honeymoon, were never worn after she died suddenly but remain in pristine condition in the collection of a Western Australian historical society. The necessity of making one's own clothes was not, however, restricted to garments for special occasions. Governments knew that this had to become an everyday normality, and throughout the 1940s the development of advice groups and clothing agencies was taken extremely seriously. An article from *The Listener*, published in March 1943, advised that a newly formed Women's Group on Public Welfare met frequently in London to provide clothes advice centers that would "tell you the best way of unpicking old clothes and making new ones out of them."[8] Such groups went to great lengths to cater to women of all sewing abilities, but while the sessions were advertised with a social as well as educational rationale, their underlying message was clear: frivolity had to make way for austerity. Frequent among these articles and advertisements was the suggestion that "party frocks" should be dismantled and turned into sensible daytime dresses. However, many commentators also acknowledged a popular underlying theme that, in the words of Joanna Chase's 1941 *Sew and Save*, "every woman wants to be well-dressed." Chase's book is an accessible blend of both the practical and realistic, reassuring women that a smart and elegant appearance need not be compromised by the restraints of rationing. To achieve this she recommends the acquisition of a well-made suit that can be worn in many different ways, and that every woman should consider buying second-hand from a dress agency. "You will not only save money this way," she enthuses, "but often get a better-styled, better-made garment than a new one at the same price."[9]

Dinner/evening ensemble,

c.1935, McCord Museum, Montreal

—

This formal Norman Hartnell ensemble consisting of dress and fur-trimmed jacket epitomizes the glamour and chic of a fashion-conscious woman in the 1930s. Navy was a very popular shade for eveningwear, seen frequently in the collections of notable designers. The accessories shown—a single strand of pearls and high, single-strapped shoes—are a good indication of how this dress would have been worn.

Deep V necks at both front and back were popular for eveningwear during the decade.

By the early 1930s, the trend was for short, fur-trimmed jackets for eveningwear, sitting alongside the popular "cape" style. Long roll collars, such as that seen here, were common, and a jacket like this would probably be lined in satin. The rise of synthetics meant that fur as a symbol of wealth and status was no longer as strong as it had been. Nevertheless, real fur was still a prized accessory and would become more so during the straitened war years.

The dress is made from navy velvet, a fabric recommended for evening dress but especially for the older woman. As Australian newspaper *Barrier Miner* put it in June 1936, "there is something particularly gracious and dignified about a velvet dress worn by a white-haired woman, especially if it is allied with fur." [10]

The ankle-length hem on this example illustrates a new mode of thinking for eveningwear. Evening dresses were now significantly longer than those worn for day and even sometimes, as in this example, sported a small train as well (on some styles this could be detachable, though here it is built into the body of the gown). Designer Norman Hartnell was one of the first to capitalize on this approach, becoming known for long and luxuriant styles that epitomized the growing return to a more traditional femininity. [12]

The uneven hemline and sweep of the skirt on this dress are described in an Australian newspaper from 1931, discussing an outfit worn by the film star Carol Lombard: "Of unrelieved black velvet, the frock is adaptable for either formal evening or dinner wear, and sweeps the floor in an uneven hemline falling from a fully flared skirt at the natural waistline." [11]

Evening dress,

c.1935–45, Powerhouse Museum, Sydney

◆

This gown is a good example, epitomizing the long line that had become essential for eveningwear. The heroine of E.M. Delafield's *Diary of a Provincial Lady*, published in 1930, declares with horror that "I have nothing whatever to wear in London. Read in *The Daily Mirror* that all evening dresses are worn long… not one of mine comes even half-way down my legs." [13]

Padded shoulders give a wide, boxy appearance that continued into the following decade.

Floaty *capped sleeves* create a liquid effect in keeping with the shimmering, moving quality of the rayon-satin weave.

The liquid gold of this rayon-satin weave, which at first glance looks like far more delicate *lamé* (a fabric woven with metallic yarns) is representative of a mid to late 1930s craze for metallic fabrics. Probably fueled by the sparkling and shimmering effect it provided on-screen for film costumes, it became a popular choice for evening wear. As one newspaper's fashion column put it, "You'll be a shining light if you throw restraint to the winds and choose one of the gold, silver, copper, bronze fabrics, that look like solid beaten metal." The same writer also acknowledged that many readers would be purchasing rayon, rather than silk or satin, and commented that "Rayon, a typical product of the times, has a character of its own in weave, touch, and color. It has… endless resources." [14]

The turn down collar closely resembles a shirt front and embodies elements of a shirtwaist effect on this evening dress. *Shirtwaist dresses* became popular in the 1930s and were a practical daywear choice, being—in effect—a long fitted shirt with collar, sleeves, and front button fastening. It was less usual to see such a style adapted for eveningwear, although it did gain more popularity after being endorsed by actress Sylvia Sidney in 1934.

Glass paste is used to replicate semiprecious gems in the center of this belt, which emphasizes the simulation of a separate blouse and skirt.

This skillfully bias-cut skirt clings to the wearer's hips and thighs. The method of bias cutting, largely fueled by couturiere Madeleine Vionnet in the early twentieth century, involves cutting the fabric across the grain so that it hangs diagonally, rather than in a straight line. This slinky silhouette became an incredibly fashionable cut during the 1930s.

High-heeled, low-cut shoes with bar straps were worn with these slinky, bias-cut evening dresses.

Jeanne Lanvin evening dress,

1941, North Carolina Museum of History, Raleigh

◆

Designers like Madame Grès (also known as Alix Barton) popularized a trend for Grecian-inspired evening gowns, using pleated and tucked silk and crêpe fabrics to produce long, fluid lines. This ballgown by Jeanne Lanvin picks up on those influences, creating a graceful and feminine silhouette composed of French silk chiffon with rhinestone detailing.

....

The sleeves are cut with extra fabric, enabling an elegant draped effect at the back.

A columnar line and draped shoulders— the front ends seemingly caught and held together by rhinestone brooches—make this dress reminiscent of the loose classical styles of ancient Greece and Rome, but particularly of those appropriated in the nineteenth century by artists such as Lord Leighton (below), which would go on to influence reinterpretations of classical dress into the twentieth century.

In the manner of many evening dresses from the late 1930s onward, this gown features a low waist, the skirt flaring down from the hips. In 1945, one fashion column expressed the advantages of this silhouette, stating that "emphasis on the hips makes the waist appear smaller." [15]

Frederic, Lord Leighton, Figure Studies, c.1870–90 (detail), National Gallery of Art, Washington, D.C.

Despite its easy appearance, the internal structure of this dress is fairly intricate, and its shape would have been maintained through the wearing of knickers, bra, girdle, and slip.

Rows of tiny square rhinestones adorn each pleat edge on the bodice. Made from glass or paste, this method of decoration had grown since the 1930s and was used in place of precious gems. Rhinestones (commonly referred to as *paste or diamante* in Europe) were always backed with a metallic layer of gold or silver, meaning that light bounced off the glass of the rhinestone and sparkled as the wearer moved. [16] Further use of rhinestones is seen in the two leaf-shaped brooches that sit on the décolletage, highlighting the placement of the sleeves.

In March 1945 the New York designer Madame Eta, heavily influenced by Grecian styles, spoke of an important practical element of her recent collection: "It is a fresh development of design, based on bits of ancient Greek motif and fluid simplicity of line, made to enhance the modern figure, yet conform to current wartime restrictions to conserve material." [17] These considerations must be taken into account when assessing any style produced during wartime, and a similar aim at simplicity—both aesthetic and practical—can be seen here in Lanvin's design.

Aqua linen day dress,

early 1940s, Swan Guildford Historical Society, Australia

◆

This dress was made by its incredibly svelte owner, a bride, in anticipation of her honeymoon during the early years of the war. Tragically, she died before commencing her married life, so the dress lies pristine and unworn for posterity. [18] Its survival is propitious since it is such an excellent example of popular shape, line, and color from the period.

Slight gathers at the shoulder create a square look to the sleeves, contributing to the classic boxy silhouette of the period.

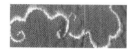

White hand-embroidered scrolls decorate the collar, cuffs, and skirt.

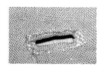

Nine hand-stitched buttonholes with white *Bakelite* buttons fasten the dress at center back.

A wide waistband of the same fabric emphasizes this wearer's tiny waist.

Square-shaped pockets were common on day dresses and outerwear. Here, there is no functioning pocket insert, but the shape balances the outfit by mirroring the wide, square shoulders and straight sleeves.

The bride was right on trend when it came to the soft aqua color she chose for this dress. The press reported a propagation of "soft pastel shades, borrowed from Nature," some specially chosen by experts as, the *Daily Mail* explained, "a take-me-away-from-the-war tonic." These rather poignantly termed "tonic colors" ranged from the "cheerful blue of the sunny sky" to "the soft beige of the seashore." [19] The gentle shade of this aqua was evocatively christened "Opaline Green" by the British Colour Council, which designated names for a range of colors used across industries and government. [20]

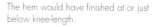

The hem would have finished at or just below knee-length.

Bone linen day dress,

early 1940s, Swan Guildford Historical Society, Australia

◆

Made by the same owner as the previous aqua linen dress, this princess-line example was hand sewn and embroidered in anticipation of a honeymoon holiday. It is representative of 1940s shape and aesthetics, particularly the sweetheart neckline and wide padded shoulders.

Sweetheart necklines are so called because they mimic the top of a stylized love-heart shape. The two curved sections also echo the contours of a woman's bust. There is some debate over exactly when and where this style of neckline originated, but it was at its most popular during the 1940s and into the second half of the twentieth century. It is frequently seen today as a neckline used for formal strapless dresses, particularly bridal.

The shape of the neckline is mirrored in these deep scalloped sleeve cuffs.

Eight shaped panels of fabric, four at the front and two at the back of the dress, create a princess-line cut.

It is very likely that the bride would have used a commercial pattern to construct this dress. Many options were available in Australia through newspaper promotions and advertisements, with some publications offering a "daily pattern" for readers. These could be bought through mail order, though some papers and magazines—such as *The Australian Woman's Weekly*—offered full instructions and images of the completed garment.

These hand-embroidered flowers and leaves, sitting high on the shoulder of the bodice, masquerade as a corsage. This was a cheap and therefore popular way of adding interest to an outfit, an example of wartime trends in the production and consumption of fashion. Throughout the 1940s, embroidery transfers were also available, and an easy way to buy them was through newspaper promotions. A Sydney publication in September 1943, for example, advertised "A touch of embroidery... Transform bolero, jacket or dress with these sprays in lazy-daisy and single stitch in wool, cotton or silk." [21] One shilling and threepence would buy a transfer pattern of twelve floral motifs, with suggested stitches and color schemes. Pattern kits like this made self-decorating something that almost anyone could attempt, with varying levels of detail and intricacy.

A real spray of flowers is seen in this bridal corsage, pinned to a bolero jacket (c.1945–48).

Chapter 10
1947–1959

Although 1947 is a hallmark point in fashion history, being the year Dior's "New Look" implored women to put aside their drab wartime wardrobes and embrace a degree of glamour, the reality for most was far less optimistic. Despite its victory over fascism, Britain was left in a supremely unstable position in 1945, and rationing was to remain for another nine years, meaning that the make-do-and-mend attitude that arose from necessity was still a prime concern for the government.

France, however, enjoyed a substantial economic boom after the immediate postwar dust had settled. It was determined to reassert its dominance in the world of couture, and designers like Christian Dior therefore felt there was reason to be sanguine. He chose to express this through the creation of a substantial and luxurious skirt, worn with jackets and tops emphasizing a nipped-in waist, soft shoulders and the effortless femininity of bygone days. This style, paving the way for the shape of the 1950s, captured the public's imagination across Europe and was adopted in toned-down versions even in the United Kingdom. This photograph, taken by a street photographer in London in the late 1940s, shows a woman wearing such a variant on the New Look: a pleated ankle-length skirt teamed with a wraparound cardigan and simple court shoes. This is Dior's classic *Bar* suit adapted for everyday wear in a time of economic austerity and illustrates the importance fashion still held in the wake of these conditions. Such was the impact of Dior's creation on the imagination of the public that one woman wrote, in January 1948: "The 'new line' seems to have ousted points problems, the poor quality of coal and even the weather, when women are talking." [1]

However, its reception was by no means entirely positive. The new silhouette caused feelings of dismay for many women, and in America those most vehemently opposed (at least a few thousand) formed protest groups—the largest known as the Below the Knee Club. They publicly protested what they saw as a return to restrictive clothing, joining other voices across the world that asked why Dior was so keen to hide women's legs. Criticism ranged from the long skirts being "dangerous" to, in the words of a former model, suggestive of the designer having read "too many historical novels." This was a serious protest on the part of many women, who believed the trend was a step backward in terms of female equality and emancipation. Men, too, were no more enthused: their dislike of the New Look was based mainly on the amount of money they would have to spend on fabric, if their wives chose to embrace the look. Their group, dubbed the League of Broke Husbands, at one point consisted of 30,000 members. [2]

In the midst of this skirt controversy, rival designers saw a chance to respond by bringing out their own alternatives to the New Look. Costume designer-turned-couturier Adrian, introduced in Chapter 9, announced in New York at the end of 1947 that his latest collection would feature short daytime skirts, their hems around fourteen inches from the

ground. This, the *Alexandra Herald and Central Otago Gazette* reported, would "reassure those women who do not care for the new exaggerated look. In an Adrian ensemble they can retain their elegant and streamlined appearance and not feel dated." Adrian lost no time in getting Dior's critics on side, the newspaper stating that he "believes implicitly in the female figure almost as Nature made it. Woman, he says looked her best during the war when designers were creating clothes to suit her life." [3] The suits, in particular, that Adrian provided in 1947 fed into this style and did retain popularity as a point of difference. However, Dior's New Look was ultimately popular in part *because* it was harking back to a more distant past, lining garments with stiffening fabrics such as taffeta to accentuate the waist and the volume of the hips and bust. Through doing this, he hoped he would achieve "the return to an ideal of civilised happiness." [4] This was historical escapism, nostalgia; which Hardy Amies acted upon when he created cleverly tailored suits that offered the appearance of fullness and effortless curve without using nearly as much fabric as the likes of Dior and Balenciaga. Two examples, from 1947 and 1950, respectively, can be seen in this chapter.

America, in a somewhat different economic situation in the immediate postwar years, also took a lead in the direction of high fashion. The New Look was as popular there as across Europe, thanks to the great publicity the style received across the world. However, during the war years, the nation had, partly due to necessity, been successful in promoting and assisting its own designers (particularly in the arena of sports and casual wear), and the reemergence of French couturiers at the end of the decade was not going to stop that. Certainly America seems to have offered a broader range of choice for the "everywoman," recognizing that not everyone fitted into the style aesthetic (neither physically nor emotionally) that was required by French couture. Broader acceptance of ready-to-wear clothing, aided in America by the creation of a standardized sizing system, made the latest fashions accessible to all. Moreover, the end of the war had not dulled the continuing popularity of paper patterns and home dressmaking, and women could create day, evening, and cocktail dresses as well as shirts, skirts, and nightwear, adapting the patterns to suit personal taste.

World War II had played a part in spurning new transnational influences, and this continued into the 1950s and 1960s. America is frequently mentioned in the pages of European newspapers and fashion magazines of the period, and one issue of Britain's *Sunday Times* of April 6, 1952, sings the praises of "the new young Paris designer, Hubert de Givenchy, (who) . . . is yet another example of American influence in fashion." The writer goes on to mention Givenchy's flair for "separates . . . so obviously designed for American taste . . . [but] everybody, not just Americans, loved them." [5] These separates, an American idea new to Europe, enabled women to mix and match individual bodices and skirts from their wardrobe and create fresh, individual looks. As seen in Chapter 7, the concept was not new: during the nineteenth century, it was possible to make and purchase a single bodice

RIGHT
For women still adjusting to post-war life, dress remained relatively conservative and feminine smartness was expected at all times. c. 1956, England, author's family archive

that could be transformed for either day or evening wear. Throughout the twentieth century so far, other designers had also popularized the convenience of separates ensembles, but Givenchy's emphasis reinforced the idea that the bodice and skirt did not need to match or complement each other in any sense. They did not need to form "a dress" as such. The stress was on individuality over maintaining the traditional convention of the dress as a single garment. Crucially in this case, it also meant that the idea of an evening dress could expand and become much more diverse, befitting the formality or informality of the occasion.

Separates were also prominent in the continuing rise of the female suit. Throughout World War II, these had been a popular and practical choice, favored in Britain by the Board of Trade and its Utility Clothing Scheme. With more and more women actively seeking careers, suits remained in demand and could be purchased in a wide variety of styles. *The Bulletin*, published in Oregon, wrote in 1948 of the styles available in the department stores of North America. These ranged from "the flared suit, usually with short, fitted jacket . . . the tuxedo suit, with long, slim revers" to "the bustle suit . . . the swallowtail suit, with graceful cutaway jacket" and "the ballerina suit, popular with the young crowd."[6] The two suits analyzed in this chapter both showcase this variation in design and scope of choice. The silhouettes shown here are also indicative of sensible and ingenious wartime thrift, despite their couture labels.

The archetypal image of the 1950s woman, with wide skirt stiffened by layers of net and starched petticoats, sweetheart neckline, and perfectly coiffured hair is not representative of the varied styles during that decade. Although this continuation of Dior's hourglass figure certainly underpinned most style choices, slim pencil skirts and sheath dresses became just as popular, and were worn side-by side for much of the decade. Marilyn Monroe famously used the look to great effect in *How to Marry a Millionaire* (1953) and *The Prince and the Showgirl* (1957). The term "little black dress," still employed today, was often used in conjunction with the sheath style. Another design, the Trapeze style, was introduced in 1958 by Yves Saint Laurent (who took over the Dior fashion label after the designer's death the previous year).[7] Shaped something like a trapezoid, this garment illustrated yet another alternative aesthetic. It was cut narrowly at the shoulders and then flared out, creating a loose, almost architectural effect that was a world away from nipped-in waists and full, billowing skirts. The trapeze— along with similarly unfitted styles, loosely termed "chemise" dresses—was a ready successor to Balenciaga's early sack dress, a shift style that was appropriated by Mary Quant in the 1960s and became an essential fashion staple of that decade.

Suit by Hardy Amies,

1947, McCord Museum, Montreal

◆

Despite this outfit's practicality, it is already possible to see a softer, more sloping outline compared to the hard and blunt edges seen in wartime fashion. This is achieved with rationing still in mind: smaller details requiring large pieces of fabric have been exemplified, such as the wide triangular lapels and shaped pockets seen here.

The broad shoulder line is still prominent, but it is now somewhat softer and beginning to slope.

The nipped-in waist of Dior's New Look is referenced here in the curvaceous cut of the jacket. Meanwhile, the padded hips of Dior's famous look are suggested in these thick pockets that add shape and width.

Suits like this were popular choices for formal wear, including weddings: indicating that a traditional wedding dress was no longer the only option for modern brides. This image from November 1946 shows a postwar British bride wearing a suit that, although cut on far simpler lines than the Amies example, shows a similar aesthetic.

Large, stylized lapels are a feature of the jacket and evidence Amies's fondness for exaggerated pocket and collar detail.

An attraction of double-breasted jackets is their ability to provide a flattering, lengthening effect on both men and women, and that is certainly achieved here. From the back, the jacket is quite plain but achieves its close fit with two seams reaching from shoulder to hem.

Sleeves are cut close to the shape of the arm, ending in a close-fitting, unembellished cuff.

This slim pencil skirt is slightly longer than seen during the previous six years, sitting at below knee level. It is equally as plain at the back as it is at the front, featuring only a modest slit to the left-hand side.

Portrait, c.1946–47
(Author's family archive)

Day suit by Hardy Amies,

c.1950, McCord Museum, Montreal

◆

The era of "the dress" as the only daytime option for women was becoming ever more remote, as the popularity of suits like this shows us. This suit is made from English Worsted wool, a common fabric used to make high-quality tailored garments.

Shoulders are now more sloping, and the boxiness of the 1940s is disappearing.

Single-breasted fastenings were common on utility day suits, and the trend is continued with this early postwar example. Clothes were still subject to rationing at this time, and this suit uses more fabric overall than the previous example—so some economy was necessary to make its production feasible.

By 1950, jacket lapels for women were generally becoming smaller, rounder, and narrower, sitting high up and close to the neck. Indeed, examples such as this one can be compared to very similar styles seen on official WAAF uniform tunics and early 1940s utility garments.

The two sections of layered knife pleats give this skirt an extra level of interest and, crucially, heighten the effect of fullness at a time when fabric was still in scant supply. They also highlight Amies's own aesthetic, and his keenness to experiment with different combinations and sequences of pleats in one garment. [8]

Australian division uniform of the Women's Auxiliary Air Force (WAAF), 1943–45 (detail), Evans Head Living History Society, New South Wales

Articles discussed the various merits and drawbacks of these uniforms, often full of praise for the fact that "the WAAF uniform," as one article claimed, "is so far ahead of civilian clothes that it has come to stay. Post-war suits will be modeled on the skirt, blouse, and tunic pattern." [9]

Wedding dress,

1952, Powerhouse Museum, Sydney

◆

This dress was made for Sydney socialite Betty McInerney for her marriage on May 31, 1952. The designer, Beril Jents, was a renowned couturier whose clientele included such stars as Elizabeth Taylor and Dame Margot Fonteyn.

Betty McInerney's dress is a couture garment and an excellent example of high fashion in the early 1950s. However, it does not represent what most postwar brides would have been wearing. This photograph from 1950 shows a more common design, based on bridal styles of the late 1940s with its wide cape-collar, slight V waist, and earphone headdress with veil. (Author's family archive)

The silk-satin roses adorning this peplum were handmade and, according to the designer, "so heavy we had to build a frame of twisted wire and chiffon in the shape of a half-moon to take the weight." [12] The 1950s saw the reintroduction of stiffened petticoats, sometimes referred to as *crinolines*, and this dress seems almost nineteenth century in the complexity of its construction and the excess of materials needed to sustain its shape.

The bodice originally had long sleeves, which the bride later removed so that the gown could be worn as an evening dress. [10]

The bodice is draped and fitted over the bust, supported by lengths of boning inserted at each side.

Detachable overskirts were popular for formal wear in the early years of the 1950s. More affordable and accessible bridal dresses would often featured detachable trains, which, when removed, left a slim streamlined evening dress suitable for use after the wedding. A similar idea is described in a Queensland newspaper from June 1953: "The long detachable... train, buttoned in front at the waist, was fully scalloped and edged with pleated tulle." [11]

The flower-covered peplum leads into layers of chiffon forming a train, supported by organza and taffeta underskirts and crinoline bands. The chiffon is cut on the cross to give a smooth flare to the skirt. [13]

Green faille dress,

c.1952, Shippensburg Fashion Museum & Archives, Shippensburg, Pennsylvania

◆

According to museum records, this dress was purchased by the wearer from store Dress-eteria (the name dresseteria originally meaning a shop selling ready-made clothes, in which customers served themselves) in Wilkes-Barre, Philadelphia, and is likely to be a "first copy of a designer original." It combines several details typical of the era to create a fashionable early 1950s silhouette. [14]

A broad, long collar, tapering toward the bust, draws attention to a small waist and to the equal width of the shoulders with the skirt hem.

This dolman sleeve is cut as one with the bodice, with a seam only visible on the underside. The sleeves continue long and close to the arm, ending just above the wrist with a turned-up cuff.

On early coat styles like this, skirts were often worn full and flared. Here, the fabric falls in tight pleats from a natural waistline, but it was also common to see dropped waist designs in the early years of the decade.

This dress is made from heavy-weight *faille*, a sturdy material well suited to outerwear. This, coupled with certain details—the front-fastening buttons, belt, and broad collar—make it easy to understand why the label *coat dress* (or *walking dress*) was sometimes applied to these tailored styles. "The one-piece dress that looks like a coat... acts exactly like a suit," said the Washington-based *Spokesman-Review* in 1953, "looking equally well on the street and at an important luncheon." [15] Most importantly, it "offers a complete change from living-in-a-suit and is the answer for the woman who feels she wears a dress more successfully than a suit." Another publication from the same year commented that the coat dress "is a hybrid of the open front shirtwaist frock and an actual light Spring coat . . . the best of them look like coats and, indeed, can often be worn over a printed Summer frock... they are a coat when you want them to be." [16]

It was also advertised as an affordable as well as practical fashion, as the *Sydney Morning* Herald reported in July 1952: "The coat dress is one of the most important, most elegant fashions of 1952. That's why it's so wonderful to see it at such a low price . . . it can be worn any hour of the day or night . . . a New York design for only £9'19'6." [17] In the United States, an advertisement for a store in Kansas in 1952 lists a "black faille coat dress" as $59.95, reduced to $38 in a "pre-Thanksgiving clearance." [18]

Court shoes like these were a popular and elegant footwear choice. Throughout the decade it was fashionable to wear a tailored dress or suit with matching gloves, handbag, shoes, and hat. [19]

Summer day dress,

1954, Swan Guildford Historical Society, Western Australia

◆

This frock features an intricate floral design with dark red roses and white plum blossom set on a gray background.[20] It is unlined and made from a very lightweight nylon fabric, perfectly complementing the blazing West Australian summer. It is likely that this dress was homemade, probably from a readily available commercial pattern.

....

The sleeves are cut from a single rectangle of fabric, one end forming the top section of the neckline.

A wide gathered panel, inserted several inches below the neckline created by the sleeve, creates an interesting stepped effect. The row of gathers also mirrors the gathering at the hem, bringing varying elements of the garment together.

The dress fastens at the side with a metal zipper, concealed by a flap of fabric.

The comparatively short skirt (sitting at just below knee level) is gathered into very narrow pleats, giving more volume to the thin, crisp fabric and mirroring the gathered detail at the neck.

The waistline is set at the natural position, complementing the sought-after hourglass figure of the period.

The fullness of the skirt would have been achieved by frilled petticoats, stiffened with tulle, crinoline (the original term meaning a wool and horsehair fabric), cambric, or new synthetic materials such as *crintex*: defined by a newspaper in1952 as "crinoline laminated with a non-woven material called masslinn."[21]

Day dress,

c.1954, Swan Guildford Historical Society, Australia

◆

This lightweight floral summer frock is made to a popular style and shape, conforming closely to the ballerina-length skirt, made moderately full, and the very short sleeves that could be seen throughout the decade.

....

The crossover neckline is open to the waist.

This dress is made from pale blue patterned *bubble nylon*, a new innovation that was quite a novelty in the early years of the decade. The merits of nylon in general were discussed frequently, with one newspaper article (illustrating the "uncrushable" qualities of bubble nylon among others) listing the many benefits of this new fabric technology: "Nylon... is in the limelight again—this time in frocks which are now appearing in Perth. Frocks of nylon fabrics... are uncrushable, quick drying, need no ironing or even pressing... The fabric is so soft and feminine that it lends itself to soft lines and many gathers or tucks without being bulky." [22] This is shown in some key structural qualities of this dress.

The bodice is gathered into a fabric insert at the waist, approximately 8.5 inches wide. This detachable belt is made from the same fabric as the rest of the dress.

Floral prints such as this were popular for summer dresses, described in one contemporary publication as having "lots of casual elegance without being fussy or overdone." [23]

The original owner of the dress and a friend, Perth, Australia, mid 1950s

Short cap sleeves, cut as one with the bodice in a Magyar style, extend just enough to cover the shoulder and very top of the arm.

Evening dress and jacket designed by Christóbal Balenciaga,

1954, Paris, Powerhouse Museum Sydney

◆

Spanish designer Balenciaga's curvy balloon silhouette (which could also incorporate detachable balloon-shaped sleeves) created a dramatic and impeccable line. The style also took advantage of new conveniences in technology, fastening at center back with a metal zipper hidden under a silk panel.

....

This outfit would have been accessorized with court shoes and a wide, flat hat with face veil.

Three-quarter or bracelet-length sleeves are cut with the jacket in the *dolman* style. The front is wraparound, crossing over and tying around the waist. [25]

Balenciaga favored dark, solid colors such as black and deep blue. The single use of one shade here is characteristic of his aesthetic and approach.

To achieve necessary fullness, the skirt would probably have been worn over layers of net petticoats.

The skirt is gathered to the waist and gathered again at the hem, shaping and enhancing the balloon effect that was so central to this design. The dress originally featured a silk ruffle at the hem, which has since been removed.

Under the wraparound jacket, the dress bodice is boned and strapless, fitting snugly to the torso and draped in the designer's trademark architectural style. [24] Alongside slim straps such as those seen in the portrait below, strapless designs were becoming ever more popular. One publication declared in 1950 that "the highlight of recent mid-season collections in London was the pre-dominance of strapless fashions for afternoon and evening as well as for beachwear." In line with this example, though, the article continues to reassure that "most models had little matching or contrasting jackets in bolero or coolie style to make them completely adaptable." [26]

Denis Barnham, *Portrait of Kathleen Margaret Rudman*, 1954 (Borland family archive)

Chapter 11
1960–1970

One of the key sartorial influences for this decade was youth. A simmering revolution was brewing concerning the emergence of fashions specifically for those teetering between childhood and adulthood. Prior to the 1950s, an adolescent would be dressed as a child until, for girls, around the age of fifteen or sixteen when she was given her first "grown-up" outfit. Now, however, as young people were being catered to in other areas of life—particularly music—manufacturers saw an opportunity, and clothes for adolescents were produced and marketed for the first time. This earnest new outlook for young people's fashion was sent up particularly well in the Beatles's debut feature film *A Hard Day's Night* (1964). In one scene, waiting to rehearse in a busy London studio, band member George Harrison stumbles upon a production office for a television program aimed at teenagers. Mistaking him for a new recruit, the director asks for "your opinion on some clothes for teenagers." Harrison obliges and is shown some shirts, reacting with disgust: "I wouldn't be seen dead in them. They're dead grotty." The director replies "of course [they are] ... but that's what you'll want!" After insulting the professional "trendsetter" hired by the company, Harrison exits, leaving the director and his assistant to wonder: "You don't think he's a new phenomenon, do you ... an early clue to the new direction?" [1] Such conflict was quite new, as was the choice that went with it, but for women emerging from adolescence into 1960s adulthood, this element of choice represented a freedom that had never existed before.

It also affected fashion houses, since designers found they could no longer set trends without first considering what was happening within "street" style. *Street fashion* came to mean styles that were developed by young, fashionable men and women, usually in urban centers, making the availability of the latest fashions more accessible than ever before. Independent boutiques such as Granny Takes a Trip and—most famously—Mary Quant's Bazaar, inspired a range of other "mod" stores including Miss Selfridge and Foale and Tuffin. The favored location for many of these boutiques was Carnaby Street, the center of "swinging London" and the home of young, dynamic fashion trends. Considering women's wear, one of the most important shifts in the development of the dress was the mini. Largely credited to Mary Quant and Andre Courrèges (though in fact with far broader origins), its development mirrored changing attitudes to gender and to popular perspectives of the female body. She has commented that by developing the mini, she was only responding to demand: "The Chelsea girls had really terrific legs ... If I didn't make the clothes short enough, they would shorten them more." [2] In this respect, Quant was reacting directly to street style and influence and tailoring her designs accordingly. Simultaneously, in the world of high-end couture, Yves Saint Laurent also recognized that street style was a pivotal part of the future direction of fashion and, consequently, incorporated elements into his collections. [3] As a result of this gradual move toward the new pop culture and away from traditional elitism in fashion, women gradually became less constrained by convention. For young women in particular,

RIGHT
Capri pants worn
in Rhodes, Greece,
late 1950s, private
collection

different cultural and even sexual attitudes could be expressed through clothing choices, and experimentation in dress was a key means of self-expression. In an era punctuated by controversial conflicts abroad, by growing sexual liberation, and by a new fluidity in the way gender roles were perceived, clothing became a glaring indicator of an individual's political, social, and sexual standpoint.

Dresses and skirts still made up a substantial part of most women's wardrobe; by the end of the 1960s trousers were no longer seen by all as an oddity but instead added further choice and variation. The *Daily Mail* went so far as to suggest in 1960 that trousers "are ousting skirts for top glamour." The writer wishes to "defy any man to say that they're unfeminine. Women are wearing them when they want to look their most seductive." [4] This does not mean that all of society suddenly regarded trousers as acceptable for women—reactions to Yves Saint Laurent's "Le Smoking" evening ensemble as late as 1967 were evidence enough of widespread distaste—but it does mean that the 1960s is an era in which we can begin to dimly see the dress take on its contemporary role as just another option among many. It was one frequently worn for best and often denoted smartness and a sense of occasion, and this attitude has not changed. Ever on the rise in terms of its influence, youth fashion was especially successful in furthering the trend for trousers, and this photograph depicts a fashionable outfit worn by a Greek girl of around fifteen years of age. She wears a pair of white Capri pants, named after the holiday destination of Italian designer Emilio Pucci who is credited with their invention. Images like this provide valuable documentation of the increasing "ordinariness" of such garments in everyday women's lives.

Nevertheless, throughout the 1950s and 1960s the concept of women's fashion was still very much tied up with the idea of some kind of skirt, whether as separates or as a dress. A skirt was absolutely required in professional circumstances, and it would not be until the 1980s that the idea of a trouser suit for work became commonplace. By the end of the 1960s, the mini dress was a fashion staple, but its antithesis had arrived on the scene in 1966 in the form of the maxi dress. Harking back to images of romantic charm, this floor-length garment often was composed of floral fabric, edged with lace, and featured long, puffed sleeves with yoked bodices. In the UK, designers such as Laura Ashley became synonymous with the look. However, alongside this overtly feminine revival, the 1960s is also the period in which we first see the term *unisex* used and applied to items that could be worn by either men or women. Although the clothing of each sex has always borrowed elements of the other, never before this point had clothes been made *specifically* to be worn by both.

Black satin evening gown,

c.1963–65, Shippensburg Fashion Museum & Archives, Shippensburg, Pennsylvania

◆

This slinky evening gown brings to mind the chic elegance of Audrey Hepburn, and continues an often-seen use of bustle effects in eveningwear during the 1940s and 1950s. Designers like Balenciaga and Victor Stiebel used drapery, puffs, and pleats to recreate the feminine curves of the nineteenth century. However, this dress was worn only infrequently by its owner because, her husband commented, the bustle made it uncomfortable to sit for any period of time—especially in the car going to and from evening parties. [5] The dress was bought from retailer Katy O'Connell's of Hagerstown in Maryland. According to Hagerstown's Daily Mail, Katy O'Connell herself was something of a couturier and a minor celebrity in the area, offering public talks and Katy's Dos and Don'ts fashion advice to local women. [6]

A broad turn-over neckline dips to a deep V at the back, where the zip fastening can be seen.

Strapless bodices, especially popular since the 1950s, continued into the 1960s on evening dresses in particular. Their prevalence in eveningwear meant that fashion columns often devoted segments to discussing how to wear strapless: "Underpinnings are… crucial to fit. If a dress does not have a built-in bra, it should be fitted over the evening bra to be worn with it… from every angle, a strapless dress demands erect carriage. You can't slump for a second and expect the dress or your figure to stay on course." [7] For these reasons, the bodice needed to be fitted snugly to the torso and, ideally, supported and shaped with boned inserts.

Incorporating a bow into bustle drapery was a fun and contemporary way of emphasizing the style. This bow is attached just below the waistline with snap fasteners, allowing access to the zip.

The floor-length skirt is narrowly cut, hugging the thighs and allowing the bustle to be the main focus of the dress. Throughout the decade, fashion writers spoke of a return to "slinky" eveningwear—some referring to trends of the 1920s, 1930s, and 1940s as comparison: "For evening, the 'with it' gal will be a recall of the slinky sirens of the 1930s flicks, with lots of skin showing front and back." [8] Another talked of current designs as having "all the glamour of the 1940s updated to 1969." [9] The seductive black evening gown worn by Rita Hayworth in *Gilda* (1946) can certainly be seen in details of the dress shown here.

Underneath the bustle bow, the black panel—forming a shallow train—hangs loose.

Coat and mini dress by Andre Courrèges,

1965, England, Powerhouse Museum, Sydney

◆

Courrèges's Space Age collection debuted in the spring of 1964, bringing angular lines and stark white and silver color combinations into fashion. This ready-to-wear ensemble relates to this aesthetic but also ties into another key aspect of his approach: attainable, commercial fashion choices for modern young women.

Underneath the coat, this bright yellow woolen dress has a stand-up collar that is surrounded by a wide yoke across the shoulders. This style recalls little girls' clothing, an aesthetic that increased in popularity during the remainder of the decade. [10]

Rows of *topstitching* on the seams of both dress and coat help to emphasize their clean and linear cut.

The white belt is made from vinyl, a variant of polyvinyl chloride, or *PVC*. The fact that this shiny and hard-wearing material had its origins in a laboratory gave it a "futuristic" appeal that was intensely modern, and lent itself perfectly to the space-age aesthetic of designers like Courrèges and Pierre Cardin.

Belt loops mirror the shape of the false pocket flaps, oval belt buckle, and jacket lapels. Soft, curved edges were a prominent feature of many types of design during the decade, seen in furniture and homewares as well as in clothing.

Banded hemlines were a feature of Courrèges's space-age aesthetic. Often applied as separately made bands of fabric to the hem of a skirt, some examples featured contrasting colors including the space-age favorite, silver. [11]

This *A-line* skirt is fitted at the hips and gradually flares, in this case only very slightly, towards the hem

These flat-soled, shiny boots are similar to those promoted by Courrèges for his 1964 collection. Their inspiration was taken from the clothing worn by astronauts.

Evening dress,

1965-70, Swan Guildford Historical Society, Australia

◆

It was not all about mini skirts in the 1960s. This striking lime-green and polka dot evening dress is typical of long styles seen in the middle of the decade, of a length that would resurface as the maxi during the late 1960s and into the 1970s. Made from polyester and viscose, it was purchased by the wearer from Habe Garments in Sydney. [12]

....

Six buttons, covered with the same green fabric as the skirt, decorate the center front of the bodice. The actual fastening for the dress is through a long zip at the back. [13]

These sleeves, tight to the elbow and then a flared circular cut, could be seen throughout the 1960s and into the 1970s. A thin length of pale yellow ribbon at the elbow highlights the style.

Sheer, filmy fabrics—particularly when used on just one part of a garment—were popular in the mid 1960s. *The Australian Women's Weekly* promoted their use in 1965, as well as proclaiming that "prints, stripes and polka dots" were enjoying a resurgence. [14]

The floor length of this A-line skirt was quite fashionable for eveningwear and in 1964–65 was being recommended as a suitable choice for evening and formal functions.

This high waist with an inverted V line is a nod to empire styles that became popular again during the decade and into the 1970s (see images below). These were often recommended to home dressmakers, who were frequently advised to use multiple fabrics and textures. Various sources from the mid 1960s suggest that a contrast bodice would be the correct fashion on an empire-line evening dress, and this was also a favored approach of designer John Bates (as the label Jean Varon), who helped popularize the empire line.

Empire line maxi dresses from the early to mid 1970s, England (Author's family archive)

"Going away" dress and jacket,

1966, Swan Guildford Historical Society, Australia

◆

The clear similarity of this princess-line dress to Chinese cheongsam (also known as qipao or the *Suzie Wong dress* after the 1960 film) is referential of Australia's proximity to, and level of influence from, its neighboring Asian countries. [15] Tight-fitting styles such as this were first developed in Shanghai in the 1920s. Originally, and into the 1960s, styles were often made in silk or satin fabrics, in imitation of traditional Chinese designs. This example, however, shows the use of light turquoise linen.

The coat's only fastenings are hooks and eyes at the collar. From there the fabric hangs straight to the hem, with two darts at each side of the bust providing some shape.

Both dress and coat have a standing collar, similar to that seen on the Nehru style, fundamentally a man's garment and popularized by the image of Indian prime minister Pandit Jawaharlal Nehru. The Chinese Mao suit is sometimes synonymously referred to.

The neckline fastens with press studs, leading into a double row of self-fabric scrolling applique.

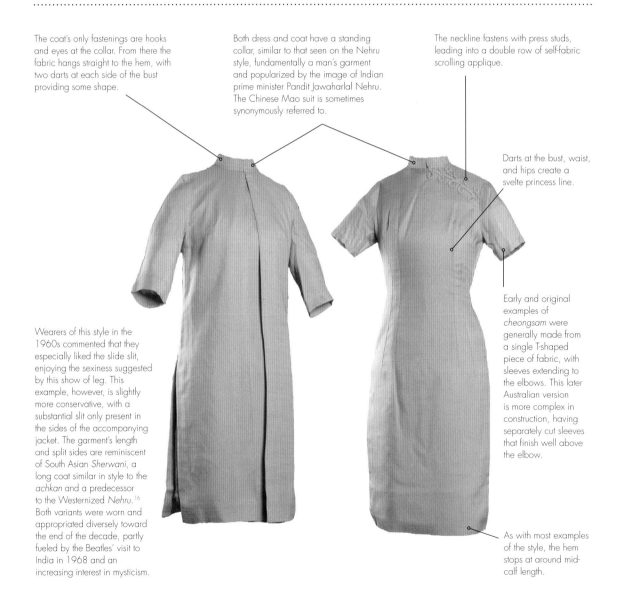

Darts at the bust, waist, and hips create a svelte princess line.

Wearers of this style in the 1960s commented that they especially liked the slide slit, enjoying the sexiness suggested by this show of leg. This example, however, is slightly more conservative, with a substantial slit only present in the sides of the accompanying jacket. The garment's length and split sides are reminiscent of South Asian *Sherwani*, a long coat similar in style to the *achkan* and a predecessor to the Westernized *Nehru*.[16] Both variants were worn and appropriated diversely toward the end of the decade, partly fueled by the Beatles' visit to India in 1968 and an increasing interest in mysticism.

Early and original examples of *cheongsam* were generally made from a single T-shaped piece of fabric, with sleeves extending to the elbows. This later Australian version is more complex in construction, having separately cut sleeves that finish well above the elbow.

As with most examples of the style, the hem stops at around mid-calf length.

Orange and teal silk print dress,

mid-late 1960s, Shippensburg Fashion Museum & Archives, Shippensburg, Pennsylvania

◆

This dress was worn by the wife of the president of the Canadian Hotel Association. As such, she traveled widely, attending numerous functions, and wore this dress with matching scarf to formal association luncheons. It was paired with light green shoes and a handbag. The dress was created by dressmaker Adele Bloss, cost approximately $110, and its bright floral print, low waist, and knee-length skirt are extremely representative of the era. [17]

The word *psychedelic* has become synonymous with the 1960s, referring to the effect of recreational drug use and the perceptual distortions that occur as a result of substances like LSD. This type of experience was expressed through art and music, and "psychedelic prints" like the one seen here were hugely popular, both among those who had experimented with drugs and those who had not.

The image built up around "flower power" late in the decade centered on antiwar protests and the hippie movement. The focus on flowers as powerful, natural symbols of peace was also expressed through the counterculture of psychedelia, and fashionable prints combined traditional floral designs (popular throughout the decade) with bright, almost synaesthesic combinations of color and shape that suggested the hallucinatory experience of a drug trip. Here, the bright orange background with petals and stems in neon pink, turquoise, baby blue, purple, mustard and black represent no real flower combinations found in nature, but the synthesis of these perfectly exemplifies the cultural and artistic influences of the age.

Matching dress-and-scarf combinations were popular and versatile, with the scarf worn around the neck, as seen here, or used as a hair accessory.

Bishop sleeves, seen here, are a style cut full at the wrist and gathered into a cuff. In this example, the cuff is long and close-fitting, fastened with two self-covered buttons.

The low waist, often referred to as a "dropped torso" or "dropped waist" by fashion writers, was frequently used. An American "Fashion Tips" column recommended the look for younger women in particular, commenting on the "fall (but never the decline) of the waist... Young rebels look deliciously long and willow in dropped waist dresses." [18] The continuing influence of the 1920s and the flapper is evident in both the style and in this comment.

A single inverted pleat in the skirt front adds extra movement.

Red mini dress,

c.1968–70, Swan Guildford Historical Society, Western Australia

◆

This dress was purchased at a store called Lavender, located in Melbourne in the late 1960s.
Made from a synthetic winter-weight fabric, it was purchased for a university choral society dinner and
worn in Western Australia from the late 1960s into the early 1970s. [19]

The bodice is closely fitted to the bust with darts at each side.

Square necklines were popular for both day- and eveningwear toward the end of the decade, and high collarless styles were recommended by fashion pages for daywear.

The dress illustrates trends discussed by readers in the *Australian Women's Weekly* magazine. Asking for dresses that had "long sleeves and a square or oval neckline," women were advised by the magazine's fashion column to opt for square necklines, "newer than oval," wrist-length sleeves, and a slightly defined waist. [20] In this case, the waistline is also raised to an empire line, suggested by the placement of the strips of white braid.

The striking vertical and horizontal white lines of this example bring to mind the paintings of Piet Mondrian and consequently of the *Mondrian dress*, the well-known cocktail dress produced, in1965, by Yves Saint Laurent in homage to the artist. This design was reinterpreted in many ways since the appearance of the original, with high street shops quick to produce their own affordable versions for a far broader customer base.

The short skirt has a slight A-line, leading into a flare at the hem.

Yellow crepe dress,

1960s–early 1970s, Shippensburg Fashion Museum & Archives, Shippensburg, Pennsylvania

◆

This brightly colored sleeveless dress represents the simple but dynamic lines of 1960s mini dresses. Its A-line skirt and empire waist are typical of the fashionable cut at this time, and the feather trim adds a fun and very popular finish to the skirt.

The fabric used for this dress is a lightweight crepe. Easy to wear and to care for, synthetic fabrics were in demand throughout the decade and suited the youthful, carefree attitude often expressed in clothing.

Two darts on the bust add definition to the torso, leading into a high empire waist.

Delicate feather trim is the only ornamentation on this dress—along with the back bow—and as such it makes a statement, drawing the eye to the above-knee length of the hem. It also highlights a connection to 1920s fashions, frequently seen throughout the 1960s, with simple, sleeveless sheaths and extensive use of feathers and feather boas. The design here is also suggestive of styles produced by Givenchy for the actress Audrey Hepburn, including a plain white dress that featured a band of red coq feathers at the hem.

This wide, high boat neckline falls into a deep V at the back, where it is met by a center back zip fastening. There is a self-fabric bow at the center back waistline. [21] This V back and bow combination was a relatively popular one during the decade, suggested in fashion columns as a suitable style for both grown women and young girls.

Feathered hems were also referenced as a 1920s inspiration: "You don't have to remember the Roaring '20s to wear flapper dresses, feathers on your hem, long tunics and short hair-dos—it's part of the spring look for 1966. Virtually every collection… has borrowed some, or all, of the '20s influence." [22]

Glossary of Terms

Aesthetic dress (nineteenth and twentieth centuries): Also referred to at the time as *artistic dress*, this desire for naturalness and less restriction, influenced by the designs of William Morris and Liberty's of London, was propagated by Oscar Wilde and his Aesthetic Dress Movement. In Wilde's words, "the value of the dress [should be] … simply that every separate article of it expresses a law," and the emphasis was on soft velvets and loose gathering to create less structured clothing based on historical examples (particularly medieval).

Apron dress (twentieth century): A lightweight cotton dress with a fitted bodice, a slightly gathered skirt, and a long, rectangular panel inserted down the center front. This panel, which is usually be ruffled or edged with lace, has decorative ties that fasten around the waist, forming the apron.

Bandeau (twentieth century): A band of fabric tied around the forehead, often worn as an evening accessory during the 1920s.

Basque (seventeenth century): The tabbed section of a bodice that helped to shape the torso. Worn with a skirt.

Bergere hat (eighteenth century): Large, wide-brimmed round hat with a very shallow crown, this style was developed from a rural accessory and became especially popular c.1750–70.

Bertha (nineteenth and twentieth centuries): A wide collar encircling and sitting on the edge of the shoulders.

Bias cut (twentieth century): Fabric cut diagonally against the grain. This produced a figure-hugging effect before the widespread use of stretchy manmade materials and is still a popular technique today.

Bishop sleeve (nineteenth century): Popular during the 1840s, this was a long sleeve fitting snugly to the arm at the top and graduating into a wide cuff gathered at the wrist.

Bombast (seventeenth century): Padding or stuffing for clothes, often made from wool.

Brunswick (eighteenth century): An informal (usually un-boned) three-quarter-length jacket worn with a petticoat. A floor-length version was known as a *Jesuit.*

Busk (seventeenth century): A long, flat strip of whalebone, wood, or metal that was inserted down the front of a bodice to add stiffness and to improve the posture of the wearer.

Butterfly sleeves (twentieth century): Short, loose sleeve with very wide opening, gathered at the armhole.

Caraco (eighteenth century): A woman's jacket mirroring the bodice of a dress (specifically a robe à l'anglaise) worn with a petticoat as a two-piece outfit. It was fitted to the wearer's torso and was often made in the same fabric as the wearer's petticoat.

Cartwheel ruff (sixteenth and seventeenth centuries): Introduced and worn between c.1580 and 1610 the cartwheel variation was the ruff at its most extreme width. It could measure up to 18 inches in diameter and required the use of a supportive prop, worn around the neck underneath the ruff.

Chemise (twentieth century): "Unfitted" styles of dress influenced by designers such as Balenciaga and Dior, who attempted to introduce a new aesthetic in the 1950s. It did not catch on seriously until the end of the decade, although the styles were highly influential for the "sixties look" that was to follow.

Chopines (seventeenth century): Tall wooden shoes that created a "platform" for the wearer, well away from the mud and muck of the streets. These were derived from earlier "pattens" and were perhaps the inspiration for early forms of clog.

Cloche (twentieth century): A close-fitting cap commonly made from felt, often brimless, encapsulating the hair and mirroring the bobbed cut so typical of the 1920s.

Coat dress (twentieth century):
Popular toward the end of World War I, the coat frock was what its name suggests—a lightweight fitted garment usually belted and with a high neck. This combined practical with elegant to create suitable professional garb for the newly professional woman.

Coif (sixteenth and seventeenth centuries): A fabric cap, closely fitting the shape of the head.

Corsage (nineteenth and twentieth centuries): A spray of flowers pinned to the front of a dress or worn around the wrist.

Corset (nineteenth century onwards): An undergarment stiffened with whalebone, worn on the torso and shaped to compress the waist. Used to enable the fit of fashionable dresses. See also stays.

Crêpe de chine (twentieth century):
Popular in the 1930s, crêpe de chine is a fabric made with an all silk warp and weft, creating an attractive sheen.

Crinoline (nineteenth century):
Originally the term meant a textile made from horsehair, used to stiffen petticoats. Soon it became used to describe the cage crinoline petticoat of the late 1850s–60s, which was constructed of rows of steel hoops to create a domed effect.

Damask: A silk fabric featuring contrasting floral- or fauna-based designs.

Drop-front dress (also known as apron-front dress, nineteenth century): A dress with either a detachable or free-hanging front panel that was pinned or buttoned to the front shoulder straps. This method of fastening left the back of the dress smooth and undivided.

Engageantes (eighteenth century):
False sleeve ruffles worn with various dress styles throughout the 1700s. The most elaborate and expansive examples are often seen worn with sack gowns (robes à la française).

Falling band (seventeenth century):
Instead of a ruff, these soft collars were worn around the neck and featured long hanging ends extending onto the chest.

Flapper (twentieth century): A young woman of fashion who enjoys flouting convention and sampling everything that is new and modern. Her clothes are flamboyant and up-to-the-minute, with short skirts and low necklines, with a demeanor inviting reckless behavior.

Fontange (seventeenth century):
The decorative part of a tall headdress composed of lace and gauze, arranged on a wire frame. Popular during the last twenty years of the 1600s, it was also known as a commode—the original name for the wire structure supporting the fontange.

Forepart (sixteenth century): A richly decorated underskirt, often made from a contrasting fabric, designed to show under an open skirt.

French farthingale (sixteenth and seventeenth centuries): Also described as the wheel or drum farthingale, this petticoat created a drastically different silhouette toward the end of the 1500s. Its series of hoops, identical in width from waist to floor, produced a broad plate-like structure from which skirts fell straight to the ground.

Furbelow (seventeenth century):
Ruffled trim or flounce adorning a garment.

Gallants (seventeenth century):
Ribbon bows attached to the bodice and skirt at various points, highlighting cuffs, shoulders, and necklines and, later in the century, indicating newly draped and looped-up sections of skirt.

Garibaldi blouse (seventeenth century): Designed to be worn with a plain day skirt, the Garibaldi blouse joined an emergence of "separates" for women in the nineteenth century. Originating in the military, it was made with full, low-set sleeves gathered at the wrist and high neck. The term could also be used independently to refer to a jacket, bodice, and sleeve type.

Gaulle (chemise à la Reine, eighteenth century): A muslin gown styled, as the name suggests, from the chemise—a woman's principal undergarment. The shape is gathered and maintained by a sash around the waist, and examples frequently show billowing sleeves and frilled necklines made from the same light fabric.

Girdle (twentieth century): A supportive garment worn around the lower torso and hips, used in the 1920s and 1930s to help create, first, the boyish silhouette and, then, the svelte figure needed under slinky bias-cut gowns.

Go-go boots (twentieth century): A fashionable low-heeled, calf-length boot worn with mini dresses and skirts in the 1960s.

Gored skirt: A skirt constructed from triangles of fabric that create a flattering, waist- and hip-hugging silhouette.

Half boots (nineteenth century): A practical alternative to the dainty slippers worn indoors and for eveningwear, these were sturdy leather boots finishing at around calf-length.

Hanging sleeves: Gown oversleeves that hang open to the wrist or floor, sometimes with edges held together with ribbon ties.

Hobble skirt (twentieth century): c.1910–14; skirts that tapered to produce extremely narrow hems—when walking the effect was likened to a "hobbling" gait.

House dress/coat (twentieth century): A simple cotton dress worn for household chores and shopping.

Indienne (eighteenth century): The term used for almost any printed fabric imported from the East.

Japonisme (nineteenth century): A surge of enthusiasm for Japanese textiles, painting, furniture, and interior design that flowed through Britain to America at the end of the century. This developed largely in response to the opening of Japan's trade routes with Europe in 1854.

Kirtle (sixteenth century): Could refer simply to an underskirt, and sometimes a bodiced petticoat worn to provide extra warmth.

"Kitty Foyle" dress (twentieth century): Named after the eponymous heroine of the 1940 film starring Ginger Rogers. This was a day dress made from a dark, plain fabric with contrasting white collar and, sometimes, white cuffs, buttons, and other detail.

Lamé (twentieth century): Popular eveningwear fabric woven with metallic threads.

Leg-of-mutton sleeves (nineteenth century): Very wide, puffed balloon-shape upper sleeves, narrowing from the elbow. Also known as a gigot sleeve.

Mantua (seventeenth century): A loose, initially informal garment with sleeves cut in one piece with the front and back. Pleated at the shoulders, the fabric fell to the waist and was held in place by a sash and pins. This was to develop into the "sack" gown in the early years of the eighteenth century.

Mini dress (twentieth century): A very short dress, its hemline sitting well above the knee. Usually cut straight in the form of a shift dress, it could be sleeved or sleeveless and often featured a high, round neckline, sometimes collared.

Mod (twentieth century): 1960s term meaning "modern," "in fashion"—particularly in relation to clothes.

Pagoda sleeve (nineteenth century): Wide, bell-shaped sleeves, usually worn over a false sleeve and sometimes partially open at the seam; they are held together by decorative bands or ribbons.

Paletot (nineteenth century): A long, fitted jacket worn over crinoline and, later, bustle styles.

Paned sleeve (sixteenth and seventeenth centuries): Constructed from several individual panels that, when worn, hang open and allow the rich (often contrasting) fabric beneath to be visible.

Paniers (eighteenth century): A hoop skirt (later, a pair of smaller "pocket hoops") designed to hold out the sides of a skirt in a rectangular shape.

Partlet (sixteenth century): A separate neck and chest covering featuring long sleeves.

Paste (1930s): Glass made to look like precious stones, set into jewelry. Also known as diamante and rhinestone.

Pattens (seventeenth century): Footwear similar to chopines (see Chapter 2).

Peg skirt (twentieth century): Similar to the hobble skirt in its construction, this skirt emulated wooden clothes pegs with widely cut hips tapering to a narrow end at the ankles.

Peg-top dress (twentieth century): Inspired by World War I styles, this look was adopted by more mature women rather than the teenage trendsetters of the 1950s and 1960s. They were cut full across the hips, tapering down the leg to produce a hobble skirt effect around the ankles. They could also be made in a knee-length variety, popular as a cocktail dress.

Pelerine (nineteenth century): Shoulder-length cape often trimmed with fur and made from a thick lustrous fabric, such as velvet.

Pelisse (nineteenth century): Long high-waisted jacket to be worn in colder months.

Pet-en-lair (eighteenth century): Similar in function to the caraco, the pet-en-lair was a jacket made in the style of a robe à la française or sacque gown, complete with Watteau pleats and three-quarter-length sleeves.

Petticoat (sixteenth- twentieth centuries): Skirts were referred to as *petticoats* throughout the eighteenth century. *Under-petticoats* were those worn beneath for warmth and volume. Into the nineteenth century, the term came to mean only a skirt worn as a foundational garment.

Pierrot (eighteenth century): A (usually) long-sleeved jacket characterized by a ruffle at the back. This was worn during the latter years of the century and is similar to the casaquin, a short fitted jacket with flared pleats in the place of the pierot's ruffle.

Pigeon—pouter or pigeon-fronted—bodice (twentieth century): Gathered, puffed front section of a blouse that hung slightly over the waist. This helped to create the fashionable "mono-bosom" of the early twentieth century.

Pillbox hat (twentieth century): A small brimless hat with a flat crown and straight sides, popularly worn by Jackie Kennedy.

Playsuit (twentieth century): Rompers and "playsuits" associated with American designer Claire McCardell (1905–58) were short once-piece bifurcated summer outfits for casual wear. They offered women a sporty, relaxed garment exclusively for leisure time and were the epitome of the easy and fun clothing that was becoming readily available on the American mass market.

Poodle skirt (twentieth century): Originating in America in the 1950s, this simply constructed circle skirt has become a popular 1950s emblem. Usually made from felt, it got its name from the fabric poodle dog motif sewn near the hem. The term *bobby-soxer* was often used to refer to girls who wore them with sweaters and short socks.

Rayon (twentieth century): Often known contemporaneously as artificial silk, rayon was a manmade fiber created from regenerated cellulose.

Rebato (seventeenth century): Derived from the ruff, a standing collar attached to the neckline of a bodice or gown, c.1580–1630s.

Reticule (nineteenth century): Small purse, often closing with a drawstring, used to carry items such as money, keys, and handkerchiefs.

Robe de style (twentieth century): An alternative to the low-waisted flapper style, often made for older women who wanted a more substantial version of the look.

Robe à l'anglaise (eighteenth century): Gown with close-fitted torso with a long, full skirt, usually worn without paniers. The skirts were often worn draped à la polonaise. Also sometimes known as an English bed gown, nightgown, or close-bodied gown

Robe à la circassienne (eighteenth century): A variant on the polonaise, but decorated with specifically oriental trimmings and accessories.

Robe à la française (eighteenth century): A one-piece gown, usually open-fronted, worn with a stomacher and decorated petticoat. Worn over a corset and paniers to hold out the sides of the skirt.

Robe à la polonaise (eighteenth century): A gown with a cutaway bodice and a skirt drawn up into draped sections, displaying a (usually) contrasting petticoat beneath.

Robe à transformation (nineteenth century): This innovative idea became popular during the period in question, usually consisting of a bodice and skirt that could be worn for both day and evening affairs (an 1890s example can be seen in Chapter 7). By adding longer sleeves and removing a chemisette/neck covering, a demure afternoon dress could become an alluring evening ensemble and, for purely practical consideration, meant that garments could have a far longer life.

Robe à la turque (eighteenth century): A dress inspired by Middle Eastern or so-called oriental fashions. Usually loose fitting, it is often recognizable through its use of short oversleeves, colorful sashes about the waist, and a rich overall color scheme.

Round gown (eighteenth century): Popular during the late eighteenth century and first years of the nineteenth century, this was a high-waisted closed robe with the bodice and skirt joined as one.

Sack dress (twentieth century): A short, loose, waistless dress introduced by Christóbal Balenciaga.

S-bend corset (twentieth century): Also called the straight-fronted corset, this garment did what its name suggests: molded a woman's torso into a subtle S shape by pushing the chest forward and

hips back. It was particularly popularized by the Gibson Girl style: an idealization of femininity initiated by cartoonist Charles Dana Gibson (1867–1944).

Scoop neckline (twentieth century): A wide, round, low-cut neckline on a dress or separate.

Shirring (nineteenth and twentieth centuries): Tightly gathered rows of fabric for decorative and shaping purposes.

Shirtwaist (nineteenth century): A woman's tailored blouse (American terminology).

Short stays—or half stays (nineteenth century): A corset or "pair of stays" made to cover and support only the bosom and ribcage, thus focusing on the fashionable line featuring free waist and hips. Longer varieties were also worn.

Slashing—dagges (sixteenth and seventeenth centuries): The practice of cutting—in pinked or plain "slashes"—the surface of a fabric as a means of decoration.

Smocking (sixteenth century onward): Similar to shirring; an embroidering technique used to enable stretch in fabric. This remains popular in children's clothing.

Spanish farthingale (sixteenth century): A petticoat consisting of a series of circular hoops, starting narrowly at the hips and getting progressively wider toward the floor, forming a distinctive conical shape. This can be seen from the Tudor era and, with slight modifications,

throughout succeeding years until the final decade of the sixteenth century. Its first appearance was at around the end of the fifteenth century.

Spencer (nineteenth century): Short jacket with long sleeves cut to cover the high-waisted bodice, worn over day and evening dresses. It was named after Earl Spencer (1758–1834) who experimented with a similar style by removing the tails from a coat.

Spoon bonnet (nineteenth century): A high-brimmed bonnet with raised peak, exposing the wearer's profile more fully than previous styles. The inside of the brim was usually decorated with ribbons, flowers, and lace.

Stays (sixteenth–nineteenth centuries): A boned corset worn under a gown to give shape and structure and to create the fashionable line. Often known contemporaneously as a "pair of bodies," which could also refer to the bodice of a dress. The word corset would not come into common parlance until the nineteenth century.

Surplice bodice (nineteenth and twentieth centuries): Crossed-over V-shaped neckline.

Swiss waist (nineteenth century): An under-the-bust boned garment (not a corset) worn on top of a daytime ensemble, usually a blouse and skirt.

Tippet (sixteenth century onward): A shoulder cape, short in length.

Trapeze dress (twentieth century):
Trapezoid-shaped garment cut narrowly at the shoulders and then flaring out over the waist and hips. It was created for the house of Dior in 1958 by designer Yves Saint Laurent.

Twin set (twentieth century): Seen throughout the 1950s and into the 1960s, this sophisticated look consisted of a fitted cardigan and slim line skirt, often worn with a row of pearls.

Utility clothing (twentieth century): A wartime government initiative aiming to economize on fabric and produce fashionable, but primarily functional, clothing for British citizens. A similar initiative in the United States was known as the L-85 Regulation. In America, the utility suit was known as the victory suit.

Virago sleeve (seventeenth century): Wide paned sleeves tied into puffed sections along the arm (see Anthony van Dyck's *Lady with a Fan* in Chapter 2).

Wiggle dress (twentieth century): Another term for the 1950s sheath dress: fitted and slim line with a hem narrower than the width of the hips. As with the hobble skirt of four decades earlier, the wearer is forced to take mincing "wiggling" steps.

Wrapper (nineteenth century): An informal garment (a "house" dress) worn at home, usually during the earlier part of the day. Wrappers fastened up the front and could be worn without a corset, making them largely unsuitable for public wear.

Zibellini (sixteenth century):
A luxury accessory worn as a tippet or held throughout the fifteenth and sixteenth centuries. It consisted of a pelt of a pine marten, often ornamented with gold and jewels to simulate the facial features of the animal. (The "fur of sables" mentioned in Elizabeth I's sumptuary decree are zibellini.)

Zouave jacket (nineteenth century):
A short jacket in the bolero style, fashionable during the 1860s, that was worn open with its front sides curving and tapering to the waist.

Notes

Preface

[1] Elsa Schiaparelli in Kahm, Harold S., "How to be Chic On a Small Income," *Photoplay Magazine*, Aug. 1936, p. 60.

[2] Luther Hilman, Betty, *Dressing for the Culture Wars: Style and the Politics of Self-Presentation in the 1960s and 1970s*, The Board of Regents of the University of Nebraska, 2015 (eBook).

[3] Gabor, Zsa Zsa, "Always at Your Best," *Chicago Tribune*, Sept. 25, 1970, p. 8.

Introduction

[1] "De Givenchy, a New Name in Paris," *Life*, March 3, 1952.

[2] Ovid in Robert Selbie, *The Anatomy of Costume* (London : Mills & Boon, 1977), p.21

[3] Paul McCartney, *Memory Almost Full*, Mercury Records, 2007.

[4] Quentin Bell, *On Human Finery* (Berlin: Schocken Books, 1978), p.234.

[5] Ruth M. Green, *The Wearing of Costume: the changing techniques of wearing clothes and how to move in them, from Roman Britain to the Second World War* (London: Pitman, 1966), p.151.

[6] Ibid, p.4

Chapter One

[1] Fagan, Brian, *The Little Ice Age: How Climate Made History*, New York: Basic Books, 2000, p. 53.

[2] Aughterson, Kate, *The English Renaissance: An Anthology of Sources and Documents*, London: Routledge, 1998, pp. 164–67.

[3] Ashelford, Jane, *A Visual History of Costume: The Sixteenth Century*, New York: Drama Book Publishers, 1983.

[4] Cotton, Charles, *Essays of Michel Seigneur de Montaigne: The First Volume* (facsimile), London: Daniel Brown, J. Nicholson, R. Wellington, B. Tooke, B. Barker, G. Straban, R. Smith, and G. Harris, 1711, p. 409.

[5] Köhler, Carl, *A History of Costume*, New York: Dover, 1963, p. 237.

[6] Wace, A.J., *English Domestic Embroidery—Elizabeth to Anne*, Vol. 17 (1933) *The Bulletin of the Needle and Bobbin Club*.

[7] Latteier, Carolyn, *Breasts: The Women's Perspective on an American Obsession*, New York: Routledge, 2010, p. 32.

[8] Landini, Roberta Orsi, and Niccoli, Bruna, *Moda a Firenze, 1540–1580: lo stile di Eleonora di Toledo e la sua influenza*, Oakville: David Brown Book Company, 2005, p. 21.

[9] Mikhaila, Ninya, and Malcolm-Davies, Jane, *The Tudor Tailor: Reconstructing 16th-Century Dress*, London: Batsford, 2006, p. 22.

[10] Yarwood, Doreen, *Outline of English Costume*, London: Batsford, 1977, p. 13.

[11] Davenport, Millia, *The Book of Costume: Vol. I*, New York: Crown Publishers, 1948, p. 446.

[12] Cumming, Valerie, Cunnington, C.W., and Cunnington, P.E., *The Dictionary of Fashion History*, Oxford: Berg, 2010, p. 88.

[13] Yarwood, Doreen, *European Costume: 4000 Years of Fashion*, Paris: Larousse, 1975, p. 124.

Chapter Two

[1] Waugh, Norah, *The Cut of Women's Clothes, 1600–1930*, London: Faber & Faber, 1968, p. 28.

[2] Cunnington, C. Willett, and Cunnington, Phyllis, *Handbook of English Costume in the Seventeenth Century*, London: Faber & Faber, 1972, p. 97.

[3] *The Needle's Excellency: A Travelling Exhibition by the Victoria & Albert Museum— Catalogue*, London: Crown, 1973, p. 2.

[4] Pepys, Samuel, and Wheatly, Benjamin (eds.), *The Diary of Samuel Pepys*, 1666, New York: George E. Croscup, 1895, p. 305.

[5] Otavská, Vendulka, Ke konzervování pohřebního roucha Markéty Františky Lobkowiczové, Mikulov: Regionální muzeum v Mikulově, 2006, s. 114–20.

[6] Ibid.

[7] Ibid.

[8] Ibid.

[9] Pietsch, Johannes, "The Burial Clothes of Margaretha Franziska de Lobkowitz 1617," *Costume*, vol. 42, 2008, pp. 30–49.

[10] Cunnington, C. Willett, and Cunnington, Phyllis, *Handbook of English Costume in the Seventeenth Century*, London: Faber & Faber (proof copy), 97.

[11] Waugh, Norah, *The Cut of Women's Clothes: 1600–1930*, London: Faber & Faber, 2011 (1968) p. 45.

[12] Eubank, Keith, and Tortora, Phyllis G., *Survey of Historic Costume*, New York: Fairchild, 2010, p. 261.

[13] Mikhaila, Ninya, and Malcolm-Davies, Jane, *The Tudor Tailor: Reconstructing 16th-Century Dress*, London: Batsford, 2006, p. 18

[14] Eubank. Keith, and Tortora, Phyllis G., *Survey of Historic Costume*, New York: Fairchild, 2010, p. 241.

[15] Powys, Marian, *Lace and Lace Making*, New York: Dover, 2002, p. 5.

[16] Rothstein, Natalie, *Four Hundred Years of Fashion*, London: V&A Publications, 1984, p. 18.

[17] De La Haye, Amy, and Wilson, Elizabeth, *Defining Dress: Dress as Meaning, Object and Identity*, Manchester: Manchester University Press, 1999, p. 97.

[18] "Mantua [English]" (1991.6.1a,b), in *Heilbrunn Timeline of Art History*. New York: The Metropolitan Museum of Art, 2000–. http://www.metmuseum.org/toah/works-of-art/1991.6.1a,b (October 2006)

[19] Cunnington, C. Willett, and Cunnington, Phyllis, *Handbook of English Costume in the Seventeenth Century*, London: Faber & Faber (proof copy), p. 181.

[20] Cumming, Valerie, *A Visual History of Costume: The Seventeenth Century*, London: Batsford, 1984, pp. 102–22.

[21] Cavallo, Adolph S., "The Kimberley Gown," *The Metropolitan Museum Journal*, vol. 3, 1970, pp.202–05.

[22] Waugh, Norah, *The Cut of Women's Clothes: 1600–1930*, London: Faber & Faber, 2011 (1968) p. 111.

Chapter Three

[1] Ribeiro, Aileen, *Dress in Eighteenth-Century Europe, 1715–1789*, New Haven/London: Yale University Press, 2002, p. 4.

[2] Fukai, Akiko, *Fashion: The Collection of the Kyoto Costume Institute: A History from the 18th to the 20th Century*, London: Taschen, p. 78.

[3] Nunn, Joan, *Fashion in Costume, 1200–2000*, Chicago: New Amsterdam Books, 2000 (1984), p. 93.

[4] Thornton, Peter, *Baroque and Rococo Silks*, London: Faber & Faber, 1965, p. 95.

[5] Anderson, Karen, Deese, Martha, and Tarapor, Mahrukh, "Recent Acquisitions: A Selection, 1990–1991," *The Metropolitan Museum of Art Bulletin*, vol. 9, no. 2, Autumn 1991, p. 54.

[6] Waugh, Norah, *The Cut of Women's Clothes, 1600–1930*, London: Faber & Faber, 2011 (1968), p. 68.

[7] Watt, James C.Y., and Wardwell, Anne E., *When Silk was Gold: Central Asian and Chinese Textiles*, New York: Metropolitan Museum of Art, 1997, p. 213.

[8] Powerhouse Museum item descriptions and provenance, registration number: H7981. http://from.ph/249639

[9] Schoeser, Mary, *Silk*, New Haven: Yale University Press, 2007, p. 248.

[10] Waugh, Norah, *The Cut of Women's Clothes, 1600–1930*, London: Faber & Faber, 2011 (1968), p. 76.

[11] Fukai, Akiko, *Fashion: The Collection of the Kyoto Costume Institute: A History from the 18th to the 20th Century*, London: Taschen, 2002, p. 78.

[12] Takeda, Sharon Sadako, *Fashioning Fashion: European Dress in Detail, 1700–1915*, Los Angeles: Los Angeles County Museum of Art, 2010, p. 78.

[13] Cavallo Adolph S., and Lawrence, Elizabeth N., "Sleuthing at the Seams", *The Costume Institute: The Metropolitan Museum of Art Bulletin*, vol. 30, no. 1, August/September 1971, p. 26.

[14] Ribeiro, Aileen, *A Visual History of Costume: The Eighteenth Century*, London: Batsford, 1983, pp.128–30.

[15] Fukai, Akiko, *Fashion: The Collection of the Kyoto Costume Institute: A History from the 18th to the 20th Century*, London: Taschen, p. 83.

[16] Lewandowski, Elizabeth J., *The Complete Costume Dictionary*, Plymouth: Scarecrow Press, 2011, p. 41.

[17] Naik, Shailaja D., and Wilson, Jacquie, *Surface Designing of Textile Fabrics*, New Delhi: New Age International Pvt Ltd Publishers, 2006, p. 8.

[18] Fukai, Akiko, *Fashion: The Collection of the Kyoto Costume Institute: A History from the 18th to the 20th Century*, London: Taschen 2002, p. 202.

[19] Lewandowski, Elizabeth J., *The Complete Costume Dictionary*, Plymouth: Scarecrow Press, 2011, p. 253.

Chapter Four

[1] Le Bourhis, Katell (ed.), *The Age of Napoleon: Costume from Revolution to Empire, 1789–1815*, New York: The Metropolitan Museum of Art/Harry N. Abrams, 1989, p. 95.

[2] "Miscellany, Original and Select," *Hobart Town Gazette* (Tas.: 1825–27), April 5, 1826: 4. Web. April 16, 2015. http://nla.gov.au/nla.news-article8791181

[3] Curtis, Oswald, and Norris, Herbert, *Nineteenth-Century Costume and Fashion, Vol. 6*, New York: Dover, 1998 (1933), p. 188.

[4] Austen, Jane, *Northanger Abbey*, 1818, Cambridge: Cambridge University Press, 2013, p. 22.

[5] Brooke, Iris, and Laver, James, *English Costume from the Seventeenth through the Nineteenth Centuries*, New York: Dover, 2000, p. 178.

[6] McCord Museum item catalogue and provenance, M982.20.1.

[7] Ibid.

[8] Cumming, Valerie, Cumming, C.W., and Cunnington, P.E., *The Dictionary of Fashion History*, Oxford: Berg, 2010, p. 97.

[9] Starobinski, Jean, *Revolution in Fashion: European Clothing, 1715–1815*, New York: Abbeville Press, 1989, p. 151.

[10] McCord Museum item catalogue and provenance, M990.96.1.

[11] Yarwood, Doreen, *Illustrated Encyclopedia of World Costume*, New York: Dover, 1978, p. 268.

[12] Nunn, Joan, *Fashion in Costume: 1200–2000*, Chicago: New Amsterdam Books, 2000, p. 121.

[13] McCord Museum item catalogue and provenance, M982.20.1.

[14] Steele, Valerie, *Encyclopedia of Clothing and Fashion*, New York: Charles Scribner's Sons, 2005, p. 392.

[15] Bradfield, Nancy, *Costume in Detail: 1730–1930*, Hawkhurst: Eric Dobby, 2007 (1968), pp. 121–35.

[16] Cumming, Valerie, Cunnington, C.W., and Cunnington, P.E., *The Dictionary of Fashion History*, Oxford: Berg, 2010 (1960), p. 279.

[17] Cumming, Valerie, *Exploring Costume History: 1500–1900*, London: Batsford, 1981, p. 67.

[18] Powerhouse Museum item catalogue and provenance, 87/533.

[19] Byrde, Penelope, *Nineteenth Century Fashion*, London: Batsford, 1992, p. 48.

[20] *La Belle Assemblée, or, Bell's Court and Fashionable Magazine—A Facsimile*, London: Whitaker, Treacher and Co., 1831, p.187.

[21] Waugh, Norah, *The Cut of Women's Clothes: 1600–1930*, London: Faber & Faber, 2011 (1968), p. 149.

[22] Powerhouse Museum item catalogue and provenance, A10017.

Chapter Five

[1] Raverat, Gwen, *Period Piece: A Victorian Childhood*, London: Faber & Faber, 1960, p. 260.

[2] *The Workwoman's Guide by a Lady*, London: Simkin, Marshall and Co., 1840, pp. 108–112.

[3] Ibid.

[4] *A Hand-Book of Etiquette for Ladies, by an American Lady*, New York: Leavitt and Allen, 1847.

[5] Waugh, Norah, *Corsets and Crinolines*, London: Routledge, 2015 (1954), p. 79.

[6] Bloomer, Amelia, in *The Lily*, March 1850, p. 21, quoted in Solomon, W.S., and McChesney, R.W., *Ruthless Criticsm: New Perspectives in U.S. Communication History*, Minneapolis: University of Minnesota Press, p. 74.

[7] Dickens, Charles, *The Mystery of Edwin Drood*, London: Chapman & Hall, 1870, p. 177.

[8] "The Dressing Room," *Godey's Lady's Book*, 1851.

[9] Miller, Brandon Marie, *Dressed for the Occasion: What Americans Wore*, Minneapolis, MN: Lerner Publications, 1999, pp. 36–38.

[10] Waugh, Norah, *Corsets and Crinolines*, London: Routledge, 2015 (1954), p. 93.

[11] McCord Museum item description and provenance, M976.2.3.

[12] Bradfield, Nancy, *Costume in Detail: 1730–1930*, Hawkhurst: Eric Dobby, 1968 (2007), p. 141.

[13] *A Sense of Style: Shippensburg University Fashion Archives & Museum Newsletter*, no. 49, Spring 2013, pp. 4–6.

[14] *The Workwoman's Guide by a Lady*, London: Simkin, Marshall and Co., 1840, pp. 108–112.

[15] Watts, D.C., *Dictionary of Plant Lore*, Atlanta, GA: Elsevier, 2007, p. 2.

[16] *The New Monthly Belle Assemblée: A Magazine of Literature and Fashion*, January to June 1853, London: Rogerson & Tuxford, p. 334.

[17] Reeder, Jan Glier, *High Style: Masterworks from the Brooklyn Museum Costume Collection at The Metropolitan Museum of Art*, New York: The Metropolitan Museum of Art, 2010, p. 22.

[18] Foster, Vanda, and Walkley, Christina, *Crinolines and Crimping Irons: Victorian Clothes: How They Were Cleaned and Cared For*, London: Peter Owen Publishers, 1978, p. 19.

[19] Yarwood, Doreen, *Outline of English Costume*, London: Batsford, 1967, p. 31.

[20] Museum catalogue item and provenance, Swan Guildford Historical Society.

[21] Waugh, Norah, *The Cut of Women's Clothes, 1600–1930*, New York: Routledge, 2011 (1968), p. 139.

[22] Powerhouse Museum item catalogue and provenance, A9659.

[23] Ibid.

[24] *Marysville Daily Appeal*, no. 135, December 5, 1869, p. 1.

[25] McCord Museum item catalogue and provenance, M969.1.11.1-4.

[26] Condra, Jill, and Stamper, Anita A., *Clothing through American History: The Civil War through the Gilded Age, 1861–1899*, Santa Barbara: Greenwood, 2011, p. 96.

[27] Waugh, Norah, *The Cut of Women's Clothes: 1600–1930*, New York: Routledge, 1968 (2011), p. 149.

[28] Item catalogue and provenance, Swan Guildford Historical Society.

Chapter Six

[1] Brevik-Zender, Heidi, *Fashioning Spaces: Mode and Modernity in Late-Nineteenth Century Paris*, Toronto: University of Toronto Press, p. 10.

[2] "The Ladies Column," Alexandra and Yea Standard, Gobur, Thornton and Acheron Express (Vic.: 1877–1908), August 5, 1887: 5. Web. December 3, 2015. http://nla.gov.au /nla.news-article57170466

[3] Haweis, Mary, *The Art of Beauty*, New York: Garland Publishing, 1883 (1978), p.120.

[4] "Letters to the Editor: Various Subjects Discussed: A Lady's Views on Fashionable Costume," *New York Times*, August 8, 1877.

[5] Waugh, Norah, *Corsets and Crinolines*, Oxford; Routledge, 2015, p. 83.

[6] Author unnamed, "Bustles," *The Evening World* (New York), December 26, 1888, p.2. www.loc.gov.

[7] Author unnamed, "The Fashions," *The New York Tribune*, June 20, 1871, quoted in the *Sacramento Daily Union*, June 28, 1871 (California Digital Newspaper Collection, Center for Bibliographic Studies and Research, University of California, Riverside, http://cdnc.ucr.edu).

[8] Author unnamed, "New York Fashions," *Sacramento Daily Union*, March 13, 1872 (California Digital Newspaper Collection, Center for Bibliographic Studies and Research, University of California, Riverside, http://cdnc.ucr.edu).

[9] McCord Museum item catalogue and provenance, M971.105.6.1-3.

[10] Powerhouse Museum item catalogue and provenance, A8437.

[11] Author unnamed, "Fashion Notes," *Otago Witness*, Issue 1296, September 1876, p. 19. National Library of New Zealand, viewed August 26, 2014. http://paperspast.natlib .govt.nz/.

[12] Powerhouse Museum item catalogue and provenance, A8437

[13] Sherrow, Victoria, *Encyclopedia of Hair: A Cultural History*, London: Greenwood Press, 2006, p. 387

[14] "The Ladies," *The Sydney Mail and New South Wales Advertiser* (NSW: 1871–1912), January 24, 1880: 156. Web. June 7, 2015. http://nla.gov.au/nla.news-article161877917

[15] Cumming, Valerie, Cunnington, C.W., and Cunningham, P.E, *The Dictionary of Fashion History*, Oxford: Berg, 2010, p. 11.

[16] Amneus, Cynthia, *A Separate Sphere: Dressmakers in Cincinnati's Golden Age, 1877–1922*, Costume Society of America Series, Cincinnati Art Museum/Texas Tech University Press, 2003, pp. 86–102.

[17] "Paris Fall and Winter Fashions," *Sacramento Daily Union*, October 26, 1878, vol. 7, no. 211 (California Digital Newspaper Collection, Center for Bibliographic Studies and Research, University of California, Riverside, http://cdnc.ucr.edu).

[18] *The Queen*, 1883, quoted in Buck, Anne, *Victorian Costume and Costume Accessories*, London: Herbert Jenkins, 1961, p. 72.

[19] Haweis, Mary, *The Art of Beauty*, 1883, New York: Garland Publishing, 1978, p. 120.

[20] Powerhouse Museum item catalogue and provenance, A8070.

[21] Ibid.

[22] Maynard, Margaret, *Fashioned from Penury: Dress as Cultural Practice in Colonial Australia*, Cambridge: Cambridge University Press, 1994, p. 127.

[23] "Ladies' Page," *Australian Town and Country Journal* (Sydney, NSW: 1870–1907), November 4, 1882: 28. Web. June 7, 2015. http://nla.gov.au/nla.news-article70992507

[24] "Ladies Column," *South Australian Weekly Chronicle* (Adelaide, SA: 1881–89), March 1, 1884: 15. Web. December 16, 2015 .http://nla.gov.au/nla.news-article93151399

[25] "Feminine Fashions and Fancies," *The South Australian Advertiser* (Adelaide, SA : 1858–89), July 23, 1883: 10 Supplement: Unknown. Web. December 16, 2015. http://nla.gov.au/nla.news-article33766418

[26] "The Ungraceful, Wobbling Hoops Again," *The Courier-Journal* (Louisville, Kentucky), July 5, 1885, p. 14.

[27] "The Ladies," *The Sydney Mail and New South Wales Advertiser* (NSW: 1871–12), January 15, 1881: 90. Web. December 17, 2015. http://nla.gov.au/nla.news-article161883913

[28] "The Fashions," *Daily Alta California*, April 3, 1887 (California Digital Newspaper Collection, Center for Bibliographic Studies and Research, University of California, Riverside, http://cdnc.ucr.edu).

[29] *Demorest*, New York, 1887 April pp. 374–377.

[30] Bloomingdale Brothers, *Bloomingdale's Illustrated 1886 Catalogue: Fashions, Dry Goods and Housewares*, New York: Dover Publications, 1988, pp. 51–56.

Chapter Seven

[1] Condra, Jill (ed.), *The Greenwood Encyclopedia of Clothing through World History, Vol. 3: 1801 to the Present*, Westport: Greenwood, 2008, p. 75.

[2] *Birmingham Daily Post*, 1899, University of Bristol Theatre Collection: HBT/TB/000022.

[3] Nunn, Joan, *Fashion in Costume, 1200–2000*, Chicago: New Amsterdam Books, p. 185.

[4] "By Gladys: Boudoir Gossip on Frocks AND Fashions," *Observer*, vol. XI, no. 756, June 24,1893, p. 14, National Library of New Zealand, viewed December 15, 2015, http://paperspast.natlib.govt.nz/

[5] "Traveling Gowns and Notions," *The New York Times*, April 16, 1893.

[6] Object provenance catalogue, Swan Guildford Historical Society, WA.

[7] Ibid.

[8] "Spring Novelties," *Australian Town and Country Journal* (Sydney, NSW: 1870–1907), August 15, 1896: 34. Web. December 16, 2015. http://nla.gov.au/nla.news-article71297069

[9] " World of Fashion," *Bairnsdale Advertiser and Tambo and Omeo Chronicle* (Vic.: 1882–1918), January 12, 1895: 2 Edition: morning., Supplement: Supplement to the Bairnsdale Advertiser. Web. December 16, 2015. http://nla.gov.au/nla.news-article86387500

[10] "Paris Gowns and Capes," *The New York Times*, March 26, 1893, p. 16.

[11] Takeda, Sharon Sadako, *Fashioning Fashion: European Dress in Detail, 1700–1915*, Los Angeles: Los Angeles County Museum of Art, 2010, p. 113.

[12] "Our English Letter," *The Queenslander* (Brisbane, Qld : 1866–1939), December 7, 1901: 1095. Web. June 22, 2015. http://nla.gov.au/nla.news-article21269013

[13] Australian Dress Register: Wedding Dress of Mrs. Rebecca Irvine, 1905, Manning Valley Historical Society, ID: 415.

[14] Ibid.

[15] Nunn, Joan, *Fashion in Costume: 1200–2000*, Chicago: New Amsterdam Books, 2000, p. 184.

[16] McCord Museum item catalogue and provenance, M984.150.34.1-2.

[17] Adam, Robert, *Classical Architecture: A Complete Handbook*, New York: Harry Abrams, 1991, p. 280.

[18] Australian Dress Register: Hilda Smith's black silk satin and lace dress, 1908–1912, Griffith Pioneer Park Museum, ID: 232.

[19] "The Importance of a Sash," *The Brisbane Courier* (QLD: 1864–1933), December 27, 1911: 15 Supplement: Courier Home Circle. Web. September 3, 2015. http://nla.gov.au/nla.news-article19743295

[20] Powerhouse Museum item catalogue and provenance, 86/610.

[21] *Delineator*, New York, November 1908, p. 670.

[22] Powerhouse Museum item catalogue and provenance, 86/610.

[23] "Fashion Notes," *Examiner* (Launceston, Tas.: 1900–54), September 9, 1911: 2 Edition: DAILY. Web. December 16, 2015. http://nla.gov.au/nla.news-article50492419

[24] "A Lady's Letter from London," *The Sydney Mail*, September 3, 1898, p. 12.

[25] "Ladies' Column," *Bendigo Advertiser* (Vic.: 1855–1918), May 20, 1899: 7. Web. December 16, 2015. http://nla.gov.au/nla.news-article89820861

[26] 1900 "Dress and Fashion," *The Queenslander* (Brisbane, Qld.: 1866–1939), 7 April 7, p. 654, Supplement: The Queenslander, viewed September 2, 2014. http://nla.gov.au/nla.news-article18544394.

[27] "The Autumn Girl and Her Autumn Coat," *The Chicago Tribune*, August 26, 1900, p. 55.

[28] McCord Museum item catalogue and provenance, M976.35.2.1-2.

[29] *Delineator*, New York, September 1911, pp. 160–169.

[30] McCord Museum item catalogue and provenance, M976.35.2.1-2.

[31] Ibid.

[32] De La Haye, Amy, and Mendes, Valerie, *Fashion Since 1900*, London: Thames & Hudson, 2010, p. 20.

[33] "Age of Sloppy Dress," *Maryborough Chronicle, Wide Bay and Burnett Advertiser* (Qld.: 1860–1947), May 12, 1914: 5. Web. December 16, 2015. http://nla.gov.au/nla.news-article150875205

[34] McCord Museum item catalogue and provenance, M983.130.3.1-3.

[35] Ibid.

[36] Ibid.

Chapter Eight

[1] "The New Costume: Eking out the Paris Cloth Ration—From Our Own Correspondent," The Daily Mail, August 18, 1917, from the Digital Archive: Gale–Cengage Learning, The Daily Mail, 2015.

[2] "Fashion: Dressing on a War Income," *Vogue*, vol. 51, no. 5, March 1, 1918, pp. 54, 55, and 126.

[3] Waugh, Evelyn, *Brideshead Revisited: The Sacred and Profane Memories of Captain Charles Ryder*, London: Penguin, 1945 (1982) p. 172.

[4] Roe, Dorothy, "The Picture Frock is Back Again," *Milwaukee Sentinel*, October 14, 1934, p. 8.

[5] de Montebello, Philippe, "Foreword," in Koda, Harold, and Bolton, Andrew, *Chanel: The Metropolitan Museum of Art*, New Haven: Yale University Press, 2005, p. 12.

[6] Lowe, Corrine, "Fashion's Blue Book," *The Chicago Daily Tribune*, May 21, 1918, p. 14.

[7] Donnelly, Antoinette, "Short Skirts or Long—Heels Must Be Invulnerable," *The Chicago Sunday Tribune*, October 16, 1918, p. 2.

[8] Tortora, Phyllis G., *Dress, Fashion and Technology: From Prehistory to the Present*, London: Bloomsbury, 2015, p. 136.

[9] Koda, Harold, *Goddess: The Classical Mode*, New York: The Metropolitan Museum of Art, 2003, p. 219.

[10] "Mariano Fortuny: Evening Ensemble (1979.344.11a,b)," in Heilbrunn, *Timeline of Art History*, New York: The Metropolitan Museum of Art, 2000–. http://www.metmuseum.org/toah/works-of-art/1979.344.11a,b (December 2013)

[11] Item catalogue and provenance, North Carolina Museum of History, H.1978.17.1.

[12] "A Frock For Seven Shillings." *Sydney Mail* (NSW: 1912–38), November 2, 1921: 22. Web. December 17, 2015. http://nla.gov.au/nla.news-article162034166

[13] Item catalogue and provenance, Swan Guildford Historical Society, WA.

[14] Wells, Margery, "Gay Embroideries Sound the Season's High Note," *The Evening World*, September 25, 1923.

[15] "For Australian Women," *Table Talk* (Melbourne, Vic.: 1885–1939) July 20, 1922: 4. Web. December 7, 2015. http://nla.gov.au/nla.news-article147420574

[16] Dr. Jasmine Day, Curtin University, December 2015.

[17] Powerhouse Museum item catalogue and provenance, 2008/8/1.

[18] "Dress Decorations," *The Queenslander* (Brisbane, Qld.: 1866–1939), November 28, 1929: 52. Web. December 17, 2015. http://nla.gov.au/nla.news-article2292174.

[19] "The Vogue for Beige," *Sunday Times* (Perth, WA: 1902–54), November 10, 1929: 39 Section: First Section. Web. December 17, 2015. http://nla.gov.au/nla.news-article58366337

[20] Item catalogue and provenance, Swan Guildford Historical Society, WA.

[21] "Dress Hints," *Albury Banner and Wodonga Express* (NSW: 1896–1938), February 15, 1924: 15. Web. December 17, 2015. http://nla.gov.au/nla.news-article101523864

[22] "The Uncertain Waist-Line," *Queensland Figaro* (Brisbane, Qld.: 1901–36), January 19, 1929: 6. Web. December 17, 2015. http://nla.gov.au/nla.news-article84904764

[23] "Paris Tells Its Beads," *Truth* (Brisbane, Qld.: 1900–54), February 5, 1928: 18. Web. 17 December 17, 2015. http://nla.gov.au/nla.news-article206147705>

[24] "Evening Modes," *Sunday Times* (Perth, WA: 1902–54), 6 November 6, 1927: 36. Web. December 17, 2015. http://nla.gov.au/nla.news-article60300520

Chapter Nine

[1] "Feminine Garb more Romantic and Expensive: Luxury New Keynote of Fashion," *Chicago Sunday Tribune*, August 17, 1930, p. 17.

[2] Polan, Brenda, and Tredre, Roger, *The Great Fashion Designers*, Oxford: Berg, 2009, p. 59.

[3] "Daily Mail Atlantic Edition," July 22, 1931, "Spruce Up! Is Dame Fashion's Warning," from the Digital Archive: Gale–Cengage Learning, The Daily Mail, 2015.

[4] De la Haye, Amy, *The Cutting Edge: 50 Years of British Fashion, 1947–1997*, London: V&A Publications, 1996, p. 16.

[5] Anderson, David, "British to Add Cut in Living Standard; Dalton Says It Will Take More Than Year to Reach Strict War Economy Level," *The New York Times*, March 4, 1942.

[6] McEuen, Melissa, *Making War, Making Women: Femininity and Duty on the American Home Front, 1941–1945*, Athens: University of Georgia Press, 2010, p. 138.

[7] Bedwell, Bettina, "Saving Clothes Is Fashionable in England: Ration System Abroad Makes It Imperative," *Chicago Sunday Tribune*, October 11, 1942.

[8] Drew, Ruth, "The Housewife in War Time." *Listener* [London, England], March 11, 1943: 314. *The Listener Historical Archive 1929–1991*. Web. May 26, 2014.

[9] Chase, Joanna, *Sew and Save*, Glasgow: The Literary Press, 1941—HarperPress, 2009, pp. 1–2.

[10] "Winter Evening Wear." *Barrier Miner* (Broken Hill, NSW: 1888–1954), June 4, 1936: 5. Web. December 17, 2015. http://nla.gov.au/nla.news-article47910634

[11] "Black Velvet Gown," *The Times and Northern Advertiser*, Peterborough, South Australia (SA : 1919 - 1950) 30 Jan 1931: 4. Web. 17 Dec 2015 http://nla.gov.au/nla.news-article110541726

[12] Pick, Michael, *Be Dazzled!: Norman Hartnell: Sixty Years of Glamour and Fashion*, New York: Pointed Leaf Press, 2007, p. 49.

[13] Delafield, E.M., *The Diary of a Provincial Lady* (eBook), e-artnow, 2015.

[14] "Evening Glory," *The Inverell Times* (NSW: 1899–1954) May 2, 1938: 6. Web. December 17, 2015. http://nla.gov.au/nla.news-article185833902

[15] "Novelties in Designs for Evening Dress," *The Courier-Mail* (Brisbane, Qld.: 1933–54), December 31, 1945: 5. Web. December 3, 2015. http://nla.gov.au/nla.news-article50255268>

[16] Leshner, Leigh, *Vintage Jewelry 1920–1940s: An Identification and Price Guide*, Iola, WI: Krause Publications, p. 10.

[17] "Greek Influence," *Daily Mercury* (MacKay, Qld.: 1906–54), 5 March 5, 1945: p. 6. Web. 2November 29, 2015. http://nla.gov.au/nla.news-article170980779

[18] Item catalogue and provenance, Swan Guildford, Historical Society, WA.

[19] "The Daily Mail," February 6, 1941, "Forget War Modes," from the Digital Archive: Gale–Cengage Learning, The Daily Mail, 2015.

[20] *The British Colour Council Dictionary of Colour Standards: A List of Colour Names Referring to the Colours Shown in the Companion Volume*, London: The British Colour Council, 1934.

[21] "The Housewife in War Time," March 11, 1943, "The Listener," from the Digital Archive: Gale–Cengage Learning, The Listener, 2015.

Chapter Ten

[1] Pochna, Marie France, *Christian Dior: The Man Who Made the World Look New*, New York: Arcade Publishing, 1994, p.178.

[2] "Woman's World," *Alexandra Herald and Central Otago Gazette*, November 19, 1947, p. 3.

[3] Christian Dior, *Christian Dior: The Autobiography*, London: Weidenfeld and Nicolson, 1957, p. 41.

[4] Ibid.

[5] *The Sunday Times* (April 6, 1952), "Transatlantic Fashion Trend," from the Digital Archive: Gale–Cengage Learning, The Sunday Times, 2015.

[6] "Women's Suits for Easter in Wide Choice of Colours," March 17, 1948, *The Bend Bulletin*, Oregon, Bend, p. 14.

[7] Nunn, Joan, *Fashion in Costume, 1200–2000*, Chicago: New Amsterdam Books, 2000, p. 226.

[8] Amies, Hardy, *Just So Far*, London: Collins, 1954, p. 88.

[9] "Woman's World," *The Mail* (Adelaide, SA: 1912–54), January 9, 1943: 10. Web. 17 December 17, 2015. http://nla.gov.au/nla.news-article55869851

[10] Powerhouse Museum item catalogue and provenance, 2003/59/1.

[11] "Wedding Bells," *The Central Queensland Herald* (Rockhampton, Qld.: 1930–56), June 25, 1953: 29. Web. December 17, 2015. http://nla.gov.au/nla.news-article77228054

[12] English, Bonnie, and Pomazan, Liliana, *Australian Fashion Unstitched: The Last 60 Years*, New York: Cambridge University Press, 2010, p. 50.

[13] Powerhouse Museum item catalogue and provenance, 2003/59/1.

[14] Catalogue, Fashion Archives and Museum, Shippensburg University, Pittsburgh: #S1984-48-012 Lineweaver.

[15] "New Patterns Feature Classic and High Style," *The Spokesman-Review*, October 1, 1953, p. 5.

[16] Hampton, Mary, "Coat Dress Is Alternate for Suit, Materials, Styles Vary," *The Fresno Bee/The Republican* (Fresno, California), March 27, 1952, p. 28.

[17] *The Sydney Morning Herald*, July 20, 1952, p. 8.

[18] "Chasnoff pre-Thanksgiving Clearance: Dresses," *The Kansas City Times* (Kansas, Missouri), November 21, 1952, p. 13.

[19] Mitchell, Louise, and Ward, Lindie, *Stepping Out: Three Centuries of Shoes*, Sydney: Powerhouse, 1997, p. 56.

[20] Item catalogue and provenance, Swan Guildford Historical Society, WA.

[21] "Spring Issues a Call to Colors—and a Pretty Look!" *The Van Nuys News* (Van Nuys, California), March 17, 1952, p. 24.

[22] "They Won't Be Crushed," *The West Australian* (Perth, WA: 1879–1954), November 8, 1951: 9. Web. December 17, 2015. http://nla.gov.au/nla.news-article48998780

[23] "Dress Sense," *The Australian Women's Weekly* (1933–82), November 17, 1954: 43. Web. December 17, 2015 .http://nla.gov.au/nla.news-article41491009

[24] Powerhouse Museum item catalogue and provenance, 89/250.

[25] "Fine Wools Featured for Summer Wear in Paris and London," *The Mercury* (Hobart, Tas.: 1860–1954), June 20, 1950: 14. Web. December 17, 2015. http://nla.gov.au/nla.news-article26710285

[26] Powerhouse Museum item catalogue and provenance, 89/250.

Chapter Eleven

[1] Lester, Richard, and Owen, Alun, *A Hard Day's Night*, United Artists, 1964.

[2] Cochrane, Lauren, *Fifty Fashion Designers That Changed the World*, London: Conran Octopus: 2015, p. 34.

[3] English, Bonnie, *A Cultural History of Fashion in the 20th and 21st Centuries: From Catwalk to Sidewalk*, London: Bloomsbury, 2013, p. 2.

[4] *The Daily Mail* (Friday October 28, 1960), "Unstoppable . . . This March of Women in Trousers," from the Digital Archive: Gale–Cengage Learning, Illustrated London News, 2015.

[5] *A Sense of Style: Shippensburg University Fashion Archives & Museum Newsletter*, no. 51, Spring 2015, p. 8.

[6] "Women's Club Tea Spiced With Talk By Local Fashion Adviser," *The Daily Mail* (Hagerstown, Maryland), April 14, 1966, p. 8.

[7] Miller, Mary Sue, "Strapless Gowns Must Fit Nicely," *Denton Record-Chronicle* (Denton, Texas), November 22, 1965, p. 5.

[8] Miller, Mary Sue, "The Now Dress Is the Softest," *The Daily Journal* (Fergys Falls, Minnesota), February 18, 1968, p. 6.

[9] "Total Look in Fashions Is Varied," *Statesville Record and Landmark* (Statesville, North Carolina), 28 July 28, 1969, p. 3.

[10] Pitkin, Melanie (Assistant Curator), "Design & Society," Powerhouse Museum, Statement of Significance: 89/250.

[11] Ibid.

[12] Item catalogue and provenance, Swan Guildford Historical Society, WA.

[13] Ibid.

[14] "Paris Says . . . Look Ultra-Feminine This Spring Season," *The Australian Women's Weekly* (1933–82), September 1, 1965: 21. Web. December 17, 2015. http://nla.gov.au/nla.news-article46239642

[15] Wilson Trower, Valerie, "Cheongsam: Chinese One-Piece Dress," *Berg Encyclopedia of World Dress and Fashion, Vol. 6: East Asia*, http://dx.doi.org/10.2752/BEWDF/EDch6023.

[16] Condra, Jill (ed.), *Encyclopedia of National Dress: Traditional Clothing Around the World: Vol. I*, Santa Barbara: ABC-CLIO, 2013, p. 571.

[17] Item catalogue and provenance, Fashion Archives and Museum, Shippensburg University, #S1979-01-002.

[18] "Fashion Tips," *The Indiana Gazette* (Indiana, Pennsylvania), September 7, 1966, p. 8.

[19] Item catalogue and provenance, Swan Guildford Historical Society, WA.

[20] "Dress Sense," *The Australian Women's Weekly* (1933–82), November 26, 1969: 68. Web. December 17, 2015. http://nla.gov.au/nla.news-article44027834

[21] Item catalogue and provenance, Fashion Archives and Museum, Shippensburg University, #S1981-45-001.

[22] Smith, Kelly, "Spring Fashion Is a 1920's Flapper," *Standard-Speaker* (Hazleton, Pennsylvania), January 14, 1966, p. 15.

Bibliography

Adam, Robert, *Classical Architecture: A Complete Handbook*, New York: Harry Abrams, 1991.

Amies, Hardy, *Just So Far*, London: Collins, 1954.

Amneus, Cynthia, *A Separate Sphere: Dressmakers in Cincinnati's Golden Age, 1877–1922*, Costume Society of America Series, Cincinnati Art Museum/ Texas Tech University Press, 2003.

Anderson, Karen, Deese, Martha, and Tarapor, Mahrukh, "Recent Acquisitions: A Selection, 1990–1991," *The Metropolitan Museum of Art Bulletin*, vol. 9, no. 2, Autumn 1991.

Arnold, Janet, *Patterns of Fashion: 1660–1860: Vol. 1, Englishwomen's Dresses and Their Construction*, London: Macmillan, 1985.

Arnold, Janet, *Patterns of Fashion: 1860–1930: Vol. 2, Englishwomen's Dresses and Their Construction*, London: Macmillan, 1985.

Arnold, Janet, *Patterns of Fashion: 1560–1620: Vol. 3, The Cut and Construction of Clothes for Men and Women*, London: Macmillan, 1985.

Ashelford, Jane, *A Visual History of Costume: The Sixteenth Century*, New York: Drama Book Publishers, 1983.

Austen, Jane, *Northanger Abbey*, 1818, Cambridge: Cambridge University Press, 2013.

Aughterson, Kate, *The English Renaissance: An Anthology of Sources and Documents*, London: Routledge, 1998, pp.164-67.

Bell, Quentin, *On Human Finery*, Berlin: Schocken Books, 1978.

La Belle Assemblée, or, Bell's Court and Fashionable Magazine—A Facsimile, London: Whitaker, Treacher and Co., 1831.

Bloomingdale Brothers, *Bloomingdale's Illustrated 1886 Catalogue: Fashions, Dry Goods and Housewares*, New York: Dover Publications, 1988.

Boucher, François, and Deslandres, Yvonne, *A History of Costume in the West*, London: Thames & Hudson, 1987.

Bradfield, Nancy, *Costume in Detail: 1730–1930*, Hawkhurst: Eric Dobby, 2007 (1968).

Brevik-Zender, Heidi, *Fashioning Spaces: Mode and Modernity in Late-Nineteenth Century Paris*, Toronto: University of Toronto Press.

Brooke, Iris, *English Costume of the Seventeenth Century*, London: Adam & Charles Black, 1964.

Byrde, Penelope, *Nineteenth Century Fashion*, London: Batsford, 1992.

Byrde, Penelope, *Jane Austen Fashion: Fashion and Needlework in the Works of Jane Austen*, Los Angeles: Moonrise Press, 2008.

Cavallo, Adolph S., "The Kimberley Gown," *Metropolitan Museum Journal*, vol. 3, 1970.

Chase, Joanna, *Sew and Save*, Glasgow: The Literary Press, 1941; HarperPress, 2009.

Cochrane, Lauren, *Fifty Fashion Designers That Changed the World*, London: Conran Octopus, 2015.

Conan Doyle, Arthur, *The Adventures of Sherlock Holmes: The Copper Beeches* (1892), in *The Original Illustrated Strand Sherlock Holmes*, Collingdale, PA: Diane Publishing, 1989.

Condra, Jill, *The Greenwood Encyclopedia of Clothing Through World History: 1501–1800*, Westport, CA: Greenwood Publishing Group, 2008.
Condra, Jill (ed.), *Encyclopedia of National Dress: Traditional Clothing Around the World: Vol. I*, Santa Barbara: ABC-CLIO, 2013.

Cotton, Charles, *Essays of Michel Seigneur de Montaigne: The First Volume* (facsimile), London: Daniel Brown, J. Nicholson, R. Wellington, B. Tooke, B. Barker, G. Straban, R. Smith, and G. Harris, 1711, p. 409.

Cumming, Valerie, *A Visual History of Costume: The Seventeenth Century*, London: Batsford, 1984.
Cumming, Valerie, Cunnington, Willett C., and Cunnington, P.E., *The Dictionary of Fashion History*, Oxford: Berg, 2010.

Cumming, Valerie, *Exploring Costume History: 1500–1900*, London: Batsford, 1981.

Cunnginton, Willett, C., *English Women's Clothing in the Nineteenth Century: A Comprehensive Guide with 1,117 Illustrations*, New York: Dover, 1990.

Cunnington, Phyllis, and Willett, C., *Handbook of English Costume in the Seventeenth Century*, London: Faber & Faber (proof copy).

Curtis, Oswald, and Norris, Herbert, *Nineteenth-Century Costume and Fashion, Vol. 6*, New York: Dover, 1998 (1933).

Davenport, Millia, *The Book of Costume: Vol. I*, New York: Crown Publishers, 1948.
Delafield, E.M., *The Diary of a Provincial Lady*, e-artnow, 2015 (e-Book).

De La Haye, Amy, and Mendes, Valerie, *Fashion Since 1900*, London: Thames & Hudson, 2010.

De La Haye, Amy, and Wilson, Elizabeth, *Defining Dress: Dress as Meaning, Object and Identity*, Manchester: Manchester University Press, 1999.

De Winkel, Marieke, *Fashion and Fancy: Dress and Meaning in Rembrandt's Paintings*, Amsterdam: Amsterdam University Press, 2006.

Druesedow, Jean L., "In Style: Celebrating Fifty Years of the Costume Institute," *The Metropolitan Museum of Art Bulletin*, vol. XLV, no. 2, 1987.

English, Bonnie, *A Cultural History of Fashion in the 20th and 21st Centuries: From Catwalk to Sidewalk*, London: Bloomsbury, 2013.

English, Bonnie, and Pomazan, Liliana, *Australian Fashion Unstitched: The Last 60 Years*, New York: Cambridge University Press, 2010.Eubank, Keith, and Tortora, Phyllis G., *Survey of Historic Costume*, New York: Fairchild, 2010.

Fagan, Brian, *The Little Ice Age: How Climate Made History*, New York: Basic Books, 2000.

Fukai, Akiko, *Fashion: The Collection of the Kyoto Costume Institute: A History from the 18th to the 20th Century*, London: Taschen, 2002.

Geddes, Elizabeth, and McNeill, Moyra, *Blackwork Embroidery*, New York: Dover, 1976.

Green, Ruth M., *The Wearing of Costume: The Changing Techniques of Wearing Clothes and How to Move in Them, from Roman Britain to the Second World War*, London: Pitman, 1966.

Hart, Avril, and North, Susan, *Historical Fashion in Detail: The 17th and 18th Centuries*, London: V&A Publications, 1998.

Haweis, Mary, *The Art of Beauty*, New York: Garland Publishing, 1883 (1978).

Hill, John (ed.), *The Diary of Samuel Pepys*, 1666 (Project Gutenberg, e-book).

Koda, Harold, *Goddess: The Classical Mode*, New York: The Metropolitan Museum of Art, 2003.

Koda, Harold, and Bolton, Andrew, *Chanel: The Metropolitan Museum of Art*, New Haven: Yale University Press, 2005.

Köhler, Carl, *A History of Costume*, New York: Dover, 1963.

Landini, Roberta Orsi, and Niccoli, Bruna, *Moda a Firenze, 1540–1580: lo stile di Eleonora di Toledo e la sua influenza*, Oakville: David Brown Book Company, 2005, p. 21.

Latteier, Carolyn, *Breasts: The Women's Perspective on an American Obsession*, New York: Routledge, 2010.

Le Bourhis, Katell (ed.), *The Age of Napoleon: Costume from Revolution to Empire, 1789–1815*, New York: The Metropolitan Museum of Art/Harry N. Abrams, 1989.

Lee, Carol, *Ballet in Western Culture: A History of Its Origins and Evolution*, New York: Routledge, 2002.

Leshner, Leigh, *Vintage Jewelry 1920–1940s: An Identification and Price Guide: 1920–1940s*, Iola, WI: Krause Publications, 2002.

Leslie, Catherine Amoroso, *Needlework through History: An Encyclopedia*, Westport, CA: Greenwood Press, 2007.

Lewandowski, Elizabeth J., *The Complete Costume Dictionary*, Plymouth: Scarecrow Press, 2011

Luther Hilman, Betty, *Dressing for the Culture Wars: Style and the Politics of Self-Presentation in the 1960s and 1970s*, The Board of Regents of the University of Nebraska, 2015 (e-Book).

McEuen, Melissa, *Making War, Making Women: Femininity and Duty on the American Home Front, 1941–1945*, Athens: University of Georgia Press, 2010.

Mikhaila, Ninya, and Malcolm-Davies, Jane, *The Tudor Tailor: Reconstructing Sixteenth-Century Dress*, London: Batsford, 2006.

Mitchell, Louise, and Ward, Lindie, *Stepping Out: Three Centuries of Shoes*, Sydney: Powerhouse, 1997.

Naik, Shailaja D., and Wilson, Jacquie, *Surface Designing of Textile Fabrics*, New Delhi: New Age International Pvt Ltd Publishers, 2006.

The Needle's Excellency: A Travelling Exhibition by the Victoria & Albert Museum—Catalogue, London: Crown, 1973, p. 2.

The New Monthly Belle Assemblée: A magazine of literature and fashion, January to June 1853, London: Rogerson & Tuxford, 1853.

Nunn, Joan, *Fashion in Costume, 1200–2000*, Chicago: New Amsterdam Books, 2000.

Otavská, Vendulka, *Ke konzervování pohřebního roucha Markéty Františky Lobkowiczové*, Mikulov: Regionální muzeum v Mikulově, 2006, s. 114–120.

Peacock, John, *Fashion Sourcebooks: The 1940s*, London: Thames & Hudson, 1998.

Pepys, Samuel, and Wheatly, Benjamin (eds.), *The Diary of Samuel Pepys, 1666*, New York: George E. Croscup, 1895, p. 305.

Pick, Michael, *Be Dazzled!: Norman Hartnell: Sixty Years of Glamour and Fashion*, New York: Pointed Leaf Press, 2007.

Pietsch, Johannes, *The Burial Clothes of Margaretha Franziska de Lobkowitz 1617*, Costume 42, 2008, S. 30–49.

Polan, Brenda, and Tredre, Roger, *The Great Fashion Designers*, Oxford: Berg, 2009.

Powys, Marian, *Lace and Lace Making*, New York: Dover, 2002.

Randle Holme, *The Third Book of the Academy of Armory and Blazon*, c.1688, pp. 94–96.

Reeder, Jan Glier, *High Style: Masterworks from the Brooklyn Museum Costume Collection at The Metropolitan Museum of Art*, New York: The Metropolitan Museum of Art, 2010. Ribeiro, Aileen, *A Visual History of Costume: The Eighteenth Century*, London: Batsford, 1983.

Ribeiro, Aileen, *Dress in Eighteenth-Century Europe, 1715–1789*, New Haven/London: Yale University Press, 2002.

Ribeiro, Aileen, *Dress and Morality*, Oxford: Berg, 2003. Rothstein, Natalie, *Four Hundred Years of Fashion*, London: V&A Publications, 1984.

Sherrow, Victoria, *Encyclopedia of Hair: A Cultural History*, London: Greenwood Press, 2006.

Steele, Valerie, *Encyclopedia of Clothing and Fashion*, New York: Charles Scribner's Sons, 2005.

Stevens, Rebecca A.T., and Wada, Iwamoto Yoshiko, *The Kimono Inspiration: Art and Art-to-Wear in America*, San Francisco: Pomegranate, 1996.

Stevenson, Burton Egbert, *The Macmillan Book of Proverbs, Maxims, and Famous Phrases*, New York: Macmillan, 1948.

Tarrant, Naomi, *The Development of Costume*, Edinburgh: Routledge/National Museums of Scotland, 1994.
Thornton, Peter, *Baroque and Rococo Silks*, London: Faber & Faber, 1965.

Tortora, Phyllis G., *Dress, Fashion and Technology: From Prehistory to the Present*, London: Bloomsbury, 2015.

Wace, A.J., *English Domestic Embroidery—Elizabeth to Anne*, Vol. 17 (1933) *The Bulletin of the Needle and Bobbin Club*.

Watt, James C.Y., and Wardwell, Anne E., *When Silk was Gold: Central Asian and Chinese Textiles*, New York: Metropolitan Museum of Art, 1997.

Watts, D.C., *Dictionary of Plant Lore*, Atlanta, GA: Elsevier, 2007.

Waugh, Evelyn, *Brideshead Revisited: The Sacred and Profane Memories of Captain Charles Ryder*, London: Penguin, 1982 (1945).

Waugh, Norah, *The Cut of Women's Clothes, 1600–1930*, London: Faber & Faber, 2011 (1968).

Waugh, Norah, *Corsets and Crinolines*, Oxford; Routledge, 2015.

The Workwoman's Guide by a Lady, London: Simkin, Marshall and Co., 1840.

Yarwood, Doreen, *English Costume from the Second Century B.C. to 1967*, London: Batsford, 1967.

Yarwood, Doreen, *European Costume: 4000 Years of Fashion*, Paris: Larousse, 1975.

Yarwood, Doreen, *Outline of English Costume*, London: Batsford, 1977.

Yarwood, Doreen, *Illustrated Encyclopedia of World Costume*, New York: Dover, 1978.

Photographic Credits

A dress with a wide sailor collar, c.1917–18, author's family archive. p.134, top left

A fashionable ensemble in Cape Town, early 1930s, private collection, p.155, full

Agnolo Bronzino, *A Young Woman and Her Little Boy*, c.1540. Courtesy National Gallery of Art, Washington, D.C., p.6

Anthony van Dyck, *Lady with a Fan*, c.1628. Courtesy National Gallery of Art, Washington, D.C. p.37

Anthony van Dyck, Queen Henrietta Maria with Sir Jeffrey Hudson (detail), 1633. Courtesy National Gallery of Art, Washington, p.38

Anthony van Dyck, Queen Henrietta Maria with Sir Jeffrey Hudson (close-up detail), 1633. Courtesy National Gallery of Art, Washington, p.38, left

Antoine Trouvain, Seconde chambre des apartemens, c.1690–1708, J. Paul Getty Museum, Los Angeles, p.50, left

Appliquéd robe de style, c.1924, Vintage Textile, New Hampshire, p.142, bottom left

Aqua linen day dress, early 1940s, Swan Guildford Historical Society, Australia. Photo: Aaron Robotham, p.161

Aqua linen day dress, early 1940s (detail: buttonhole), Swan Guildford Historical Society, Australia. Photo: Aaron Robotham, p.161, left

Aqua linen day dress, early 1940s (detail: embroidery), Swan Guildford Historical Society, Australia. Photo: Aaron Robotham, p.161, right

A sleeveless day dress worn with brown fringed shawl in Wales, mid-1920s, author's family archive, p.146, right

Attic Geometric Lidded Pyxis, detail, Athens, Greece, courtesy Los Angeles County Museum of Art online Public Access, p.128, left

Auguste Renoir, Mademoiselle Sicot, 1865. Courtesy National Gallery of Art, Washington, D.C., p.89, right

Australian division uniform of the Women's Auxiliary Air Force (WAAF), 1943–45 (detail), Evans Head Living History Society, New South Wales, p.172, right

Black crêpe de chine day dress, c.1920–25, Photo: Aaron Robotham Guildford Historical Society, Australia, p.146

Black satin evening gown, c.1963–65,

Shippensburg Fashion Museum & Archives, Shippensburg, Pennsylvania, p.183

Black silk satin and lace dress, c.1908–12, Image Courtesy and Copyright of Griffith Pioneer Park Museum, Costume Collection. Photographer Gordon McCaw, p.129

Blouse and skirt: portrait by Mathew Brady, USA, c.1865, U.S. National Archives and Records Administration, p.81, right

Bone linen day dress, early 1940s, Swan Guildford Historical Society, Australia. Photo: Aaron Robotham, p.162

Brown silk moiré taffeta afternoon dress, c.1865. Collection: Powerhouse Museum, Sydney. Photo: Marinco Kojdanovski, p.89

Bustle, England, 1885, courtesy Los Angeles County Museum of Art online Public Access, p.97, top right

Cage crinolette petticoats, 1872–75, courtesy Los Angeles County Museum of Art online Public Access. p.97, top left

Cameo, 18th–19th centuries, J. Paul Getty Museum, Los Angeles, p.105, left

Taffeta dress, c.1880, France, courtesy Los Angeles County Museum of Art online Public Access, p.106

Capri pants worn in Rhodes, Greece, late 1950s, private collection, p.181

Caraco jacket, 1760–80, courtesy Los Angeles County Museum of Art online Public Access, p.48, left

Caspar Netscher, *The Card Party* (details), c.1665, Metropolitan Museum of Art, New York, p.40, right

Chantilly lace scarf, Belgium, 1870s to 1890s, courtesy Los Angeles County Museum of Art online Public Access, p.110, right

Christoffel van Sichem I, *Elizabeth, Queen of Great Britain*, 1570–80 (published 1601), National Gallery of Art, Washington D.C., p.26, full

Circle of Jacques-Louis David, *Portrait of a Young Woman in White*, c.1798, National Gallery of Art, Washington, D.C., p.69, right

Coat and mini dress by Andre Courrèges, 1965, England. Collection: Powerhouse Museum, Sydney. Photo: Andrew Frolows, p.184

Corset, c.1900, courtesy Los Angeles

County Museum of Art online Public Access, p.124, left

Cotton dress, c.1790s, Fashion Museum, Bath and North East Somerset Council/Gift of the Misses A. and M. Birch/Bridgeman Images, p.59

Cotton dress, c.1790s (detail: fabric), Fashion Museum, Bath and North East Somerset Council/Gift of the Misses A. and M. Birch/Bridgeman Images, p.59, left

Cotton gown, 1797–1805, © Victoria and Albert Museum, London, p.68

Court Dress, Fashion plate, 1807, courtesy Los Angeles County Museum of Art online Public Access, p.65

Crispijn de Passe I, Queen of England, c.1588–1603. Courtesy National Gallery of Art, Washington, D.C., p.27

Daguerreotype, 1845, J. Paul Getty Museum, Los Angeles, p.85, left

Day dress (round gown), c.1785–90 (France or England), courtesy Los Angeles County Museum of Art online Public Access, p.61

Day dress (round gown), c.1785–90 (detail: sleeve), (France or England), courtesy Los Angeles County Museum of Art online Public Access, p.61, right

Day dress, c.1893–95, Swan Guildford Historical Society, Australia. Photo: Aaron Robotham, p.120

Day dress, c.1922–24, North Carolina Museum of History, Raleigh. Photo: Eric Blevins, p.147

Day dress, c.1922–24 (detail: embellishment), North Carolina Museum of History, Raleigh, p.147, right

Day dress, c.1954, Swan Guildford Historical Society, Australia. Photo: Aaron Robotham, p.176

Day or afternoon dress, c.1900, M22148.1-2, McCord Museum, Montreal, p.123

Day suit by Hardy Amies, c.1950, M967.25.22.1-2, McCord Museum, Montreal, p.172

Denis Barnham, Portrait of Kathleen Margaret Rudman, 1954, Borland Family Archive, p.177

Detail, robe à la française, 1760s, courtesy Los Angeles County Museum of Art online Public Access, p.87, right

Dinner/evening ensemble, c.1935, M991X.1.29.1-2, McCord Museum,

Montreal, p.158

Dress, c.1836–1841, M976.2.3, McCord Museum, Montreal, p.84

Dress, c.1836–1841 (detail: embellishments), M976.2.3, McCord Museum, Montreal, p.84, left

Dress, c.1870–73, M971.105.6.1-3, Canada, McCord Museum, Montreal, p.101

Dress, 1897, courtesy Los Angeles County Museum of Art online Public Access, p.122

Dress, 1897 (detail: bodice front), courtesy Los Angeles County Museum of Art online Public Access, p.122, left

Dress, c.1918–19, Kent, England, author's family archive, p.140

Dress, late 1920s, Kästing family archive, p.150, left

Dress of black Chantilly lace and pink satin, c.1888, M20281.1-2, Canada, McCord Museum, Montreal, p.110 and p.111, full

Dress of light blue mousseline de laine, c.1854–55, M973.1.1.1-2, McCord Museum, Montreal, p.86

Dress with exchange sleeves c.1895–96. Collection: Powerhouse Museum, Sydney. Photo: Penelope Clay, p.121

Elisabeth Vigée Le Brun, Marie-Antoinette, after 1783, National Gallery of Art, Washington D.C., p.48, left

Empire-line maxi dresses from the early to mid 1970s, England, author's family archive, p.185, top right

Empire-line maxi dresses from the early to mid 1970s, England, author's family archive, p.185, bottom right

Evening coat of gray satin, Paris, c.1912, M21578, McCord Museum, Montreal, p.133

Evening dress, c.1815, M990.96.1, McCord Museum, Montreal, p.72 and p.17, full

Evening dress, 1868–69, M969.1.11.1-4, Paris, McCord Museum, Montreal, p.90

Evening dress, 1965–70, Swan Guildford Historical Society, Australia. Photo: Aaron Robotham, p.185

Evening dress, c.1873, M20277.1-2, Paris, McCord Museum, Montreal, p.102

Evening dress, 1910-12. Collection: Powerhouse Museum, Sydney. Photo: Jane Townsend, p.130

Evening dress, c.1923. Collection: Powerhouse Museum, Sydney. Photo: Sotha

Bourn, p.148

Evening dress, c.1925–29, Paris. Swan Guildford Historical Society, Australia. Photo: Aaron Robotham, p.149

Evening dress, c.1925–29 (back view), Paris. Swan Guildford Historical Society, Australia. Photo: Aaron Robotham, p.149, right

Evening dress, c.1928, M20222, Paris, McCord Museum, Montreal, p.150 and p.151, full

Evening dress, c.1935–45. Collection: Powerhouse Museum, Sydney, p.159

Evening dress and jacket designed by Cristóbal Balenciaga, 1954, Paris. Collection: Powerhouse Museum Sydney. Photo: Sotha Bourn, p.177

Evening dress inspired by Poiret, Germany, c.1918–20, private collection, p.143, full

Follower of Titian, Emilia di Spilimbergo, c.1560. Courtesy National Gallery of Art, Washington D.C., p.24, right

For women still adjusting to postwar life, dress remained relatively conservative and feminine smartness was expected at all times. c. 1956, England, author's family archive, p.169

Frans Hals, Portrait of a Woman, c.1650, Metropolitan Museum of Art, New York, p.39, right

Frederick Randolph Spencer, Portrait of Lady, United States, 1835, courtesy Los Angeles County Museum of Art online Public Access, p.84, right

Frederic, Lord Leighton, Figure Studies, c.1870–90 (detail). Courtesy National Gallery of Art, Washington D.C., p.160, left

George Haugh, The Countess of Effingham with Gun and Shooting Dogs, 1787, Yale Center for British Art, Paul Mellon Collection, New Haven, Connecticut, p.131, left

George Healy, Roxana Atwater Wentworth (detail), USA, 1876. Courtesy National Gallery of Art, Washington, D.C., p.103, right

German family portrait, c.1915–16, Kästing family archive, p.134, bottom left

Gilbert Stuart, Mary Barry, c.1803–05. Courtesy National Gallery of Art, Washington D.C., p.68, right

"Going away" dress and jacket, 1966,

Swan Guildford Historical Society, Australia. Photo: Aaron Robotham, p.186

Green faille dress, c.1952, Shippensburg Fashion Museum & Archives, Shippensburg, Pennsylvania, p.174

Green silk dress, c.1845, Shippensburg Fashion Museum & Archives, Shippensburg, Pennsylvania, p.85

Hats and mantles, fashion plate from "Le Bon Ton: Journal des Modes," Paris, 1837, author's collection, p.67

Hendrik Goltzius, Hieronymus Scholiers, c.1583. Courtesy National Gallery of Art, Washington D.C., p.26, right

Hendrik Goltzius, Portrait of Lady Françoise van Egmond, Holland, 1580, courtesy Los Angeles County Museum of Art online Public Access, p.26, right

Jacobs, William Leroy, Artist. Woman in a Blue Dress. [Between in 1917, 1870] Image. Retrieved from the Library of Congress, 2010716861 (Accessed May 07, 2016), p.144, left

Jacques Wilbaut, Presumed Portrait of the Duc de Choiseul and Two Companions (detail), c.1775, J. Paul Getty Museum, Los Angeles, p.76, left

James McNeill Whistler, The Toilet, 1878, showing the expanse of froth and fills in a fashionable train. National Gallery of Art, Washington D.C., p.99

Jean-Antoine Watteau, Studies of Three Women (detail), c.1716, J. Paul Getty Museum, Los Angeles, p.51, left

Jeanie and Gordon Hogg, c.1946–47. Hogg family archive, p.171, left

Jeanne Lanvin evening dress, 1941, North Carolina Museum of History, Raleigh. Photo: Eric Blevins, p.160

Lanvin evening dress, 1941 (detail: fabric), North Carolina Museum of History, Raleigh. Photo: Eric Blevins, p.160, right

John Bell, fashion plate (carriage visiting costume), England, 1820, courtesy Los Angeles County Museum of Art online Public Access, p.73, right

John Smith after Jan van der Vaart, Queen Mary, 1690. Courtesy National Gallery of Art, Washington, D.C., p.43, left

Joseph B. Blackburn, Portrait of Mrs. John Pigott, c.1750, courtesy Los Angeles County Museum of Art online Public Access, p.9, left

Lady Curzon's evening dress, 1902–03,

Fashion Museum, Bath and North East Somerset Council/Gift of Lady Alexandra Metcalfe and Lady Irene Ravensdale/Bridgeman Images, p.124

Lady Curzon's evening dress, 1902–03 (detail: embellishment), Fashion Museum, Bath and North East Somerset Council/Gift of Lady Alexandra Metcalfe and Lady Irene Ravensdale/Bridgeman Images, p.124, right

Maiden from a Mirror Stand, bronze, 500–475 B.C., The Walters Art Museum, Baltimore, p.144, left

Mantua, c.1690s, Britain, Metropolitan Museum of Art, New York, p.43

Marketa Lobkowicz burial gown, c.1617, © Regional Museum, Mikulov, Czechoslovakia, p.36

Marketa Lobkowicz burial cloak, c.1617, © Regional Museum, Mikulov, Czechoslovakia, p.36, left

"Munitions factory worker May Goodreid in belted coat, trousers and long boots. Wales, c.1915-16, author's collection," p.117

Muslin dress, c.1800–05 (probably India), courtesy Los Angeles County Museum of Art online Public Access, p.69

Net and silk evening dress, 1918, North Carolina Museum of History, Raleigh. Photo: Eric Blevins, p.144

New Look variant, c.1947–49, author's family archive, p.167, full

Nicolas Bonnart, Recuil des modes de la cour de France—La Sage Femme, c.1678–93, courtesy Los Angeles County Museum of Art online Public Access, p.41

Nicolas Bonnart, Recueil des modes de la cour de France—La Belle Plaideuse, c.1682–86, courtesy Los Angeles County Museum of Art online Public Access, p.42.

Open robe and underskirt, England or France, 1760–70. Collection: Powerhouse Museum, Sydney. Photo: Kate Pollard, p.53

Orange and teal silk print dress, mid to late 1960s, Shippensburg Fashion Museum & Archives, Shippensburg, Pennsylvania, p.187

"Oxford" wedding shoes, USA, c.1890, courtesy Los Angeles County Museum of Art online Public Access, p.119, right

Pale blue silk mantua gown, c.1710–20. © Victoria and Albert Museum, London, p.51

Peter Lely, Portrait of Louise de Keroualle, Duchess of Portsmouth, about 1671–74, Oil on canvas, 125.1 × 101.6 cm (49 1/4 × 40 in.) The J. Paul Getty Museum, Los Angeles, p.9, left

Peter Paul Rubens, Marchesa Brigida Spinola Doria, 1606, courtesy Samuel H. Kress Collection, National Gallery of Art, Washington D.C., p.36, right

Pierre-Auguste Renoir, La Promenade, 1870, J. Paul Getty Museum, Los Angeles, p.95

Plaid silk dress, 1878, England, courtesy Los Angeles County Museum of Art online Public Access, p.105

Portrait, c.1909–12, author's family archive, p.129, left

Portrait, c1945–48, author's collection, p.162, right

Red mini dress, c.1968–70, Swan Guildford Historical Society, Australia. Photo: Aaron Robotham, p.162

Robe à l'anglaise, 1780–90 (detail: bodice front), courtesy Los Angeles County Museum of Art online Public Access, p.59, right

Robe à l'anglaise, 1785–87, French, Metropolitan Museum of Art, New York. Image source: Art Resource, New York, p.57

Robe à la française, c.1765, courtesy Los Angeles County Museum of Art online Public Access, p.47

Robe à la française (detail), 1750–60, courtesy Los Angeles County Museum of Art online Public Access, p.104, right

Robe and petticoat, 1770–80 (detail), courtesy Los Angeles County Museum of Art online Public Access, p.55, right, and detail: trimming, p.130, left

Sack Gown, c.1770–80 (detail), courtesy Los Angeles County Museum of Art online Public Access, p.53, right

Shot taffeta robe à la française, c.1725–45, courtesy Los Angeles County Museum of Art online Public Access, p.52

Shot taffeta robe à la française, c.1725–45 (detail: back bodice view), courtesy Los Angeles County Museum of Art online Public Access, p.52, left

Shot taffeta robe à la française, c.1725–45 (detail: bodice front and stomacher), courtesy Los Angeles County Museum of Art online Public Access, p.52, right, and p.109, top right

Silk and satin reception dress, c. 1877–78, Britain, Charles Frederick Worth/Cincinnati Art Museum, Ohio, USA/Gift of Mrs. Murat Halstead Davidson/Bridgeman Images, p.104

Silk and satin redingote, c.1790, courtesy Los Angeles County Museum of Art online Public Access, p.58

Silk and wool wedding dress, 1882, Australia. Collection: Powerhouse Museum, Sydney. Photo: Penelope Clay, p.107

Silk day dress and cape, c.1830–40. Collection: Powerhouse Museum, Sydney. Photo: Ryan Hernandez, p.77

Silk dress, c.1785–90, courtesy Los Angeles County Museum of Art online Public Access, p.60

Silk dress, c.1785–90 (detail: skirt hem), courtesy Los Angeles County Museum of Art online Public Access, p.60, right

Silk faille robe à la française, England, c.1765–70, courtesy Los Angeles County Museum of Art online Public Access, p.54

Silk faille robe à la française, England, c.1765–70 (fabric detail), courtesy Los Angeles County Museum of Art online Public Access, p.54, left

Silk faille robe à la française, England, c.1765–70 (detail: bodice and stomacher), courtesy Los Angeles County Museum of Art online Public Access, p.54, right

Silk mantua, c.1708, England, Metropolitan Museum of Art, New York. Image source: Art Resource, New York, p.50

Silk robe à l'anglaise with skirt draped à la polonaise, c.1775, courtesy Los Angeles County Museum of Art online Public Access, p.55

Silk robe à l'anglaise with skirt draped à la polonaise, c.1775 (detail: bodice front), courtesy Los Angeles County Museum of Art online Public Access, p.55, left

Silk satin wedding dress, 1834. Collection: Powerhouse Museum, Sydney, p.76

Silk taffeta afternoon dress, c.1876. Collection: Australia, Powerhouse Museum, Sydney. Photo: Sotha Bourn, p.103

Silk taffeta promenade dress, 1870, American, courtesy Los Angeles County Museum of Art online Public Access, p.100

Silk taffeta promenade dress, 1870 (detail: bodice front), American, courtesy Los Angeles County Museum of Art online Public Access, p.100, left

Silk taffeta promenade dress, 1870 (detail: side), American, courtesy Los Angeles County Museum of Art online Public Access, p.100, right

Silk twill evening dress, 1810, M982.20.1, McCord Museum, Montreal, p.70

Silk twill robe à l'anglaise, France, c.1785, courtesy Los Angeles County

Museum of Art online Public Access, p.56

Silk twill robe à l'anglaise, France, c.1785 (detail: bodice front), courtesy Los Angeles County Museum of Art online Public Access, p.56, left

Silk twill robe à l'anglaise, France, c.1785 (detail: back skirt construction), courtesy Los Angeles County Museum of Art online Public Access, p.54, right

Silk velvet gown, c.1550–60, Museo di Palazzo Reale, Pisa, p.24

"Silver tissue dress," c.1660, Fashion Museum, Bath and North East Somerset Council/Lent by the Vaughan Family Trust/Bridgeman Images, p.40

"Silver tissue dress," c.1660 (detail: close-up), Fashion Museum, Bath and North East Somerset Council/Lent by the Vaughan Family Trust/Bridgeman Images, p.40, left

Similar light summer dresses in the German countryside, 1903, p.127, left

Spencer jacket and petticoat, 1815, courtesy Los Angeles County Museum of Art online Public Access, p.71

Stomacher detail, robe à la française, c.1745, courtesy Los Angeles County Museum of Art online Public Access, p.52, right, and p.109, top left

Striped silk taffeta wedding dress, c.1869–75, Swan Guildford Historical Society, Australia. Photo: Aaron Robotham, p.91

Striped silk taffeta wedding dress, c.1869–75 (detail: peplum), Swan Guildford Historical Society, Australia. Photo: Aaron Robotham, p.91, top right

Striped silk taffeta wedding dress, c.1869–75 (detail: skirt hem), Swan Guildford Historical Society, Australia. Photo: Aaron Robotham, p.91, bottom right

Studio of Gerard ter Borch the Younger, *The Music Lesson*, c.1670. Courtesy National Gallery of Art, Washington D.C., p.33, full

Suit, c.1918, M2004.163.1.1-2, McCord Museum, Montreal, p.139

Suit by Hardy Amies, 1947, M970.26.54.1-2, McCord Museum, Montreal, p.171

Summer day dress, 1954, Swan Guildford Historical Society, Australia. Photo: Aaron Robotham, p.175

Summer dress, 1830, courtesy Los Angeles County Museum of Art online Public Access, p.75

Summer dress, 1830 (detail: skirt embroidery), courtesy Los Angeles County Museum of Art online Public Access, p.75, right

Summer dress, c.1904–07, Shippensburg Fashion Museum & Archives, Shippensburg, Pennsylvania, p.127

Summer dress, c.1908, M984.150.34.1-2, McCord Museum, Montreal, p.128

Taffeta day dress, 1823-25, M20555.1-2, McCord Museum, Montreal, p.73

Taffeta day dress, 1825. Collection: Powerhouse Museum, Sydney. Photo: Andrew Frolows, p.74

Taffeta dress, c.1885, France, courtesy Los Angeles County Museum of Art online Public Access, p.109

Taffeta dress, c.1885 (detail: bodice front), France, courtesy Los Angeles County Museum of Art online Public Access, p.109, top left

Tea gown by Mariano Fortuny, c.1920–29, North Carolina Museum of History, Raleigh. Photo: Eric Blevins, p.145

The original owner of the dress and a friend, Perth, Australia, mid 1950s, Swan Guildford Historical Society, Australia, p.176, right

Thomas Gainsborough, Anne, Countess of Chesterfield, c.1777–78, J. Paul Getty Museum, Los Angeles, p.57, left

Three-piece tailored costume, c.1895, courtesy Los Angeles County Museum of Art online Public Access, p.115, full

Trimming (robings) on the overskirt of a robe à l'anglaise, England, c.1770–80, courtesy Los Angeles County Museum of Art online Public Access, p.130

Tsukioka Yoshitoshi (1839–92), *Preparing to Take a Stroll: The Wife of a Nobleman of the Meiji Period*, 1888, Los Angeles County Museum of Art, p.133, left

Two-piece dress, c.1855, courtesy Los Angeles County Museum of Art online Public Access, p.87

Two-piece dress, c.1855 (detail: sleeve), courtesy Los Angeles County Museum of Art online Public Access, p.87, left

Unknown, Portrait of a Woman, daguerreotype, 1851, J. Paul Getty Museum, Los Angeles, p.86, right

Unknown, Portrait of a Young Woman, 1567, Yale Center for British Art, New Haven, Connecticut, p.25

Utagawa Kuniyoshi, *Osatao and Gonta* (detail), Japan, 19th century, courtesy Los Angeles County Museum of Art online Public Access, p.129, right

"Walking dress," 1815, France, from La Belle Assemblée, author's collection, p.71, right

Wedding dress, c.1850-60, Swan Guildford Historical Society, Australia. Photo: Aaron Robotham, p.88

Wedding dress, 1884, M968.4.1.1-2, McCord Museum, Montreal, p.108

Wedding dress c.1890, M21717.1-2, McCord Museum, Montreal, p.119

Wedding dress, 1905, Manning Valley Historical Society, New South Wales, p.125

Wedding dress, 1905 (detail: side), Manning Valley Historical Society, New South Wales, p.125, left

Wedding dress, 1905 (detail: bodice back), Manning Valley Historical Society, New South Wales, p.125, right

Wedding dress, c.1907, M2001.76.1.1-3, McCord Museum, Montreal, p.126

Wedding dress, 1952. Collection: Powerhouse Museum, Sydney. Photo: Nitsa Yioupros, p.173

Wedding photograph, May 1950, author's family archive, p.173, left

Wedding suit, 1961, UK, author's collection, p.15

Wenceslaus Hollar, Full figure of woman wearing ruffled collar and wide-brimmed hat, 1640, Library of Congress, Washington D.C., reproduction number: LC-USZ62-49999, p. 39

William Dobson, *Portrait of a Family*, c.1645, Yale Center for British Art, New Haven, Connecticut, p.31, top

Woman's Cage Crinoline. England, circa 1865, courtesy Los Angeles County Museum of Art online Public Access, p.83, right

Woman's corset, petticoat and sleeve plumpers, c.1830–40, courtesy Los Angeles County Museum of Art online Public Access, p.75, left

Woman "Peplophoros," marble, 1st Century B.C. (Hellenistic), The Walters Art Museum, Baltimore, p.144, right

Woman's Suit, 1912, M976.35.2.1-2, McCord Museum, Montreal, p.132

Woman's suit, wool, c.1898–1900, M977.44.2.1-2, McCord Museum, Montreal, p.131

Woman's three-piece costume, c.1915, M983.130.3.1-3, McCord Museum, Montreal, p.134 and p.135, full

Yellow crepe dress, 1960s–early 1970s, Shippensburg Fashion Museum & Archives, Shippensburg, Pennsylvania, p.189

Index